Nothin

Masham Church with its battlements around the spire, scene of some of my youthful adventures. Pen and ink drawing by Julia Nadal, 1982.

Nothing Easy is the autobiography of Ken Walker and covers the first forty-two years of his life, from his birth in Leeds in 1935, and through his upbringing in Masham and the running of his business in Ilkley. It tells a story of struggle, achievement and heartache.

In the era covered by the book, Ken Walker became a well-known entreprenuer with interests in haulage, plant hire and contracting. In addition, he took to motor racing on circuits throughout the UK and Western Europe, driving most things from motorbikes and Minis to Chevron B16s and Brabhams. He also turned his hand to driving buses, a mobile fish and chip lorry and tipper wagons. He reared pigs and day-old chickens, and found himself in many a scrape along the way.

Today, Ken Walker is retired and lives quietly - well almost - in Harrogate within easy reach of the Yorkshire Moors and Dales he has always loved.

Nothing Easy is the first part of his autobiography. Watch out for part two.

Front cover photos: A photograph taken in the early 1940s at a (rare) moment at school. The backgound shot showsPark Rash looking down towards Kettlewell in the Dales, scene of my motorcycle accident in 1952. Back cover photo shows me in 1972; the background is Kettlewell.

Ken Walker Publications
23 Village Farm
Bilton, Harrogate
HG1 4DH

A CIP catalogue record for this title is
available from the British Library
ISBN 978-0-9569839-0-9

Typeset in Calibri by Perry Associates,
Knaresborough

Printed and bound by The Inter Group,
Lingerfield Park, Knaresborough

Web address: www.kenwalker.org

Nothing Easy

My young life, 1935-1977
Ken Walker

This book is dedicated to the memory of Howard,
my brother, Charles Howard Walker

Acknowledgements

I started to write this in the spring of 2009 and, I suppose reflective of my age and background, it was at first in longhand. The painful process of turning this into computer text was undertaken by Beryl Alban and it is to her that I must express the fullness of my thanks. Without Beryl's help at that stage, and advice and guidance later the book would never have happened.

I am greatly indebted to my editor, Nigel Perry, for his help and guidance. I had written a story, which he took and made readable. Credit is due to my proofreader, Julie Moxon, whose interventions have given the book rigour and consistency. I give thanks, too, to Dave Whittington, who first read some of my writings when he came to fix my PC. His enthusiasm encouraged me to continue and have it published, putting together the photographs in the book and setting up my website. Friends, colleagues and counsellors all.

Contents

Introduction - Tales start at the beginning and that is what I have done here with references to my birth in May 1935 and upbringing in the small town of Masham in North Yorkshire on the edge of the Dales. That was a different world: a place with few cars, with little farm automation, and where the internet and mobile communications were beyond our imaginings. Horses did much of the work and what they didn't do sheer effort did the rest - and I gave my share. Things have changed so much in the intervening years. Will our children and grandchildren experience as many upheavals in what they consider normal?

Looking back, nothing was easy and that's why I have chosen this as the book's title. The thought, Nothing Easy, characterised much of my young years leading up to the age of forty-two. Whatever happened came about following a struggle. Nothing original there perhaps, but it conjures up the age and my youthful experiences.

I began writing the story in 2009, inspired by my friend Beryl being asked by her daughter Shirley to write down the romantic account of how her parents had met. Shirley's father, Beryl's husband, had died many years before and there was a gap in their lives which needed filling. This turned my thoughts to my own story. My mother had passed on not long before and it was time for me to record matters for posterity.

I am a true Dalesman, having lived my life for the most part in Wharfedale, Wensleydale and Nidderdale. Much of the story is set in Yorkshire and though it takes in the Fens, Lancashire, Scotland, Germany, Spain, Portugal and Italy, it is a typical Tyke's tale of the era. The landscape of the Dales and the Moors, and of small rural towns such as Masham and Ilkley in God's County are the background for much of what occurs. I hope my enthusiasm for these locations comes through. It is also a story of quarries, and bus routes, coal depots, airfields, race tracks, farms, villages and engine workshops. It is as English, I think, as fish and chips - and they figure too!

This book is intended as the first of a two-parter, and covers the period from 1935 to 1977. It is a story of growing up, of dealing with life, schooling, work and business, with periods of play thrown in too. I married, helped raise children, started and built up a business, and encountered much along the way. I have kept my opinions to a minimum but have vented them where something or someone affected me strongly. I've been told I have a good memory, and the accuracy of what I recall is important to me.

I never set out to write an autobiography but this is what has happened. Originally, I started by setting down a few incidents from my first forty-two years, what I call 'My Young Life'. Forty-two might not seem a particularly young age to some, but looking back from my eighth decade I can assure them it now does. It was intended first for the eyes of those who are near to me, though I hope that many who have never heard the name Ken Walker will find something to interest them. These initial jottings grew and grew and I realised I had some good yarns to relate; I hope it will inspire others to set down in writing their tales too.

Kenneth Walker
Harrogate 2011

CHAPTER 1
1935 TO 1942
EARLIEST MEMORIES

It Starts With a Question

The church in Healy near Masham, North Yorkshire, sits on a hillside overlooking the valley. A steep path leads up to it through a well tended graveyard. Over to the left by the wall, it is not so well tended; in fact it's a bit neglected with long grass, policeman's bonnets and nettles. But looking through them I can see a headstone, green with moss and not easy to read. It is the grave of my grandmother, Jessie Robson, who died on 11 May 1935. She did not live to see me, though I arrived four weeks early on 21 May 1935 due, my mother said, to the trauma of losing her mother. As I look at the grave I realise the neglect must be my responsibility as I am the only living member of the family who knows of it. In my hand I have a photograph given to me many years ago by my mother, perhaps even taken by her, standing where I stand now. Written on the back it says, 'Mother's grave 1935'. The picture is much different to what I see now. Then, the grave was festooned with flowers and wreaths while everything else was covered with snow, including the distant hills. My mother often told me it snowed in May the year I was born. Why her mother died so young is a question I regret never asking.

* * * * *

I was born in Leeds Maternity Hospital, Hyde Terrace, to John Leslie (always known as Leslie) and Kathleen Jessie Walker and was christened John Kenneth. From day one I was known by my middle name, just like my father. At the time my parents lived in Mark Street, a very poor rundown area of Leeds off Woodhouse Moor, close to the notorious Camp Road where the police patrolled in pairs. My sister Freda had been born two years earlier when my parents lived in Fearby, a small village close to Masham. When Freda was very ill with rheumatic fever my gran (father's mother) had stepped in and taken her from my mother as she thought her not capable of caring for the little girl. And that's where Freda stayed for years to come.

I have often wondered why my parents moved to Leeds, away from their families and friends in Masham, a small town at the foot of Wensleydale on the edge of the Yorkshire Dales. Had there been a dispute perhaps? I know my gran didn't like my mother and made life difficult for her, so that could have been one reason. Or was it just to find work? My father drove a lorry for a firm called True Time Deliveries on Kirkstall Road, Leeds.

Father's family, the Walkers, came to Masham from the Darlington/Stockton area after the 1914-1918 war. Mother's people, the Robsons, came from further north. My grandpa, Bob Robson, arrived to work as a gamekeeper for Lord Swinton in 1910, travelling back to Hexham in Northumberland three years later to get married. My mother, who was known to everyone as Kathleen except by my father who called her Kath, was born the following year. By the time of my birth, grandpa Robson was living in Healy, a village three miles from Masham.

Originating in the border counties, the Robsons and my mother's grandmother's family, the Grahams, were Reivers, the outlaw raiders of medieval and Tudor times. On the occasions, too often to describe, when I found myself in trouble as a boy my mother would blame this Northumbrian heritage. (I once took her to Netherby where the Grahams lived for many years. She stood and gazed at the old Hall, as if she had come home.)

Home in Masham
The draw of home proved stronger than the dubious attractions of Leeds and when I was just ten days old we moved back to Masham, into a tiny cottage in Red Lane. To enter you stepped off the pavement straight into the living room, which had a wooden partition to deflect the draught when the door was open. There was a small back kitchen and two rooms upstairs: one my parent's bedroom and the other a tiny box room that later became my bedroom. We had no running water and shared an outside tap with the neighbours. In the kitchen a bucket of water sat permanently on the stone window ledge and you dipped into this with a cup or jug to save going outside each time. If I went into the kitchen after dark for a drink of water I always took a torch as my mother told me of someone once taking a drink at night and swallowing a spider ... or was that Burl Ives?

There was electricity only in the front room. A single bulb surrounded by an orange tasselled lampshade hung over the table from a short length of cable attached to a ceiling joist. Later, when my mother bought an electric iron, it was plugged into the same cable through a double adaptor with light, adaptor cable and all swinging to-and-fro as she ironed. Why my father never ran a cable through to the kitchen and the rest of the house I will never know. He certainly had the knowledge to do so.

When going into the kitchen or upstairs after dark we would light a candle set in a little green holder with a handle you hooked your finger through, remembering not to set off too fast before the flame burned up or the candle would go out. The thin stair carpet over the stone steps was held in place with a mixture of wooden and brass stair rods. I have felt both wood and brass at different times across my back (the wooden ones were broader and didn't hurt as much). Also in the kitchen was a gas-fired copper boiler for washing days and bath nights. On the latter occasions the tin bath came down from its hook on the wall and was placed in front of the fire. It was fun on a cold night. Now that I think about it, I don't remember my father getting into it very often.

I slept in a little iron high-sided cot in the same bedroom as my parents. It must have been my mother who taught me to say my prayers before going to sleep at night. I prayed to be a pilot or a steam engine driver. In the years since I have driven almost everything except a steam engine, and only made pilot on a paraglider. Maybe I didn't pray hard enough!

My Father

The tiny front room had an open fire with an oven on one side and the water boiler on the other. The boiler leaked and the oven had a crack in it, but mother still managed to bake and cook meals in it, first waiting for the coal to burn red otherwise everything in the oven was smoked. A little cupboard under the stairs held my dad's tools and a box of spare valves, transformers, condensers and other materials for his radio repairs hobby. Outside the back door under the window was a small garden of about one square yard, edged round with cobblestones. Here my mother grew hollyhocks, sweet william and sweet peas in a little patch that was taller than it was wide, especially when the hollyhocks were in bloom.

Apart from repairing radios, my father was interested in servicing cars. He didn't have a workshop and when the weather was cold he would occasionally bring a car engine into the front room. A sheet of cardboard and a sack would be put down to cover the old rug in front of the fireplace, and there he would fit new piston rings or bearings. As to be expected, my mother didn't like this but had to go along with it for, like me, she was frightened of him, and would come off second best if she challenged him. When she was angry she occasionally used a stair rod on my back to relieve her frustration, I think, at his dominance.

The kitchen door had a split in one panel where my father had struck it with his fist in a rage. It had never been properly repaired, only painted over and was like that for years as witness to his temper. I often looked at it and remembered how it got there. On the wall to the right of the door hung two pictures of Highland scenes, one with a stag standing proudly, head held high, and the other with a small stream running down through the rocks with the distant mountains shrouded in mist.

One of my earliest memories was lying awake early in the morning listening to the sound of clog footsteps. The famous Theakston's Brewery was at the top of Red Lane in Masham and the workmen would pass under my bedroom window. Sometimes they would be in step marching like soldiers; at other times it would be just uneven clatter. Captain Theakston was head of the brewery and didn't wear clogs. In fact, he would have needed just one as he had a wooden leg! His chosen transport, a bicycle, was specially adapted for him with a fixed wheel so that he could peddle with one leg; the wooden one swinging stiffly on the other side. If he passed close by, you could hear his leg creaking as it dangled down.

Theakston's Brewery has done much to put Masham on the map. Founded in 1827 by Robert Theakston, the Brewery weathered many storms and, after a brief interlude, returned to the ownership of the family in 2003. In the 1990s it even spawned a second Theakston family-owned brewery, Black Sheep. Everyone in Masham knew about the Theakstons.

Aunt Doreen

My dad had two younger sisters, aunts Madie and Doreen. Aunt Doreen would often call in at home, bringing along my sister Freda who lived with her at granny's. When I was little, she would take me out in my pushchair around Swinney Lane with Freda walking at the side holding the handle. Sometimes we would collect twigs from under the trees which my mother would dry in the oven and use to light the fire. I would be only two or three-years old at this time. I liked my aunt even then and she soon became my favourite, the two of us becoming close as I grew up. She was an attractive lady with dark hair.

I was just three when I caught chickenpox and was confined to bed feeling a bit delirious. My hands were tied securely in little mittens to prevent me scratching the spots as my mother said this would leave a scar.

At the bottom of our yard was the rear entrance to Watkinson's grocery shop. I would rattle the door till someone opened it. I don't know if they were pleased to see me or whether it was to get rid of me, but they usually gave me my favourite drink: Dandelion and Burdock. However, one day I took a gulp before realising it was vinegar. They all laughed and thought it very funny, but they only caught me that once even though they tried many times. I continued to call but always sniffed the drink first. Many years later another brown liquid became my favourite. Tea? No! Coffee? No! Only one clue: the men in clogs brewed it!

The Kitchens

Next door to us lived the Kitchen family: Ronnie and Laura and their five children - three boys and two girls. They were very poor, wearing hand-me-down clothes that were passed from one to the other. They didn't have enough cups to go round, and I often saw them drinking tea from jam jars. Ronnie drank from a different shaped glass - he certainly liked his beer!

Across the yard was our toilet, shared with the Kitchens which made a total of ten people using (and occasionally misusing) it. I hated going there. Squares of old newspapers hung on a string behind the door. When I remembered, I took a torch as there was no light. The toilet smelled of cigarettes as the adults always took a smoke with them. My mother and father would light up before dashing across the yard (not together). The toilet had only one seat, not like my aunt's at Healy where there was a two-seater. Ours had a chain, though often it had not been pulled. In winter when it was frosty the place didn't smell quite as bad as there was a small paraffin lamp by the cistern lit day and night to stop the water freezing.

Laura Kitchen's father, Billy Marshall, was the 'dustbin man'. Every house had a coal fire in those days and once a week he would arrive with his horse and cart to empty the bins. There was only ash in the bins as everything else was burned on the fire. He would stop regularly at Laura's for a cup of tea, parking his horse and cart outside. As our front doors were side by side, the cart would be in front of the Kitchen's house and the horse in front of ours. I opened our door one day to see the horse blocking the footpath, so close that I could have reached out and touched its big belly. I could see the other side of the road and I wanted to run underneath between the front and back legs. I was so small and it was so big I was sure there was room! I thought about it many times, but couldn't quite pluck up the courage.

Grandfather

My grandparents, Elizabeth Daisy Walker and Thomas Ernest (known as Ernest) Walker lived close by. Clearly, this habit the male Walkers had of going by their middle name went back a few generations at least. The front part of their house looking out on the Masham Market Place was their fish and chip shop. They lived in the back and over the shop. From the back door a small yard led down to a wooden shed where the potatoes and fish were prepared for the shop. Most days I called round to see them.

I was there one Sunday when my gran ran out of sugared almonds, her favourite sweet.

"Go to the shop Kenneth and get me a quarter," she asked.

"What shop?" was my reply. "It's Sunday and they're all closed."

"Go to the back door of Bushy Leathley's. She won't mind."

I hated being sent on that errand of knocking on a back door when the shop was closed. Still, my granny was generous and always gave me a tip, so off I went. I knocked nervously at the door. Mrs Leathley eventually appeared, as usual with a fag in her mouth.

"I'd like a quarter of sugared almonds please," I asked.

"Don't you know it's Sunday?" she replied.

Trying to make friends I said, "Yes, but my granny said Mrs Bushy won't mind."

Her reply came quick. "Well you go back and tell your gran that I don't call her Mrs Fishy. Go knock on someone else's back door!" She slammed the door in my face.

I was stunned. No sugared almonds and no tip for me. I told my gran what had happened and they all had a good laugh. Unknown to me, years earlier Mr Leathley had been given the nick-name 'Bushy' when he was spotted in some bushes when courting. He was known by it but I didn't know any better when asking Mrs Leathley for a favour. When the laughter died down my gran turned to me and said, "Well Kenneth, that means that you'll have to go to Mrs Haigh's back door."

This was another errand not to my liking. Mrs Haigh was deaf, especially on a Sunday afternoon, and what is more she shouted all the time thinking that everyone else was also hard of hearing. After my third knock she appeared at the door looking none too pleased to see me; maybe I had disturbed her afternoon nap. I smiled, "Sorry to disturb you Mrs Haigh but could I have a quarter of sugared almonds?"

She said nothing as she motioned me in, leading the way through to the shop at the front of the house chuntering under her breath. Eventually she would warm to me a little and I felt that though she was annoyed with my gran for sending me, she sympathised with my position and started to chat. She was very old and like my granddad almost bald, but she didn't hide the fact under a cap. She took the few long straggly bits she had left and wound them round on the top of her head, pinning them in place. I wanted to ask her why she didn't wear a hat as I'm sure it would have been much easier and certainly would have looked better. By the time she had weighed out the sweets and two ounces of aniseed balls for me she was in full flow and I had a job to get away.

My grandfather (father's father) was a wonderful man. He didn't show much affection but did pick me up in his strong tattooed arms, covered in fine hair and freckles just as mine are now. When I was five or six he would have been in his fifties but he looked an old man to me. These days I need only look in the mirror to see him! When I was young he had a great influence on me. He had a very strict upbringing. His father was the Chief Police Superintendent at Northallerton and a strict disciplinarian. It was said that he fastened my grandfather to the end of the bed to belt him. He couldn't allow the son of the local inspector to set a bad example by misbehaving.

Before joining the Army, grandfather had been an ironstone miner, working below ground in the Cleveland Hills mines. He served in the 1914-1918 war and sometimes told me about it. He survived the Somme and Ypres and suffered for the rest of his life from gas poisoning. He would often wake up at night screaming and my granny would comfort him. He was certainly a brave man. Once, when part of his section was cut off by the Germans and they were desperate for supplies, he volunteered for the dangerous mission of bringing relief. At night he took mules through with supplies and saved them. The CO of his section received an award for my grandfather's bravery.

Granddad told me how they lived underground with the supplies, horses and stables, which as a small boy I found hard to understand. Many years later I read a book and even more years later saw a television programme which showed an underground network of tunnels. Both were just as he had described. As I gazed at the screen I felt he was watching with me.

Grandfather kept rabbits, caged birds and dogs. I remember well his advice - and over the years have often quoted him: "always have a hobby that pays." I would help him groom the rabbits and get them ready for the show in Ripon. One day he asked if I would like to show one … just imagine my excitement! "Yes I would," was my quick reply. On show days the rabbits were put in special carrying boxes with air holes, and off we went. I put my rabbit on the table in a line with many others, taking care not to let it escape. When the judge came to me he only glanced at my rabbit before passing on to granddad, who won third prize.

"Why did he show so little interest in mine?" I asked.

"It's out of condition," he said. Maybe he knew, but allowed me to show the rabbit for experience.

The Blacksmith and the Bellman
As a little boy, I liked going round to Bob Dale's blacksmith shop. My first visit was with my dad when he went to talk football. Bob helped to run the Masham football

team and my dad was a keen and, I think, quite a good, certainly fearless, left back. Old Bob chewed tobacco and when he spat, he fired it though his bushy brown moustache so fast you didn't see it until it landed at the other side of the shop or sizzled in the forge fire. It was also the way he checked the heat of the iron he was working on, but you didn't want to catch a whiff of the steam rising from it!

He was a nice man, spoke softly and had broad shoulders. *'And the muscles of his brawny arms/Are strong as iron bands,'* (as mentioned in Longfellow's poem, The Village Blacksmith). I would go round after school and pump the bellows until white sparks shot up the chimney. The first thing he made for me was a 'booler', a circular iron ring and a handle with a hook on it. You rolled the hoop then attached the hook, pushing and guiding it along while running at the side. If I needed runners for my sledge he made them. When I needed a draw bar to pull a trailer behind my bike he made that too, and never accepted a penny.

Above Bob's workshop was a loft. Occasionally, I saw an old tramp in a long brown coat carefully negotiating the rickety ladder as Bob let him sleep up there. I suppose it was warm and he didn't mind the soot. He was not clean when he went up but looked more like a chimney sweep when he came down.

I often watched Bob shoe big carthorses, standing well back from their hindquarters. He took hold of the long hair by the hoof, tapped the leg with his other hand and the horse would politely lift it. Bob held it between his legs, leaving his hands free to work. As he fitted the new shoe, smoke would rise with a smell of burning hoof. He would then hammer in the nails from the handful he held in his mouth, trim and rasp the edges, then paint the hoof with an oily substance to make it shine. It may have been linseed oil? He would then stand back, stretch and straighten his back which was bent most of the day. A smile of satisfaction would appear on his face. Another job well done!

I also watched him re-tyre a 1.5 metre cartwheel. Burton's joiners arrived with a wooden cartwheel that had been repaired, a new spoke or outer section of ash or beech neatly married to old. It was placed on a round iron table with a hole in the middle for the hub. Bob would then get a strip of iron, heat it in the forge, curve it, join it into a circle and make it fit onto the wooden wheel, all the while making several checks to get it right. It would then be reheated, hammered on all the way, then dropped into a huge water tank to shrink the iron to the wooden wheel. All this done was with only fire and a hammer - that was real skill!

Masham was and remains today a small town out in the country, sited alongside the lovely River Ure on the route from York to Wensleydale. In medieval times it was designated a Peculier within the Minster of York, which meant it had its own ecclesiastical court. Theakston's most famous ale, Old Peculier, is a reminder of this. In such places, life runs at a slower pace than in the cities. Change was gradual but none the worse for that. There were few telephones in the late 1930s and Masham still had a Town Crier, Mr Lightfoot, who was known as the *Bellman*. He carried a large hand bell, holding it upside down by the clanger as he walked between points. He would stop at each street to ring the bell, swinging it backwards and forwards as far as he could reach, while the bell clanged loudly. Doors would open and faces would pop out to hear the news called in a loud clear voice. "The water will be turned off tomorrow at 10am until 4pm for maintenance work." He would then move on to the next street to repeat the message, passing on around the town. With this news we would quickly fill buckets and bowls from the shared outside tap. Later, when the water came back on, the flow would run for a long time red with rust from the old cast iron pipes.

I don't know when the *Bellman* custom ceased, but it was reintroduced in 2002 with John Todd appointed as Town Crier.

The Fleethams
The houses on Red Lane stood on one side only, opposite a wall along Fleetham's garden. This garden ran almost the full length of the lane from the Fleetham's farmhouse facing onto Park Square to the farm buildings at the top, close to Theakston's Brewery.

I spent lots of time at this farm and enjoyed there some of the happiest moments of my early years. I think it was a wonderfully healthy environment in which to grow up and learn about the countryside: animals, nature, and the birds and the bees.

The Fleethams were an unusual family. Three sisters and a brother lived at home, none of whom were married. Wallace was my hero and I wanted to be like him. He had thick black hair, Brylcreemed down with a quiff at the front. Mrs Fleetham would put a quiff in the front of my blonde hair so that I could look like Wallace. She was old and could walk only very slowly. On sunny days, the younger Fleethams would take her out in an old wheelchair, push her up the garden path, and then park it under a large apple tree where she would sit peacefully in the shade. Her eyesight wasn't good. While she could do little in the garden she still grew enormous pumpkins on a pile of horse manure by the stables. To increase their size she fed them extra water from a jam jar. A thick thread of cotton led from the jar to a large darning needle stuck into the side of the pumpkin. I couldn't understand how this worked but she certainly got results and was convinced that doing this was the reason.

Muriel, one of the daughters, spent a lot of time at our house when my father was away in the RAF. She was a good friend and company for my mum. They would knit, smoke a Craven A cigarette and chat, or occasionally listen to a radio show. Dick Barton and Paul Temple were very popular radio programmes at this time. I remember them listening to the Beau Geste serial and they both liked plays. They always had a library book in reserve. My mother also worked on her dressmaking. I had my own little pastime, putting on my own special slide show using an old clock tin case for a projector. I pulled out the broken clockworks and installed a torch battery and bulb, cut a hole in the front for the lens, soldered two brackets, one at each side for the film to run through, and then cut cellophane paper into strips. On the cellophane I painted images and pulled this slowly through the brackets to create a movie on the wall where it was dark under the table. Later, Muriel and I started to collect stamps, a hobby I have pursued all my life until now, at seventy-five years of age, I am disposing of them.

Winters felt much colder then and as soon as it started to freeze we would go round the fields until we found a pond on which we could skate. Muriel always ensured that she went first as she was heavier than me. That's how I first learned to ice skate on an old pair of clip-on skates that came from the Sale Room in Ripon.

Though very 'busty', I think there was a bit more man than woman about Muriel. Probably, that was an advantage for all the heavy work she had to do on the farm. She would always wear green or brown cord riding breeches, brown studded boots, thick hand knitted knee-length stockings, and a green or brown well-filled woolly jumper. I liked Muriel, she was good to me, and I spent much time with her on the Fleetham's farm.

Making Hay
I always looked forward to hay time, at which I helped out using a special little fork that had the shaft cut down short. Before the mower could go into the field to cut the grass it had to be 'opened up'. A strip around the outside close to the hedge wide enough for the horses pulling the mower had to be cut by hand with a scythe. They would then go round in decreasing circles until there was only a small patch in the middle where the rabbits had run to escape the cutter. Unfortunately, some were caught in the blades. Eventually, as the centre strip shrunk they would make a dash for freedom but were often bowled over by the blast of a twelve-bore shotgun in the hands of my hero Wallace, who was a very good shot.

Best of all was 'lowance' (lunch in the Dales' dialect) when I would walk half a mile to the farmhouse and collect two baskets prepared specially for the workers. They contained delicious home-cured ham sandwiches, home-made bread and milk bottles filled with cold tea. I would trudge back to the fields, my short arms barely keeping the baskets off the ground, to be greeted with cheers. I have never since felt quite as welcome anywhere. We would squat down by the hay pikes or stacks and have a feast out in the fresh air with a hunger brought on by manual work. Sandwiches never tasted better. The horses close by would be snatching a mouthful of new hay. I can smell it now - the hay not the horses!

The Fleethams had two horses: Dinah, who had a light sandy colour and blonde mane, and Bonny, a dark almost black horse. My best treat was at the end of the day when we returned from the fields. I'd sit on the farm carts which were loaded with hay, with me on top so high I had to duck under the low branches as we trundled down the lane between the trees, the cart rocking from side to side over the potholes. It was exciting to be so high up with only the hay to cling on to. The horses always knew when it was home time and never needed urging. I remember one day the cart started with a jerk and my friend Edwin Sturdy disappeared down the back of the load. I heard a thud followed by a cry as he hit the ground. He was shaken but unhurt, and keen to get back on top for the ride. This time, though, he settled down much nearer the front.

When hay time was over, all the implements would be cleaned and working parts oiled. Any part that might rust was painted with old engine oil before being carefully stowed away in the implement shed for the following year.

Fleetham's Farm grew turnips, mangolds and winter feed for the cows. Occasionally during a wet period, they would not be able to scuffle the weeds between the rows. The weeds would then grow tall and smother the crop, and the horse couldn't pick its way between the rows of seedlings. That was when I was given an important job: I had to ride the horse as it drew the scuffler, guiding him along between the rows. I felt very important, like Roy Rogers on Trigger.

Another job I had was on threshing days when the steam traction engine and thresher came. The corn crop of oats, wheat or barley was in a stack and the thresher would pull up at the side. Men then forked the sheaves into the top of the thresher and out would come the straw at one end and the corn at the other. Straw was bundled into bales and the corn was poured into huge sacks hired from the railway and holding sixteen stone. These sacks needed the strongest men to lift them. In those days farmers helped each other, men coming from neighbouring farms for the day.

My job was to creep between the stack and the thresher with a 'scep' and place it by a screen to catch the seeds that leaked out. Well! I crept round to check my scep and was caught by the belt that ran from the engine to the thresher, knocking me unconscious. Eventually I was missed, but they couldn't find me as I was covered in straw that had fallen from the stack. But then someone noticed the scep was running over and went round to empty it, and in the process tripped over me lying unconscious in the straw. My head was cut but it was nothing serious. I soon came round and went back to work, this time remembering to duck low under the belt. In fact, I crept along on hands and knees until my confidence returned. For many years the scar did not show, but with thinning hair it does now!

When an animal died, Muriel would load it on to a trailer and take it to the gasworks where it would be thrown into the retort (furnace). Masham's little gasworks got its coal supplies delivered by rail to the station, then hauled by road to the gasworks. It made the town self-sufficient in many ways. Domestic gas and gas for street lighting (only recently changed to electricity), coke for heating schools and the blacksmith's forge, all came from the gasworks. Then there was tar for road repairs and creosote used as a preservative for hen huts, wooden buildings and fences, all derived from coal. Whenever we visited the gasworks we always brought a can of creosote back with us.

My dad drove a lorry for the quarry at Marfield. Occasionally I went with him for the ride. He would call home at midday for something to eat, parking the loaded lorry on Park Square at the end of Red Lane. I can see the lorry now, a huge black thing with water dripping out the back from the load of washed gravel.

New airfields were being constructed in preparation for the war and that is where dad delivered the gravel. I heard him telling someone about a fiddle that the drivers had been on: they went in the front of the site fully loaded, getting their ticket signed before driving straight through without tipping the load, to a café round the back. Here they killed time with a pot of tea before returning to the front of the site with the same load. This went on for some time until they were caught. Many years later I drove a quarry wagon for a short while delivering sand and gravel to building sites.

Mullard Nine-Pins

My granny bought old radios at the Ripon Sale Room for my father, her 'wonderful son'. Dad would tinker with them, changing valves, transformers and other bits, while we all kept quiet listening for the music or a voice between the crackles and whistles.

Whether I inherited the interest or he sparked it I don't know, but I became absorbed by what he did even at four or five. I would strip out the parts of old radio sets and box them up for spares. I can still see the dark blue valve box where I carefully placed those Mullard and Cossor valves with different pin numbers and configuration. Dad would ask me for a Mullard nine-pin and woe betide me if I gave him a seven-pin! He was short on patience and tolerance but I learned quickly.

Radios then had an aluminium frame and all the parts could be unscrewed like a Meccano set but bigger and better. I loved it. I soon became familiar with my father's tools, spanners and gauges, especially his set of feeler gauges - thin strips of metal used for setting spark plugs and ignition points. When his friends called he would show me off, holding the gauge size numbers down so I couldn't see them. I would hold each one in turn between my fingers and guess the thickness. Ten thou, twenty-five thou, fifteen thou (thousandths of an inch). Most of the time I was spot on, and it was one of those rare moments when I felt he was proud of me.

War Starts

The War started in 1939 and the following year my father joined the RAF. Maybe his father's WW1 experiences in France put him off the Army. I don't think he was attracted to flying and his lack of education would have almost certainly excluded him. His handwriting was very neat but the letters were not joined-up. He was more mechanically-minded, so served as an aircraft engine fitter and was, I believe, a very good one.

Dad first went to Blackpool for basic training, with drill often done on the beach and watched with amusement by the locals. When we visited we stayed in Morecambe. He then moved down to Cambridgeshire to train as a mechanic on aircraft engines, including the Rolls Royce Merlin engine that later powered both Spitfire and Lancaster aircraft.

My mother and I were now alone in our tiny cottage in Red Lane. Sister Freda still lived with our granny, growing up in a different and rather more privileged environment to mine. She could and often did hoodwink elderly grandparents, often causing friction between them. I think that my grandfather's life was made worse for having her around.

Despite her many privileges Freda had the occasional beating from our gran when she pushed her too far. Not with a stair rod, as in my case, but usually with a coat hanger applied with such force it often broke. If Freda happened to be in the kitchen at the time it could be even worse, as she would get the rubber hosepipe on her back, a short length used on washing day to fill the copper boiler from the tap. It was hung on the wall in a much too handy place by the sink. Aunt Doreen had told Freda not to cry, "Don't let her think she's hurting you." So Freda would suffer in silence, holding back the tears. Unfortunately, this made gran even more determined and with each blow she would call out, "I will make you cry, you little hussy." Freda's bad luck was that Doreen's advice would prolong the punishment.

Later gran would feel guilty and try to make amends by taking Freda to Lawson's shop just across the road to buy her something new to wear, maybe even a dress or a pair of shoes. I suppose this would ease her conscience. My gran paid for Freda to go to a private school, whereas my education would be mostly at work, with short spells at a series of different schools thrown in.

Though kind in many ways, gran was very bossy and domineering, and would push people around. My mother couldn't stand up to that sort of treatment; she had a much milder nature. When my father and mother were first married they lived with his parents for a short while, and my gran treated my mother 'like a skivvy' (to use my mother's words). After that, I don't remember a single occasion in my life when mum and gran were in each other's company.

I heard that once, years ago when my father was quite young, he got into trouble and was taken to the police station. When my granny heard she went wild and stormed across to the station where there was quite a fracas resulting in the policeman's helmet being knocked off. She told him in no uncertain terms, "You leave my son alone; if he needs chastising I will do it, not you." Whereupon, she grabbed my dad and took him home. As I knew my granny well, I believe this to be true!

Although not a regular churchgoer, my mum took me there when I was around five years old. I also went with her to the Midland Bank in Park Square and set up a bank account. I came away with one of those round money boxes with a slot for different coins.

My mother's fondness for dressmaking gave her a source of additional income. She enjoyed chatting with her customers, smoking a cigarette and, of course, the money was welcome. I don't think she charged much, but it was a bit extra for the cigs and food. Many customers were friends or locals. When they came for fittings I would hide. I was so shy I would crawl under a chair in the corner of the tiny room and stay there until they left, though occasionally I could be coaxed out with sweets. My mother continued dressmaking for most of her life. It was a sad day when in her late 70s or early 80s she had to give it up with failing eyesight.

Mum often sent me to Brayshaw's Bakery for a 4d loaf of bread, freshly baked with a sheet of tissue paper wrapped loosely around and tucked under my arm. I had to remember not to squeeze too hard as it was still warm and could shrink to half its size. The man who baked it was called Baker Jackson and later became a drinking friend of my father.

Around this time my mother had an operation on her hand which was bandaged up for some time. One day, I asked for a slice of bread and jam and she said, "You will have to get it yourself as my hand is hurting." I did, but when she wasn't watching I cut up the whole loaf, sparingly put on margarine and then the jam, stuck the slices together in pairs and stowed them away in a cake tin. Later when my mother asked where the rest of the loaf was, I proudly showed her what I'd done. "You won't have to worry now mum, there's enough for all week."

Food in Wartime and The Onion Men

My mother wasn't a very good cook and wartime rationing made things more difficult. I suppose it had never been easy for my mother as dad was a very fussy eater. He put it down to having a bad stomach, which meant there were so many things he couldn't eat and that may have been why her cooking was always so plain. I don't remember us ever sitting down at the table together for a meal. My mother always dished out dad's dinner first and he would sit in his chair by the fire with the plate on his knee.

I cannot remember us ever having a Sunday roast. The nearest was a very small piece of rolled brisket, mashed potatoes with a little milk and margarine added, one vegetable and small, round and not very high Yorkshire puddings.

Monday was washing day leaving her no time to cook, which meant cold leftover brisket and a few potatoes, fried until they were brown and crisp. Luckily, this was just how I liked them. After the war had started milk was one of the few things not rationed and we had a plentiful supply from Fleetham's Farm, so my mother often made milk puddings. My favourite was bread and butter pudding, made with bits of stale bread, a few currants or raisins, margarine, a sprinkling of sugar with a little nutmeg grated on top and baked in the oven. My special treat was to scrape the brown from around the edge of the little enamel pie dish.

One morning my mother made me a bacon sandwich, a rare treat. I took off the top slice of bread to look inside, only to find a single slim slice of streaky bacon laid across the middle of the bread. Fortunately, it was quite crisp, so I broke it into small pieces and spread it out so there was a bit with each bite. Though rationing made food difficult, I could always rely on getting a bag of chips from my gran's fish and chip shop.

The 'onion men' came to Masham every year, arriving in a large brown van which they parked in the Market Place. There were three of them. Short and stocky, they looked alike and wore the traditional French beret; I suppose they could have been brothers. I watched them prop their bicycles against the van, loading them with so many strings of onions hung over the handlebars that the tyres looked flat. When they set off they had to push the bikes, going in different directions around the town.

It was not long before the first came riding back and, before he had reloaded, the others had reappeared. They helped each other load up and went off again. This time they took longer, with perhaps one returning with a few onions unsold. But Masham had been supplied and they loaded their bicycles into the van and moved on to the next town.

Another regular visitor was the scissors grinder, but he didn't peddle or push his grinder. It was modern and looked as if it had been an Army mobile workshop still in its original khaki finish. He did a good trade with shops, tradesmen and private houses. Everyone had something to sharpen: tools, garden shears, knives and scissors. My mother always sent me with her precious dressmaking scissors, the ones only she had authority to use and woe betide anyone who used them to cut paper!

"Tell him not to take too much off them," she would say. "Keep them pointing down and don't run."

The door to the grinder's van was at the back and if I stood on the top step I could just see over the half-door and watch him at work, sparks flying in all directions from the grinder. The van engine was always running, I suppose to drive the machine.

Pig-Keeping
My grandfather always kept two pigs. It was difficult to get feed when the war started but if you joined the Pig Club you were allowed a monthly ration. Of course, if you knew a farmer you could get more. He also fed them potato cuttings and very occasionally a few leftover chips as he would never warm up anything to sell in the shop. He'd add brewers' grains from the nearby Theakston's Brewery. There was little goodness in them, but they filled the pigs' bellies for a while and kept them quiet. One pig would be sold and the other killed for home consumption. My grandfather and others who kept a pig for their own use, would only kill when there was an 'R' in the month.

It was always a special event when the pig was slaughtered (though not for the poor pig) as we all had something: fresh pork, spare ribs, liver, black pudding, lard, dripping, with some being given to neighbours. The pig would be killed, then hung in the slaughterhouse overnight to cool off and set before being cut up.

On these occasions it was my job to go to Jackson's Chemists for a block of salt and a small amount of saltpetre. I always asked for a bit more saltpetre than my granddad had ordered as any left over could be used for making fireworks! The cheapest salt came in such a large block that I could only just manage to carry it back across the Market Place. My next task was to break and crush it, ready to spread onto the parts that were to be cured - usually the two hams and one side - the remainder being eaten fresh. The parts to be salted were put in a large lead-lined wooden tray with salt rubbed into the flesh. They were covered completely with salt and left in a cool, dry place to cure for between four and six weeks.

After this they would be taken out and hung up wrapped in muslin cloths to keep the flies off, though occasionally one would get through and lay eggs in a small crevice. Here, the eggs would hatch into maggots, eating their way into the centre along the side of the bone. Eventually, the smell would give them away and the ham would be taken down, cut open, washed in salt water, the grubs removed, and then cooked and eaten as soon as possible. Only the worst bits were thrown away. Often, parts were given to friends and relations to get them consumed as soon as possible.

Such pig meat was fit to eat but usually had a taint and was known as 'blown ham'. Cured ham was hung in the kitchen. One day my grandfather took down a ham to cut a piece and slashed through an artery in his wrist. Instead of calling for help he just held the cut under the cold tap, though he lost so much blood he almost died. Later, I also kept pigs, collecting potato peelings and any waste food from neighbours, which I boiled before feeding to the pigs.

Ripon Sale Room
Granny loved going to the Sale Room in Ripon, a town about ten miles south of Masham. We all benefited from what she bought. On Thursdays Ripon Market and the Sale Room auction were held. My gran would disappear for the whole day, which was also when *Cage Birds*, one of my grandfather's favourite magazines, came out (his other was *Exchange and Mart)*. I would collect the magazine from the newsagent and then disappear to leave him to read it from cover-to-cover. First, he would turn off the electric light. The only window in the living room looked out into a small yard and didn't let in much natural light, so the electricity burned all day - except Thursdays. He would settle into my gran's rocking chair by the window, put on his glasses, and read undisturbed in the semi-darkness, occasionally falling asleep, until late in the afternoon when my gran returned with her loot from the Sale Room.

I wouldn't be far away to see what she had brought for me. It was like Christmas every week, except that I got very little at Christmas. Gran would bossily march in, turn on the light, order granddad out of *her* rocking chair and send him down to pay the taxi waiting in the yard. This was not cheap for the twenty mile round trip from Ripon.

"Another load of rubbish," he would chunter under his breath as he went down the yard, not eager to pay the taxi but keen to see what she had bought. Occasionally, he got lucky!

One day my granddad didn't respond as ordered so gran went through to the shop, took out the locked cash box, smashed it open with a mallet, then paid the taxi herself. My granddad was a strong man, but very tolerant and would give in to her wild ways.

From the Sale Room came my first camera. It needed a bit of sticky tape to cover where it was cracked, but I took good snaps, some of which I still have. It sparked my enthusiasm for photography which has remained with me all my life.

On different occasions she brought me a cricket bat, a tennis racket, boxing gloves, books, binoculars, and a football. The latter was in good condition and made from strong leather, but you couldn't inflate it as the rubber inner had perished and it was impossible to buy a new one. A friend suggested I get a pig's bladder from the slaughterhouse. This was not a great success as we couldn't pump it up very hard, but it served for a while until the bladder burst.

Gran bought various musical instruments including a ukulele, a zither and a mouth organ. I tried but couldn't play them and didn't have the patience to practise and learn. One of the best things she brought back was a Meccano set. It was well used and many parts were missing, but I loved it and spent hours playing with it.

Occasionally I went to the Sale Room with her. I remember one time when she was bidding for an item she had set her heart on. Unfortunately, so had someone else who continued to bid every time gran did. But gran was not to be put off and shouted across the crowded room, "Don't you bid against me; I'm having it," and she did! The bidder was intimidated and didn't bid again. Gran would draw herself up to her full height, throw out her large chest and usually had her own way.

The other side of her character was very generous. Granddad was careful! He needed to be with her around. Though she wasn't particularly well-educated, she spoke without a strong accent and liked to think of herself as a bit above the working class. This came out when talking to anyone outside our family circle when she would put on her best accent, not quite 'cut glass' but very different to her normal speech. Unfortunately, as the conversation went on she would forget and slip back into her normal way. As a small boy I found this amusing. I once overheard my sister telling gran about a girl at school who had been in trouble. My gran exclaimed, "What do you expect from that family? After all, you don't get strawberries from gooseberry bushes!"

Fish Scales
Granddad was bald and was never seen without his cap, and seldom without a waistcoat in which he kept a little pencil in one pocket and a small penknife in another. The weekday waistcoat usually had a few fish scales on it, collected when cutting fish for the shop. At mealtimes he would cut a slice of bread - sliced bread was still to be invented! - hugging the loaf to his chest while cutting and turning the bread, which would collect a fish scale or two in the process. My granny would go mad and without hesitation throw something at him. He would laugh, which made her even more annoyed. At weekends or on whist drive nights his gold watch and chain would appear, proudly displayed from his best waistcoat pocket, this one without fish scales. Sometimes after a meal he would take a match stalk, sharpen it to a point with his penknife, and then use it as a toothpick to clean his teeth. This would infuriate my gran who once threw a sugar basin at him in her anger.

He had another habit that could be annoying. If gran or anyone else did something he didn't agree with he wouldn't shout or make a fuss, but instead he'd first look at the offending person, then up to the sky, tut-tutting by clicking his tongue on the roof of his mouth. This would usually have more effect than making a lot of noise. It certainly wound up gran and she'd shout, "Don't you bloody tut-tut at me, Ernest."

Granddad seldom swore but I remember one occasion when he let rip. He was kneeling by the coal house door chopping sticks. We were chatting and I think I must have distracted him, because he caught his hand with the axe. He jumped to his feet and cried out, "Hell flames of buggery, set a light to it!" I was quite shocked; I had never heard him use those words before, at least not strung together. Now I come to think of it I don't think I ever heard him use them again.

Though everything was rationed in the war, it wouldn't stop my gran from pouring sugar onto the fire if it was burning low and needed a quick boost. She also loved to read tea leaves. After drinking her tea – the first lot from the saucer if it was too hot - she would turn the cup upside down on the saucer, turn it round a few times then look inside and read out loud what she saw in the leaves. With a little imagination or, as she thought, with help from above, she predicted the future. During the war my uncle Jack was in the Army, stationed in Iceland. My gran would turn over the cup, look into the tea leaves and see a ship. We would all chorus, "Jack's coming home!" Strange as it may seem she was often right and what she saw would come to pass.

At the bottom of the yard was a little wooden shed where granddad prepared the fish and chips for the shop. When the potato peeler was running, you had to shout over the noise. Sometimes when he was in there working alone, he could be heard two streets away singing his favourite hymn, *Jerusalem*, at the top of his voice.

I often called round to my gran's on Sunday evenings after church. All the family (granny, granddad, my two aunts and my sister) would sit and listen to the radio, a huge radiogram from the Ripon Sale Room. We heard songs from the music hall and hymns. By about eight o'clock my gran would get bored; we knew what would happen and waited patiently. Eventually she would call out, "Get the cards out Ernest." We would all cheer and the rest of the evening would be spent playing cards. I could only watch them play Halfpenny Brag or Newmarket. I suppose my gran felt she had made an effort: no gambling until after 8 pm on the Lord's Day! Gran would never touch the radio which was too newfangled for her. But one day when they were listening she turned to my granddad and said, "Slow it down a bit Ernest, I can't hear what they're saying."

There were Sunday evenings that would become musical events in the seldom-used sitting room at the front of the house above the shop. My aunt Madie would play the piano and Doreen the violin. Then Madie would change over to the accordion and we would enjoy a sing-song of all the old music hall favourites from the 1920s and 1930s. If uncle Jack Marshal happened to be home from the Army he would play his ukulele and entertain us with his George Formby impersonation, at which he was very good. To my ears his Leeds accent didn't sound far different from George's fruity Lancashire lilt. Jack was very talented and also played the mouth organ and the spoons. These were the days before television, of course, when families had not yet lost the art of entertaining themselves.

One of the best things that came from the Sale Room was my first bike. It was a red two-wheeled Hercules. My father soon had me riding it: I was too scared of him not to. He held the bike while I got on. "Press down hard on the pedals and you'll keep your balance," he said. I did as I was told. He gave me a push and off I went down College Lane, past Lightfoot plumbers shop. Cycling felt good and I was sure my dad was still behind me steadying the bike, but when I looked over my shoulder (with a wobble) I was amazed to see him twenty yards back. I was on my own and still upright, so I kept peddling as I wasn't sure how to stop without falling off. I went round the block again and back to Nicholson's yard where my father was waiting, fumbled the brakes and came to a halt almost running into him – which could have ended my cycling career the same day it started!

This was a landmark. Until now I had walked everywhere. How much easier and quicker it was to peddle my bike. It would be a few years before I got a bike you didn't need to peddle, though sometimes it needed a push start!

Cycling was often, though not always, blissful in those days. There wasn't much motor traffic in a place like Masham and everyone seemed to cycle, even for work. One person we would see out and about on his bike was 'Rabbit' Close, a seller of rabbits. Many he caught himself and others he bought from farmers and other trappers for sale to butchers in the town. We'd see him riding slowly past with rabbits hung over the handlebars, swinging to and fro. Occasionally when he had been particularly successful his bike would be overloaded and he'd have to push while walking alongside. He'd buy rabbit skins but gave only a few coppers for them. Another was Billy Gill who cycled from his house in Silver Street, past our house in Red Lane and up Swinney Lane to where he kept pigs. He made a comical sight in his brown smock coat, heels on the peddles with his toes turned out to avoid the buckets of pig food dangling from the handlebars. He went so slowly I used to think he'd stall and fall off, but he never did.

Less funny - a lot less - was Tot Best. All us little boys did what we could to avoid him. He caught me one day when I was out on my own, then a few weeks later trapped a friend and me when we were walking together down by the river. We were terrified by what he did and his threats that we shouldn't tell a soul. And I didn't until now. There's little doubt that had I mentioned it to my father he would have done Tot Best some serious harm! Thankfully, Tot is long gone.

With Grandpa in Healy
Father's departure to the RAF left mother and me on our own in Red Lane. The training to become an aircraft mechanic was rigorous and lengthy, so he didn't get home on leave very often. To make matters worse, that first winter he was away was very severe, the coldest for many years with deep snow and ice for weeks. My mother decided we would go and live with her father, Bob Robson, and her sister Peggy in Healy, a small village near Masham. As I mentioned before, mother's dad, grandpa as we called him, was head gamekeeper for Lord Swinton, who owned Swinton Park and most of the surrounding land.

That cold winter was spent in his cold house. There was just a single open fire by which we all huddled during the evenings. Our feet were not allowed on the huge fender. The brass gleamed and the fireplace shone from the black lead aunt Peggy used to clean it. I would sit and gaze into the fire, watching the coal heat up, the tar bubble and the release of a jet of gas, which would flare up briefly then die.

There was no electricity in the house. As the evenings drew in my aunt would bring the oil lamp from its daytime place on the sideboard to the centre of the table, take off the glass, light the wicks (two side by side) then replace the glass with a very low light until the glass warmed. Then, the light was turned up to full power. Even then it was little more than a glow, but adequate nevertheless. As the lamp was low on the table it cast an eerie shadow on the white wall when you moved around the room.

Grandpa had a radio that he switched on for the news then immediately switched off again. We sat in silence much of the evening. There was not much in the way of conversation with my mum and aunt quietly knitting, while grandpa sat smoking his Capstan full strength cigarettes. He was a very quiet man, and was neither friendly nor unfriendly. He never picked me up in his arms as my other granddad did. He seemed totally wrapped up in his work though he didn't talk much about that either. The few occasions on which I felt close to grandpa was watching him clean his shotguns, which I found very interesting. Perhaps he had never recovered from losing his wife. There was a photograph of them together on the mantelpiece but nobody spoke of her.

He wore traditional gamekeeper clothes of brown tweed coat, plus-fours and matching, big tweed cap that was seldom off his nearly bald head. He wore thick knee-length stockings, hand-knitted by my aunt, and top quality, strong brown leather studded boots, always polished clean. When he walked across the room his boots made an echoing sound on the stone flags.

Covering parts of the floor were mats made by aunt Peggy from old clothes cut into strips, called 'Peg Rugs'. There was a thick one on the hearth in front of the fire and one each side of the table. The remainder of the floor was uncovered, just bare stone. On the occasions he bought a newspaper, grandpa would sit and read it from cover to cover. I remember one thing he particularly enjoyed - a bar of chocolate swilled down with a cup of tea, a taste I have since inherited! There was no sign of any other drink in the house and to my knowledge he never visited a pub.

Although mum and aunt Peggy were sisters I was aware they didn't like each other. Yes they talked, but it was always cool. I'll never know why; maybe Peggy resented the fact that my mother married and went away, whereas she was left at home to look after their elderly father. Although it appeared she had little prospect of marriage, she confounded the doubters years later, and I was the one to give her away.

My aunt baked her own bread and I loved the smell. She would knead the dough, putting it into tins which were placed on the fender in front of the fire to rise, before popping the tins in the oven. The baked bread didn't look much different when it came out and was quite pale, but it tasted good as did all her baking.

For many years she was the postwoman for the area and peddled her bicycle hundreds of miles over the hilly terrain. Once a week she rode the three miles to Masham for groceries. The weather had to be very bad to stop her. She was also a dinner lady at the local Kellbank school, where I attended that winter. Later she joined the Land Army, working in the Forestry Division felling timber.

There was no running water in the house and often during that winter it was not running outside either. Though wrapped round with straw and an old sack, the little tap had to be thawed with a kettle of hot water, and the water then carried indoors. The toilet was in a little outhouse round the corner of the house and up three stone steps. It was always referred to as 'the netty'. There was a long scrubbed white wooden bench with two holes. I couldn't picture two people side by side on the toilet and when I asked, I was told that when one was full the other was used until it was emptied. They each had a lid that you removed to do your business, then shook powder from a canister of what I think was lime onto what you left behind/below.

There were even fewer telephones in Healy than in Masham but by chance there was a telephone box at the bottom of our garden on the grass verge at the roadside. The door was left permanently wedged open as there were four or five houses within earshot. Whoever heard it ring first answered and then told the person who was being called. That was neighbourly!

At the back of the house was a small hen run but there was no chance of a fresh egg in the cold weather, as both grass and hen run were regularly buried in snow. I used to clear a patch, before giving the hens their corn.

Saving Donald Greg
My school friend at Kellbank, Donald Greg, was from a large family. His father ran the corn mill. Most villages had a mill where the local farmer took his corn for milling, wheat for flour and oats to be rolled for horse feed. The mill was a huge, tall building, powered by water from a stream that ran down from the hillside. Donald showed me how to start the great water wheel. Water came down a channel from the millpond at the back. He wound the handle that lifted the sluice gate letting the water in. Then we went inside, up a number of stone steps to a small room where he opened a door to reveal part of the water wheel. The wheel looked like a series of wooden steps. Donald stood on one, his weight, though light, moved the step down and he stepped on to the next one like a treadmill, climbing faster but going nowhere. As the wheel began to turn it gathered momentum then the water took over and he would jump off. The wheel turned faster and water splashed our feet. He closed the door, turned to me and smiled proudly. "A man's job," he said. He had seen his father start the wheel many times and this was something he could now do when his father was not around. After the demonstration he went outside to turn off the water so as not to empty the pond.

During the worst of the weather that winter, Kellbank School was closed for a while and, with snow on the ground, we were happy to go sledging. One day we were enjoying ourselves on a slope at the back of the mill. As we pulled our sledges back up the hill Donald, who was walking backwards while talking to me suddenly disappeared. He had walked over the edge into the cut. There was a loud crash as the ice broke where he landed and by the time I reached the edge he was disappearing through a hole into deep icy water.

I lay on the ground and reached over the side to grab him. His face appeared through the hole already looking frozen with shock and gasping for breath. I took hold of his sleeve and helped him scramble up the steep side of the cut. As soon as he was on his feet again he got the shakes and stood trembling from head to foot, mouth open, teeth chattering. He shook and tried to speak but nothing came out.

He didn't need to as I knew exactly what he needed. I grabbed his arm and rushed him into his house which was fortunately not far away. He was immediately surrounded by his large family of brothers and sisters, though there was more laughter than sympathy as his mother undressed him and dried him by the fire. When he was sufficiently revived and wrapped in a blanket, sitting with a hot drink in his hand, he turned to me and said, "Thanks Ken, you saved my life!"

When the worst of the winter was over we returned to our house in Red Lane, Masham, and I went back to my old infant school with Miss Ebsworth. In those days, most teachers were 'Miss' and thus single; if they married they had to leave the profession. I can still see the blackboard with the large frame abacus complete with rows of coloured beads for counting and we would use cowrie shells, kept in little tins, for the same purpose. There was also plasticene for making models. My schooling was soon interrupted - as it would be many times over the years, generally by my father and the need for my labour. This time, however, it was sickness: I had caught ringworm. My gran said it must have come from the cows at *that* farm with the Fleethams, but it turned out it was a different strain. Who knows where it came from but it stayed with me for weeks. I had to go out plastered with green ointment on my head, neck, legs and arms, which was all most uncomfortable. I was not able to play with other children so I spent my time at the Fleetham's Farm. I couldn't give ringworm to the cows as it was a human strain!

War Comes to Masham
As it was wartime every window had to be covered at night with dark curtains to stop the light showing through. These had to be lined and my mother machined them for us and for many neighbours on her faithful Singer sewing machine. Tennant's Fabric Shop was at the bottom of Red Lane. Mrs Tennant could hardly see and wore very thick bottle bottom glasses. When she measured the cloth she stretched it out on the counter along a brass yard measure screwed to the counter top. She would then bend down to see, so close her nose was almost touching the measure. I think it said 'Milliners' above the shop door. They sold cloth and lots of black fabric at this time, thus doing nicely out of the war for a short period. But they were very old-fashioned, failing to move with the times and eventually closed.

The Air Raid Patrol (ARP) warden patrolled the streets at night to make sure there was no light showing, or you would get a loud knock, "Put that light out," or "Don't you know there's a war on?" Windows in schools, offices, and public buildings also had adhesive tape criss-crossed over the panes to prevent the shattered glass flying in the event of an explosion. Iron railings were cut down and carted away. Aluminium pans were collected to be melted down and reused in the war effort. People willingly handed in their aluminium items to make, as we were told, Spitfires.

Masham had its Home Guard contingent who would parade on Sunday mornings in Park Square before going on their training routine, complete with wooden weapons!

During the war new clothes could be bought only with coupons, so nothing was thrown away. A good woollen item, though out of date and style, would be unravelled and wound into balls to reuse and make a new garment. Old clothes were cut into strips and made into rugs like aunt Peggy had done in Healy. Sweets were also rationed. The coupons had an E on them for four ounces, or a D for two ounces. Each child's ration worked out at four ounces per week. I had a friend called Bernard who came to Masham on a Saturday from the farm where he lived. He always had plenty of sweet coupons and told me his family didn't eat sweets so he had spare ones to sell. I bought some from him most weeks.

One Saturday I met him. "Any coupons Bernard," I asked. "Oh! I haven't got any yet," was his reply. That seemed odd. We walked round the town together, then called in Len Timm's shop on Leyburn Road. Bernard was friendly with him (I was soon to find out why) and went round behind the counter to chat. When Len went into the storeroom at the back of the shop Bernard's hand shot into the Oxo tin where the coupons were kept and grabbed some, stuffing them into his pocket. I said nothing. He chatted for a while with Len. I bought some coconut marshmallows before we left. When he got outside he took some of the coupons out of his pocket and handed them to me, holding out his other hand for payment. I took a firm grip on the Es and Ds before I told him I wouldn't pay for stolen coupons. Later when I thought about it, I felt a little uneasy now that I knew where the coupons really came from; not his family as he had told me. I knew shopkeepers had to send the coupons to the food office every month and the following sweet quota for Len, based on coupons returned, would be reduced. His shop was small and it wasn't fair. I stopped dealing with Bernard.

Along Comes Howard

My mother became pregnant and used to send me to the food office with a ration book to collect the orange juice and cod liver oil supplied free for pregnant mothers and babies.

On 8 October 1941, when I was six years of age, my brother Charles Howard was born. In the Walker way, he was always known as Howard. Father was on leave at the time and I remember going with him to visit my mother in Ripon Maternity Hospital. I looked down at this tiny shrivelled-looking little thing with gingery hair sleeping peacefully. Would he be a rival to my place with my mother? We grew up to do many things together - including some we should not have done - and along the way had the occasional fraternal fight, as brothers do. But he has an important place in much of my story when we became adults.

A few days after mother came home with my baby brother I overheard dad say, "I'm not going back; they can come and get me," and that's exactly what happened. A few days later the Military Police arrived at Red Lane to arrest my father. His leave had run out the week before and he was AWOL (absent without leave). They stood around while he packed his kit, not letting him out of sight for a moment, then took him away. I note from his service record that he was given fourteen days' detention.

My father had brought home some small pieces of perspex used in aircraft windows, and he showed me how to make rings, crosses, pendants and other items of jewellery. This meant cutting and filing them into shape, then polishing them to look like glass. I soon learned and made many items working indoors on long dark nights. Unfortunately, this led to a mishap when I almost burned the house down.

At the side of my bed in the little back room I had a pile of books. I placed one of the largest pieces of perspex on top with a candle to read by. I must have fallen asleep without blowing out the candle. Suddenly, I woke to the crackle of burning perspex with flames going up to the ceiling. I grabbed a blanket, threw it over the fire and successfully put it out. There was an awful smell in my smoke-filled bedroom. I eased open the window which was stiff and I was frightened to make any noise. I was nearly choking, but dare not cough. It took a long time to clean up and hide the mess but I could do nothing about the scorched wallpaper and the smoke-marked ceiling. I tried hard to make it look like a minor incident and in the morning told my mother, who fortunately didn't make a fuss. She was so pleased that I had moved fast to put out the fire. The room was cleaned and given a coat of distemper, though the smell lingered for a long time. The next time my gran gave me money for running errands I used it to buy a new candle holder. It could have been much worse if my father had been at home and there's little doubt that I would have felt the stair rod on my back!

During the war we often had air raid warnings. The siren was perched on top of the police station and would scream out, rising and falling in a long wail making your stomach churn. When I was at gran's we would all crowd into a small area under the stairs until the all-clear sounded, a loud continuous tone that we all welcomed.

Masham itself was not a target but was on a flight path for German bombers going to or returning from other targets such as the Barrow-in-Furness shipyards, but one night in 1941 we were bombed. Two land mines were dropped, one flattening the White Bear pub and in the process killing two people. The other landed in Taylor's Field off Leyburn Road. The patch was visible for years simply because nothing grew there. The story goes that a German bomber had not found his target and jettisoned the bombs on his way back to base. This allowed the pilot to increase his speed to get home that bit quicker, and he wouldn't have wanted to land with bombs onboard.

On River Bank and Battlements

Masham is on the River Ure, a lovely little waterway that starts in the Dales above Hawes, eventually joining the Ouse near York before flowing to the North Sea. On the Masham side of the river is the recreation ground, with football and cricket pitches, and a bowling green. On the edge of the ground in a recess stood an old World War One gun, the thick steel and iron wheels of which were rusting away. You could still feel the rifling grooves in the great barrel.

A little way downstream stood the old corn mill, now diesel-powered. Along with two or three of my best school friends I would tiptoe carefully across the narrow timber plank that spanned the deep cut where the water from the weir had fed the mill. The water was now calm but nevertheless the cut was deep and crossing the plank was frightening for us kids. Lower down was an island where we built a den with tree branches and bits of driftwood. We had to wade across to it with water up to our knees. Heavy rain in the Dales might cause the river to rise suddenly. I was always a bit nervous, constantly eyeing the water level with visions of being cut off by a huge wave and having to climb a tree until it went down. This never happened but the thought added to the excitement. We lit fires and roasted potatoes that had originally been intended for chips at my granddad's shop. Part of the river bank close to this mill had been used as a tip and when we dug in the banking we found lots of green glass tubing about the size of a cigar. We couldn't understand how it came to be there but the mill had been used to generate electricity in the past and maybe that was where it came from. For us, they made ideal pea-shooters.

We liked to go bird-nesting but were careful not to cause undue damage. We watched the nest until there were four or five eggs, then only took one before the bird started sitting on them. This way she would not forsake the nest. However, this consideration did not apply to jackdaws, crows, magpies, and pigeons, and we took all their eggs as they were considered pests by farmers.

Many of the pigeon nests were in fir trees and difficult to get to as the branches grew thinner as you climbed higher. They would occasionally break as you neared the nest, which itself was only a little platform the size and shape of a dinner plate made from twigs. Usually, there were only two pigeon eggs and both were removed.

There were pheasants, too, on all the farms, though legally they belonged to the Swinton estate and were reared to be shot by Lord Swinton and his friends from London, many of whom were well known Members of Parliament. It was strictly forbidden to interfere with pheasant nests, but we did anyway. They were easy to find on the ground among leaves and nettles and under bushes. If the pheasant was sitting we left the eggs to hatch; if not we would test an egg. To do this we'd make a hole in each end, one larger than the other. We'd hold a dock leaf or similar then blow into the small hole and the egg and yoke would come out onto the leaf. If it was fresh we would eat some and take the rest home. Pheasant eggs are a bit smaller than hen's eggs but good to fry or use in baking. Needless to say, my gamekeeper grandpa knew nothing of this.

The local policeman was Tiny Proud, a giant over seven feet tall, but a reasonable man who had his own way of dealing with things. One day he caught three of us in an orchard helping ourselves to apples. We couldn't make a quick getaway as the fence was high and topped with barbed wire. I got caught as a barb stuck in my leg. He grabbed my two friends, while waiting for me to unhook myself. We were then marched to the police station which was, unfortunately, close by. He then started to read us the Riot Act. My leg was bleeding quite badly so I overplayed the pain a bit with a few forced tears, while holding my leg. I was pleased to hear him say, "You had better get off home and get that seen to. I will speak to you later." I limped out of the station until I was out of sight, then ran home as fast as I could.

One of the most exciting and dangerous things we did was to climb the battlements of Masham Church. The door to the steps was kept locked but, as a choir boy, I knew where the key was kept. We climbed up the narrow spiral staircase to the chamber where the bell-ringers worked and where six ropes hung down with their soft fluffy grips. The ringers said it was a skilled job. You heaved on the rope to pull the weight of the bell, then let the rope slip through your hands at the right moment or you were taken with it up to the ceiling.

We climbed more steps to the next floor where a huge box contained the clock mechanism. I pencilled my name on the box in 1941 and it was still there in the 1980s. You listened for any whirring sound that told you the clock was about to strike as you didn't want to be near the bell when it did. The next set of steps took you through the belfry and past the great bells and the huge timbers that supported them.

The last steps were narrow and steep with a trap door that opened onto the battlement chamber. Often a few pigeons would flutter out as you entered. A small door that even as a boy you had to stoop to go through led outside. As you opened this door the wind rushed through. The battlements ran around the base of the church spire with a very narrow walkway between the edge and the spire. The stonework was not very high and we would only dare crawl round on our hands and knees, occasionally stopping to have a peep over the edge. From the top you could see right across the Market Place, over the trees and miles beyond. It felt so daring, but I was always relieved to step back inside. Occasionally, we were there when the clock struck. Standing only feet away from the bell certainly made my ears ring even with my hands over them.

One of the few telephones was in the Todd's house, Masham 202, just two doors away from my grandparents' fish and chip shop. The Todds didn't like neighbours using their phone or passing on messages, so we would only go there in an emergency. The phone was fixed on the wall next to a large fish tank, at the other side of which was a huge cage housing a mouldy-looking old parrot. To use the phone you had to lift the trumpet-shaped earpiece then wind a handle to start the call.

The Todd's house fronted on the Market Place and they had a shop selling bicycles and fishing tackle. The River Ure was very popular with anglers.

Arthur Todd had a Francis-Barnett motorcycle. He would sometimes take it out for a run, 'putt putting' down the yard, smoke curling out from the twin exhausts. He only went out on fine days and it still looked like new. He was a strange character. When there was a thunderstorm he would climb up into the church battlements to watch the lightning.

Arthur's brother, Tommy Todd, had a son, John, who was about my age. John loved comics and would trade fishing tackle, hooks, lines, floats and weights for them. He was a very good artist, as were others in his family. He could paint Masham Bridge to look as if you were standing right in front of it. I tried to copy his style but failed.

The two main fishing families in Masham were the Todds and the Sturdys, with much competition between them. Edwin Sturdy was a school friend of mine. His uncle was a shoe repairer during the week, but at weekends he was one of the keenest fishermen in the town. Behind his house in the garden was a little wooden shed. Directly under the one long window was a workbench where he sat to tie his own flies. These were made from pheasant and other birds' feathers, to which Edwin's uncle would add pieces of cotton and wool. It was most interesting to watch him. He would cut a piece of feather with a little sharp penknife, tie it to the hook, then wind it round, the feathers separating and fanning out to look like hairs on a fly. He would add a little tuft of white knitting wool tied to the end of the body, and there you had what he called, 'Sturdy's Fancy' - his own fly. It was fascinating to watch in action his large hands and thick fingers more used to the trade of repairing shoes.

Learning in the Countryside
On occasions after school, I went to play with my friend Wilf Jackson. The Jacksons had a farm at Spelderbanks, a wonderful place where we had lots of fun! When John, one of his older brothers, was working in the fields, we would shout across and call him names to wind him up. Sooner or later he would lose his temper and chase us. We would run but always stayed close to the farm buildings where we could hide, with the hay loft being our favourite spot. We would bury each other in the hay and wait trembling for his footsteps climbing the ladder. John didn't grope around in the hay trying to find us, he would just stamp around in his big boots until he heard a squeal as he crushed one of us. Then he would drag us out for a beating.

There was a large granary up some steps above one of the cow byres. The granary had a dry wooden floor where the corn was stored. The corn was kept to one side, and on the other was laid out possibly the best model railway I have ever seen. It had two lines complete with stations, bridges, tunnels, a passenger and goods train, trucks for coal, milk, tank carriers, GPO, livestock and, of course, grain. It was fascinating just to stand and watch the trains go round. It was set up by Wilf's older brothers and had been handed down to him, but they would still join in and play with it.

There were two woods on the farm. On the edge of one we built a tree house but, unfortunately, Wilf fell out of it one day and broke his leg. We put him onto an old door as a makeshift stretcher and carried him to his house. When he recovered we thought we had better stay at ground level. So this time our den was a dugout, covered with branches and turf. It was cold and damp and there was no lookout to spot the enemy, so it wasn't long before we were back to the tree house, taking a little more care this time. There were guard rails and ropes around the sides and steps. Part of the fun was when we had to leave in a hurry sliding down a rope like firemen, sometimes burning our hands.

The farm had four or five hen houses placed in different locations. At teatime we would collect the eggs and then at dusk, when the hens were all inside to roost, the door flaps were closed to keep out foxes. At first light next morning, the hens were let out (but not by me as I was at home by then).

However, the day came when I was very late home, causing my mother a great deal of worry. Before I had a bike, I would walk the mile and a half to Spelderbanks with Wilf after school, then come back on my own later before dark. On this occasion it was very late when I set off towards home, so I decided to take a more direct route. Instead of using the road I followed the course of the dried-up Swinney Beck stream. It was dusk as I strode along over the cobbles. Close to home, by which time it was almost dark, at Foxholme Lane the beck runs alongside the road. I scrambled up the bank, back to the smooth surface of the road and I heard my mother's voice. She was more relieved than angry as she'd been looking for me for the past hour helped by neighbours, one of whom had cycled up Fearby Road to the farm gate. He reported back that he hadn't seen me, which caused more anxiety. Well he wouldn't have seen me striding along the beck, would he!

When I was older I shot my first rabbit at Spelderbanks. When corn was cut it was the same procedure as with hay. A man with a gun would stand at each corner of the field as the binder went round and round. The rabbits would eventually make a run for it, only to expose themselves to the waiting guns, one of which was mine. Wilf's brother John showed me how to gut and skin the rabbit and my mother made it into a stew. I was pleased to provide us with a meal. We learned how to snare rabbits, and poach pheasants at night with a torch and an air gun as they roosted in the low branches.

Growing up in the countryside was fun and coming into contact with danger in small doses at an early age was, in my opinion, a great way to learn the boundaries. When the river was in flood we went to have a look, as it was exciting to see the water bubble up under the bridge arches and rise up over the bank. Logs, branches and even trees raced by in the torrent of brown water. My father was not there to hold my hand but I knew to keep my distance. We climbed trees and dropped branches, and we crept round the church battlements, all exciting, frightening, and dangerous things to do - but that was how we learned ... and there was not an adult in sight!

For those who didn't grow up in the country I had better explain 'dropping branches'. We knew every tree in the area, but for this we had to select one with long low branches. After climbing to the top where the branches are thinner and sway in the wind, we would descend to a lower branch and crawl along it from the trunk towards the end. As we did the branch sagged with our weight. Close to the end we'd slip over the side, hang down and work our way hand over hand to the end before dropping off. By this time, if we had judged it correctly, we should have been close to the ground and could just step off. But if we had made a wrong guess we were in for a thump. Occasionally the branch broke and we would land much sooner than planned. If it didn't sag enough we were in for a long drop, so choosing the right branch was important. This game was even more fun when the branch was overhanging the river - at a well chosen spot, of course, and with few clothes on.

Explosives – Keep Out!

Troops stationed at Masham created new interest. One of their exercises was to build a pontoon bridge over the Ure just below the main road bridge. They would arrive with a convoy of vehicles, park on the strip of land by the riverside, unload mountains of equipment, then ferry out the pontoon boats one at a time. These would be tied together to span the river, with decking fixed on top. All the vehicles would be driven across to the other side and lined up. The troops would have a look at the bridge to see what a good job they had done, drink tea, then drive the vehicles back, pull up the bridge, load the sections onto the lorries and motor away in convoy. We enjoyed watching them and it was not only us schoolchildren, as many local people gathered, too.

Another military task was to build ammunition dumps. (I think another part was to find wives as two of them married my aunts, both of father's younger sisters Madie and Doreen. Madie's husband, Jack Marshall, taught me to swear. It seemed to amuse him to hear a little blonde innocent-looking boy use such words - not the worst ones, though. He always gave me money so I could buy sweets, which because he came from Leeds he called 'spice'. Doreen's husband, Colin Dixon, was called uncle Jig and was also from Leeds.)

Curved steel shelters for ammunition dumps were erected behind hedgerows and under the trees on many country lanes. These shelters were camouflaged so as not to be seen from the air and served as storage for boxes of ammunition. The ends of the shelters had only canvas flaps hanging down to keep out the rain.

I was curious to see what was in there. I didn't ask any of my school friends to explore with me as this was such a dangerous task. I had to do it alone! I rode my bike up Leyburn Road close to Marfield, left it behind a hedge and crept along the row of shelters.

Signs read, 'Danger Explosives, Keep Out'. After a last look over my shoulder, I unfastened the securing wire, lifted the canvas flap and went in. There was a narrow gap between rows of boxes, some wood and some steel. I found it easy to remove the seals and clips to open a box. I expected to find shiny brass shells and bullets, but instead discovered only little blue and white bags tied with string. I opened a blue one and found it contained small grey granules like slate coal. I put some in a tin I had brought with me. Next, I opened a white bag. Inside, there were little bits of round yellow spaghetti-like pellets. I poured some into another tin being very careful as I knew what a spark could do. I replaced the bags and closed the boxes, making them look as undisturbed as when I found them.

I was scared to look outside fearing the police or army waiting for me, but all was clear. I closed the flap and fastened it to the peg, then crept along behind the hedge to where I had left my bike. Eyes left, eyes right - the coast was clear. I jumped on my bike and peddled home with my loot. I couldn't tell anyone. I felt like a bank robber and hid the stuff in a hole in the wall round at granddad's yard, high up so it wouldn't get damp, and covered it with a stone. I left it for things to cool down - or should I say until I cooled down!

A few days later I had to test it. I had a box of matches and took a very small quantity of the materials from each tin. These I placed on a lid and, at arm's length, lit a match. Thankfully, there was no explosion, just a little 'psst'. I later learned an explosion would only occur when the materials were packed tightly into a shell and ignited. The yellow stuff was cordite, though what was in the blue bags I never found out – after all, there was no way I could have asked anyone!

Grandmother's grave at Healey, North Yorkshire 1935

My mother as a child with her parents Bob and Jessie Robson 1915

Grandfather and great Grandfather Robson

Grandmother and Grandfather Walker

Masham Football team prior to WW11 ..... Bob Dale, the blacksmith, in trilby and Dad, fifth left, standing

Mother, Sister and Myself 1937

Ken 1937

Me with little Howard and Freda 1943

Howard with the Kitchen family from next door in Red Lane, Masham

My school photo approx 5 years old

40

CHAPTER 2
1942 TO 1945
THE WAR YEARS

In late 1942, mother, Howard and I joined my father in Cambridgeshire, or as we always called it, 'down the Fen'. Freda stayed with grandfather and granny in Masham. From now on until the war ended in 1945, we would live most of the time in the Fenlands with only short breaks back at Masham. We were now in the thick of things with regular German attacks on the airfields of the flat East Anglian countryside. As I grew up in this new environment I found that plenty more adventures came my way.

Dad finished his training on the Bristol Hercules engines powering Stirling bombers and was posted to 7 Squadron as an aircraft mechanic, based at Oakington Airfield just north of Cambridge. In those early years of the war he was also attached from time-to-time to other squadrons in the area, broadening his knowledge and experience of different engines. Finally a permanent posting came towards the latter part of 1942, which was to Mepal Airfield where he remained for the rest of the war. His role was to support the Stirlings and the following year the Lancasters of 75 Squadron Royal New Zealand Air Force. Once at Mepal, father obtained permission to live out of camp in lodgings and that was our cue to join him.

Our new home was in the heart of the Fens on the Isle of Ely, lodging with the Ding family at Coveney Post Office, about three and a half miles west of the town of Ely. It is a sad fact that the Dings were a mean, miserable lot who only took us in for the money. They didn't like us (I don't think they liked anyone) and we disliked them. Matters were made worse when I punched their spoilt brat of a son on the nose. He went sprawling over the coal heap, then ran back crying to his mother, literally black and blue!

We arrived at Coveney in the middle of the night after a long journey by train from Leeds, making several changes with many stops. Having lived in the Masham countryside in peace and quiet where the loudest noise had been a cow's bellow, we quickly realised we had moved to a war zone. The noise of aircraft overhead was deafening, with many returning very low looking for the airfield. Witchford Airfield was on one side and on the other, a couple of miles further to the west along the road to Chatteris, was my father's base at Mepal Airfield.

With all these aircraft flying around, the house would vibrate. Outside, you were almost blown off your feet as the planes came over so low. That first night I didn't sleep a wink, but I quickly adjusted to all the strange, new noises, showing how soon the young can get used to change.

We didn't stay long with the Dings, though long enough for me to make a big mistake that caused much trouble and led to a beating. I hated mealtimes. Bread was rationed by the government, but Mrs Ding rationed it further to one slice each, which was enough for her wimp of a son. I dared not ask for more as she would stare at me across the table as I ate it. Mrs Ding thought I was greedy and I thought she was mean. Later, my mother would bring food up to our bedroom.

The kitchen table was on one side of the room by the window. The paraffin stove was on the other end against the wall, with the oven sitting on top of it. A chair stood at the table by the side of the oven when not needed. Instead of carrying the chair properly I sat on it, then stood holding it to my bum and walked towards the table. Crash went the oven on the floor! Whoever had put the chair away had placed it too close to the oven and the chair back had become hooked. So when I moved the chair the oven came with it, with spectacular, unintended effect. There was a dreadful row. The Dings screamed and shouted. My mum lost her temper with me, something she seldom did unlike dad. She beat me, threw me outside and slammed the door, trying to make good the damage and appease the Dings. Across the road was an old, disused blacksmith's shop and I wandered in crying and feeling miserable. It was a long time before I was allowed back in disgrace to the house and sent to bed which was, in any event, better than being tortured by Mrs Ding's 'evil eye'.

My mother took me to church in Coveney. The priest, Father Beal, was a big man, with one eye and a patch over the other most of the time. Occasionally you would get a glimpse of the glass eye that he obviously preferred not to show. He lost his eye at Dunkirk and was invalided out of the Army, becoming the priest at Coveney Church. We liked him even though he was stern with a military air about him. If you were not at church on a Sunday, he called round at your house to find out why.

He ran his little place of worship on high church lines. I joined the choir and was proud to walk round the church swinging the incense burner, though not so proud of my next job: pumping the bellows for the organ. I found it quite tiring for a long hymn, and it reminded me of pumping the bellows for the blacksmith in Masham. (More than 40 years later I took my mother back. Father Beal was long gone, although we did find his grave in the churchyard and his picture in the vestry. The little church was much the same but there was no smell of incense, which must have died with him. The incense burner hanging on the wall was now unused. We took it down and my mother took a photograph of me holding it. We enjoyed stirring old memories and my mum loved the visit.)

Before we left the Dings there was another mishap, though not quite as bad as the incident with the oven. In winter when my father came home, I would go out and cover the car engine inside the bonnet with an old blanket and a coat. This would prevent the damp Fen air getting on the ignition and plugs overnight. After tea my father said he would go to Mepal Airfield and asked did I want to go with him. "Yes please," was my swift response; anything to escape Mrs Ding's evil eye for a while. It was a dark, cold evening when we set off. After about a mile there was a strange, burning, smouldering smell, and smoke began to appear round our feet. I had forgotten to take off the covers from the engine. Immediately, my father blamed me, saying it was my fault! Just as flames started to appear at the side of the bonnet dad pulled off the road. Never squeamish, he opened the bonnet, grabbed the covers, threw them on the ground and we both stamped out the flames. Fortunately, there was no damage to the engine and we were able to continue on our way, while my father chuntered on at *me* for my forgetfulness.

Fog on the Fens

Most of Cambridgeshire is flat and low, the Fens especially, making this ideal country for airfields for Germany-bound bombers. One problem that flyers faced, though, was fog. I recall standing with my mother on the edge of the fields at dusk watching the fog creep round. In the distance was Ely Cathedral, 'the Ship of the Fen' as it was locally known, which became first surrounded and then swallowed up in the grey mist. As it became thicker you could see only a few yards. Even the farmhouse and buildings near us were lost, until all I could see was my mother beside me. Then it was time for us to disappear indoors!

Driving conditions during the winter were dreadful. Fog would creep round at dusk and get thicker after dark. It would then freeze. There were no heaters or de-misters on the old cars. My father would wedge a matchbox under the bonnet so that warm air from the engine could escape and hit the windscreen. This didn't work when it was very cold. I have sat freezing for miles while dad drove with his door open, standing on the running board and peering over the door into the gloom with his left foot on the accelerator.

While we lived at the Dings I went to the school in Coveney. The local boys made fun of my Yorkshire accent, which led to a few fights. The schoolmaster, Mr James, was Welsh with quite a strong accent of his own, though none of the boys were brave enough to make fun of him. Being another outsider meant he liked and protected me as much as he could. Things improved when some London evacuees arrived. They were not as vulnerable as there were five of them. I joined them, north and south becoming allies against the East Anglians. One of the London girls, Irene Lewis, was lovely and we would play chase and kiss.

A local boy called Donald Gray lived in a council house at Wardy Hill. He came from a very poor family and always wore old clothes. At school one day a woman gave him a bundle to take home for the family. Next day when he came to school I noticed he was wearing two pairs of short trousers.

"Why two pairs Donald, it's not winter yet?" I asked.

"Well I like these." was his reply. "If I leave a pair at home my mother will sell them!" I told him, "When you go home after school give me one pair and I'll keep them safe until you need them - and don't worry Donald, I won't wear them."

I was pleased when we finally left the Dings and moved to Wentworth, lodging in an enormous, rundown old Rectory. The large kitchen had a long row of bells with wires running through tubes in the walls to every room in the house. I tried every one of them. In each room I pulled the handle then ran to the kitchen to see if the bell was still shaking. Many didn't work.

These new lodgings meant a change of school, just when I was settling in at Coveney. Now I had to go to school at Witchford, which meant starting all over again as a foreigner with a strange accent. I tried to fit in and would often say silly things to get attention or cause a laugh.

I was in trouble one day and sent to stand in the front porch. As I stood there I soon became bored. I looked around and found a handle on the wall. Investigating further I saw it was connected to a rod that ran up the wall in a rusty tube to the bell on top of the porch. It had long since broken and was not in use, but in my boredom I found that if I stood on a chair and pushed the handle up the rod would reach the bell. Standing on tiptoes on the chair I gave the rod an almighty push. There was a loud clang as the bell rang out for the first time in many years. I got down off my chair, put it back where it came from and faced the corner where I had been told to stand. I practised an innocent look for when I had to face the music! The teacher burst in; she couldn't believe her ears.

"Who rang the bell?' she asked. There was no answer to that so I kept quiet. My next word was, "Ouch!" as the cane landed on my fingers. I was in more trouble, but it caused a laugh with the other kids and my stock rose in the popularity stakes.

Monty the Dog

When we came out of school one day a circus was setting up in a field close by. It was not open but we went across to have a look and walked in to see the animals. One of the circus ladies was sitting outside her caravan with a spaniel and its litter of seven puppies. They looked lovely, coloured black and white with shiny coats.

"Does anyone want one?" she asked. "Free to a good home. The mother is a circus dog who does tricks and they will grow up to do the same."

Naturally, I was first in the queue and didn't give much thought to what my mum and dad would say. "Yes I'll have one," I said. Across the road was a little grocery shop. I ran in and asked for a cardboard box, big enough to carry the puppy home. The old lady went to the back and returned with a soap box. "That'll make him smell nice," she said.

I ran back to the circus field, panicking in case the circus lady had given them all away. She hadn't and put a lovely little pup in my box. He filled it perfectly and was snug for the trip home. "Make sure you look after him," she said. I tucked the box under my arm carefully after giving him a cuddle (he had a nice puppy smell). Now home to face the music!

For once there was no music, much to my amazement. My parents loved him. He was christened 'Monty' after Field Marshall Montgomery. He was supposed to be my dog but soon went everywhere in the car with my dad. The thought did cross my mind that as well as liking him, my father found him a good guard dog in the car, maybe putting off the military police from searching it for aviation fuel or black market goods. Occasionally, Monty would stand on his back legs as if starting a circus trick but he never completed it. I think he was only playing but we all thought him extra clever because he came from the circus. After the war he came back with us to Masham and lived many more years.

Next door to our home in the old Rectory was a farm. I overheard my mother telling dad one day that the baby of the farmer and his wife had died. It had been smothered by a cat curling up and sleeping on it in the pram. She told him the farmer, Jeff Langley, was so upset and angry that he took his twelve-bore shotgun and killed every cat he found in the village.

Sometimes on my way home from school I would ride my bike round by Mepal Airfield along the perimeter fence, looking for dad, The aircraft were not kept inside but were located on dispersal points all round the airfield, being prepared for action and loaded with bombs. Occasionally, I got a wave from dad or one of his mates. My dad also played football for the station team and was proud to play with such internationals as Tommy Lawton and Billy Liddle, two well known footballers who were also in the RAF at the time.

Ebenezer Farm

We didn't stay long at Wentworth and our next move was to Ebenezer Farm, West Fen, to live with the Spencer family, Charlie and Doris, and their children David and Dorothy. It was much better for us to live in a large farmhouse and the Spencers were much more welcoming than the Dings. It also meant I could move back to Coveney Primary School and pick up again with my old friends. However, there was one small problem: every day I had to cycle three miles each way to Coveney School along farm roads that were either dusty and dry, or very muddy when wet. The first time it rained I set off from school on my bike but didn't get far before the wheels became completely clogged with mud and wouldn't go round. I had to carry the bike all the way home. I told my dad and he looked at it and showed me how to set the mudguard so that it almost touched the wheel like a scraper. The mudguard would stop the mud clogging the wheel. It worked and I had no more trouble in the wet. Coveney would continue to be the school I attended until war's end and we returned to Yorkshire.

When I was growing up in Masham we stole apples from orchards that had probably less than a dozen trees, but here in Cambridgeshire, and particularly in Chiver's Orchards, there were rows of fruit trees that ran for miles and miles. I hadn't seen anything like it. The land was rich and fertile, with row upon row of fruit, vegetables, sugar beet, chicory, and potatoes.

On the way home from school one day I noticed a field of strawberries and a pile of baskets, but no one was around. What an opportunity, I thought, too good to miss! My school bag could hold enough for the whole family. I parked my bike and filled my bag, picking only the best mouth-watering strawberries and not eating a single one myself. In my mind I would eat only when the bag was full. At last, I had filled it up and stood up very pleased with myself. That is, until I realised a man was standing right by my side. I was in trouble again! He made me empty all the strawberries; what I had picked filled two baskets. He then took my name and address, saying he knew Mr Spencer where we stayed and would speak to him.

"Now off you go and tell Mr Spencer what has happened," he told me sternly.

I set off on the bike towards home but watched carefully as his car disappeared into the distance, followed by a cloud of dust. I had put a lot of effort into picking those strawberries and I felt cheated. So I went back and emptied one basket into my school bag (no time for two) and peddled home as fast as I could. I confessed to Mr Spencer who laughed it off. "Don't worry my lad," he said, as he ate a strawberry. "I'll have a word with him." I don't know if he did but that was the last I heard.

The next day as I approached the field I saw men and women picking the strawberries. I kept my distance looking for the farmer who had caught me. Luckily, neither his car nor he was there, so I waved to the pickers and peddled confidently past.

Charlie's Docky

I liked Charlie Spencer. He smiled a lot and seemed happy on his farm. And so he should, as while many men his age were fighting and dying in the war, he was getting rich from black market activities. He grew vegetables, peas, carrots, potatoes and a lot of chicory that was used to make a not very nice substitute coffee. Sometimes, late in the day, there would be a large trailer stacked with boxes of vegetables parked close to the house. During the night a lorry would arrive from London and next morning the trailer would be empty. Even in London where most of the food went, you could have plenty to eat. Rationing was only for poorer people.

One day when walking through the farm buildings, I noticed new straw in one corner. There were no animals in there so why had new straw been put down? When I stepped on it blood squelched up round my boots. I kicked the straw to the side and found the reason: scrapings of pig hair and skin where one had been recently slaughtered. Charlie had been a butcher before taking over his father's farm and this was pork and ham for the London mob - and cash for the lucky farmer! My father knew Charlie had lots of money in the house and for a joke told him that all the old five pound notes were to be called in. He must have swallowed it as he sent his wife Doris into Ely every day to change the notes into half-crown and two-shilling coins, which he kept in a milk churn!

While boosting their income selling food to others, the Spencers themselves ate frugally. I watched Charlie prepare his docky (lunch, to people in Fenland). This was not sandwiches like we northerners would have. He would cut about a third of the bread loaf, make a little hollow in the middle, then put in a knob of margarine, spoon in some jam or a chunk of cheese and cover it with the bit he had cut out. This, he would wrap in a tea towel or piece of cloth and put it carefully into his dinner bag along with a milk bottle filled with cold tea or Camp coffee.

Later, I would see Charlie sit on a piece of 'black oak', as the Fens farmers called it, at the edge of one of the fields. This was pulled up during ploughing by tractors, which went deeper than the old horse-pulled ploughs. As a result they often brought up old trees, many of which had been preserved in the boggy land for thousands of years. Charlie would carefully unwrap his parcel with a look of pleasure on his face, as if opening a surprise Christmas present. He spread the tea towel on his knee, positioned the loaf on top and began the ritual. He took out his little pen-knife from his waistcoat pocket, cut a small piece of bread, and spread a little margarine on it followed by jam or cheese. He placed a morsel in his mouth and chewed slowly as if it were caviar.

Charlie was a local man and used local names and expressions, some of which I couldn't understand. One day he came into the house looking annoyed and turned to Doris and said, "Those damned Diddicoys are back in the area. I've just seen them parked at the bottom of our lane." I wondered what Diddicoys were and went outside and looked down the lane to see four Gypsy caravans parked on the grass, their horses grazing peacefully close by.

Cooking was restricted to what was available and was often done with just a few simple ingredients. One of my mother's specialities was onion pudding, made with suet, flour and grated onions, wrapped in a muslin cloth and steamed. We always enjoyed it. One day, Charlie got a whiff of it. "What is it Kathleen?"

"Try a bit," my mother said proudly. He did and loved it. "It's very good. You must show Doris how to make it," Charlie said. Doris frowned. Like my mum she was not a good cook, but a few days later she made one, though it turned out rather heavy and soggy.

"You'll need more practice Doris to get it like Kathleen's," said Charlie. I don't think Doris ever tried it again, certainly not while we were there, and that might just have been my mother's one and only compliment on her cooking, too!

Sometimes my mother took me to the pictures in Ely and there was always a newsreel. Long before television, this was the way people saw what was happening in the world and kept abreast of the situation in the war. I have vivid memories of the day the Belsen concentration camp was liberated. Nothing like it had ever appeared before. People were shocked and horrified and many sat in their seats stunned, not believing their eyes. Some couldn't take it and left the cinema. My mother told me not to look but I wanted to see and put my hands over my eyes peeping through my fingers. I can still recall those images today. Years later when on National Service in Germany, our squadron visited Bergen-Belsen.

Lighting the Goosenecks
The Black Fenlands were very different to the hilly Yorkshire Dales. Most of the area was flat with drainage ditches and dykes intersecting the fields. There were plenty of willows about, many of them well-pollarded making them appear short and stubby. Ely Cathedral was used by German aircraft as a landmark when they came over looking for our airfields. On one occasion they shot down two of our bombers returning from a raid. Apparently, another plane had crash-landed blocking the runway, so our bombers had to circle while it was removed, making them easy targets for the Nazi fighters. One bomber crashed in a field just outside Coveney. Next morning on the way to school I stopped to watch it being recovered. We were not allowed near but from the road I could see the crumpled mass with bits strewn around the field. A Queen Mary recovery vehicle stood by with its long trailer, waiting to cart away the wreckage. After school I rushed back to the site. The large

sections had been moved but I could just see the tip of a twisted propeller blade sticking out of the ground. The engine itself had sunk deep into the black Fen. A few days later when everything was cleared away, I combed the area to collect pieces of perspex from the shattered windows.

The Fenland fog must have caused many problems for aircraft coming home looking for those elusive airfield landing lights. My father told us that when it was very foggy, airmen had to run along the edge of the runway lighting the 'gooseneck' flares (paraffin lamps like a kettle with a wick sticking out). They had to run even faster to put them out if enemy aircraft were around!

Often late at night or early morning, we would hear the bombers returning from raids and recognise the sound, with perhaps one 'off-song' limping home on three or even two engines. Sometimes they might not make it, crash-landing close to the airfields. Many aircrew lost their lives just a short distance from safety.

Most of the fields had a pile of black oak wood stacked at the side, just as in Charlie Spencer's fields. This was stacked to dry out and ended up being a very cheap source of fuel. Ebenezer Farm had an inglenook open fire and Charlie would roll on a huge chunk of black oak. It would burn slowly for days and, in fact, the fire never went out all the time we lived there.

After the misery of the Dings, life was much better with the Spencers at Ebenezer Farm. After school I often helped with a few jobs round the farm. One regular task was to collect the eggs. There was a small hen house where the hens were supposed to lay but they roamed free and many would lay 'away' in an old cart or oil drum, or under the edge of a haystack. There, they would sit on them until they hatched, then reappear in the yard followed by up to a dozen chicks. My job was to find the eggs before the hens started sitting. It wasn't easy as there were so many hiding places among the buildings and corn stacks, but it was fun.

I was busy there, too, at potato-picking time. My job was to ride on the horse-drawn cart, empty the full baskets heaved up by the men and throw the empty ones back into the field for refills. There were two gangs of pickers. The local one was mainly made up of women while the other gang was of men in khaki uniforms with a diamond-shaped patch on their backs. These were Italian POW's (prisoners of war), or as they became known 'Ities', and were from the nearby camp. They were kept separated from the female group.

One of the Italians fancied a woman in the other gang and he gave me messages to pass, firstly in Italian then in English. I remember one Italian phrase: he asked her for, "un bacio d' amore". I gave the message but it meant nothing to the girl until the next time round, when I told her the English translation which had been explained to me. He was asking her for "one kiss of love". She smiled, a little embarrassed. I don't know if he ever collected, but she got the message much to the disapproval of the other women in the gang! I was just a young boy but agreed with his choice; she was lovely. That was my first lesson in Italian. Many years later I spent a lot of time in Italy and learned much more of the language.

During the war the Italians were often criticised by the British for not wanting to fight and were considered cowardly. In later years in Italy, I spoke to an old man who had been through World War Two and put this to him. He said, "The majority of us didn't want the war or to fight. We wanted to be at home with our families." Well I would hardly call this cowardly; it sounds more like good old common sense!

Dad's Motor Trade

When the war started and petrol was rationed, many people took their cars off the road and parked them up. My father would search for them around the countryside and in garages, sheds and farmyards. I heard my mother ask, "Leslie, why do you go to the pub so often with Ackroyd?" (his mate).

"Well Kath, that's where I get my information from the locals on where I can find a laid-up car." It was a half-truth really for he did find many cars this way but he also liked his pint!

On one occasion I went with him to a farm and found parked in a corner of the yard an old Austin 10. It looked a wreck. As we walked up to it, hens flew out. It was filthy and was more like a hen house than a car. The tyres were flat, the head cloth lining was torn and there was hen shit on the leather seats. I thought this would be the one to get away but, no, he bought it, and the car was eventually made roadworthy again. I remember watching my mother help tack on a RAF blanket to cover the ragged roof lining. I did my bit with the cleaning, while Ackroyd helped with the mechanical work, and it was soon running round the camp. No MOT roadworthiness test was required in those days.

For those who could get petrol there was a good market for second-hand cars. Dad found it profitable selling vehicles to officers and aircrew on the camps. One evening when he came home, he told us he'd bought a little Standard 9 from a lady in Witcham. It hadn't been driven for two years and needed cleaning and repairing to get it running again. "Tomorrow, never mind school, you will learn more with me," said my father. I did learn, but many times in my life I have lacked the confidence a good education could have given me. But his word was law and there was no point in arguing: the next day I would not be at school.

I was up early next morning getting tools, oil, paraffin and cleaning rags ready. On his way to camp, dad left me at the house where the car was being kept. A nice old lady gave me the key to the garage and later in the day I had tea and biscuits with her. The car had been given a good home in a large dry garage with heating radiators. The vehicle was covered with a dust sheet, jacked up and set on blocks of wood to save the tyres. I set to work.

The first job was to pump up the tyres to the correct pressure. Fortunately, the instruction book was in the car. Next, I went round all the grease nipples, checked the brake rods, oiled and greased the connections, and made sure the handbrake was free and hadn't been left on. I spun the wheels to make sure they could move freely. Then I took out the blocks and lowered the car onto its wheels. When it was down I began to work on the engine, checking the oil level, taking out the plugs, pouring into each cylinder a little oil and paraffin, turning the handle over to free the piston and rings, and cleaned and set the plugs to 25^{thou} and the points to 12^{thou}.

Now it was time for the cleaning. There was no polish to make the car shine so I used a mixture of paraffin and oil, applied lightly with a soft rag. This made it shine for a while though it soon collected dust.

Father arrived later with the battery charged. He fitted it and primed the petrol pump. I put in the plugs while he wound the handle. It was his turn now as it was much harder with the plugs in. It soon coughed into life after its two-year sabbatical. Smoke belched out of the exhaust; maybe I had put a drop too much oil down the plug holes, but it settled down and was soon running sweetly. We looked at each other quite pleased with ourselves. I was not yet nine years old. I think he was occasionally pleased with me but always forgot to say. We went home for tea and then back to collect the car. Later that evening I asked, "Where's Ackroyd?"

"He's on duty tonight," was the reply.

"Well how do we get it home?" I asked.

"I'll show you," said my father.

He produced a tow rope and two cushions, then pushed the driving seat as far forward as it would go, placed the cushions on top and indicated for me to get in. "See if you can reach the pedals," he said. While my legs were growing, at eight I still had far to go to reach the pedals; I was about six inches too short. "Can you reach the handbrake?"

"Yes," I said.

"Well use that," was his reply, "or you'll have to stand up. You've seen Ackroyd do it now it's your turn." He hooked up the rope. "Now, whatever you do you must use the brake to **keep the rope tight!**"

* * * * *

By coincidence, seventeen years later I would say those same words to him and so I must jump forward briefly.

At the time we lived in Burley-in-Wharfedale in Yorkshire. My father had gone to visit relatives in Redcar. At about six in the evening the phone rang; he had broken down near Thirsk and asked if I would tow him home? He was in the pub car park at Busby Stoop. That didn't sound good to me! I couldn't imagine him just sitting in a broken-down car waiting for me. I found a rope and set off. I got there an hour and a half later and spotted the car. He wasn't in it. I knew where he would be and soon found him sitting on a bar stool with, at a guess, his third pint.

"Have a drink before we set off," he said. Well, I liked a pint but right at that moment I thought at least one of us should stay sober for the coming trip. While he finished his drink I went out and coupled up the rope. He came out grinning, obviously drunk, and scrambled into the car. I felt I was wasting my breath but I had to say it, **"Keep the rope tight!"**

I might as well have said it to the rope; my dad was already tight! The journey was a nightmare. He kept running over the rope with the front wheels and I had to stop, creep underneath and untangle it from the axle, knot it and start again. He just stood there laughing. "We'll get there all right," he said. The problem was that each time I knotted it, the rope got shorter and shorter and I was expecting him to run into me. We eventually reached home without further damage, just before closing time as it happened so I was able to have a well-earned pint.

* * * * *

Back to Witcham and the tow rope. We set off. I'll keep the rope tight, I thought, and use a little bit of handbrake from the start. We didn't get far before he stopped, came round and shouted, "I can hardly get going. Take the bloody brake off till we go down a hill."

We set off again. By now it was dark. I had dim sidelights only as the car headlights had not been fitted with hoods, as required by wartime regulations, and had to stay switched off. I couldn't see the tow rope and only just managed to make out the back of dad's car in the dark. I felt us pick up speed as we came to a downhill slope. I stood up with one hand on the wheel and the other on the handbrake. I kept squeezing the brake release so the ratchet wouldn't lock on. Downhill we went with me keeping the rope tight past the airfield where the runway ended close to the road, and where the huge Lancaster Bombers would pass just feet off the ground. Fortunately, the only traffic that night was overhead as aircraft set off from Mepal to bomb Germany. (My mother was once blown off her bike there by a low-passing bomber and fell into a ditch with her shopping. The mechanics ran across to make sure she was unhurt, after which they all had a good laugh.)

The rest of our journey went well. Most of it was on level ground, like most of the Isle of Ely. My father wasn't shouting so I assumed he was pleased. He must have been as I got the job! He didn't need Ackroyd any more; I was cheaper (no one was as cheap). We made many more trips like that one, towing cars back in the dark to be cleaned, recommissioned and sold. I think my father had a good sideline along with the black market sale of ham, eggs and chicken. I remember once he was in trouble for using aviation fuel in his car but it was hushed up ... maybe the ham and eggs supplied to the guardroom helped! I went into camp many times with him and saw the Military Police check his car both in and out through the gate. Sometimes they looked under the seats and in the boot, but at other times, depending on who was on duty, he was waved straight through!

Before he sold the little Standard my mother started learning to drive. It was an ideal car for learning, but my dad was far from being the ideal teacher. Mother was nervous and was made even more so by his impatient, intolerant shouting. She soon gave up and never tried again.

The Story of Living Things
I went to Mepal Airfield with my father to help with the Christmas deliveries of ham, pork, chickens and one or two turkeys, some still alive in wooden crates. They were handed out, father took the money and then the fun started! I don't know how many of the airmen, if any, had killed and plucked a bird before but everyone seemed to be having a go. In no time at all the hut was in chaos with feathers floating around and the smell of singeing as they landed on the big pot-bellied stove

glowing in the middle of the hut. I think it was about this time that one of the pluckers discovered that birds have fleas! The hut was in uproar. We left before the fleas jumped on us but still managed to go with a few feathers stuck to our clothes. A few days later, the Christmas party was held at the airfield. It was wonderful! There were not many other children so my little brother Howard and I had lots of attention and presents.

Christmas 1943 was a special occasion for me as I was given my first book, *The Story of Living Things*. During the war such books were difficult to obtain. Mother later told me she had sent in an order months before to the Waverley Book Company. I still have the book and, though faded, it remains a treasured possession with my mother's neat handwriting inside the cover. I'm sure this marked the start of my love of books. It has been a lasting regret that I didn't have the chance to read as many school books as I should have.

My father was a hard worker at this time, though in later years as I grew up he lost the appetite when he could pass work on to me. In addition to his official job as a mechanic, his car dealing and black market activities, dad repaired tractors for local farmers.

In Masham horses did most of the work with only a very occasional Fordson tractor to help out. But here in the Black Fenlands it was nearly all tractors and they needed repairing as new ones were in short supply. Dad would strip down the engines, recondition and rebuild them. I watched him refit the bearings, scrape and check them with red lead, then fit new piston rings, carefully setting the gaps. When rebuilt, such engines were so tight it took two men with an extension tube on the starting handle to turn them over; there were no starter motors or batteries in those days. They were fired into life on petrol and turned over when warm to TVO (tractor vaporising oil). My father was a good mechanic and in great demand.

He also managed to find time to study as an aircraft engine fitter and was often attached for short periods to other squadrons, meaning he had to understand different makes. He brought home the books. I was interested and would go through them with him, followed by question-and-answer sessions with me asking the questions. He worked first on huge 14-cylinder Bristol Hercules radial engines that powered Wellingtons, Stirlings and, later, a few Lancaster Bombers. Then, he started on Pegasus and Kestrel engines. Dad was also proficient in working on the exceptionally good and successful V12 Rolls Royce Merlin engine that powered Lancasters and Spitfires. By the age of eight or nine I understood how the internal combustion engine worked and could name every part of it, even remembering the firing order of the four- and six-cylinder car engines, 5hough not the twelve and fourteen-cylinder aircraft engines. I still have his book just in case I ever have the need!

In one of the camp toilets a cleaner had written on the wall, "Will the airman with a two-speed arsehole please shit in low gear!" This seemed to amuse my dad as I heard him repeat it several times to other airmen.

War Comes to an End

Until now most of the bombing raids on Germany had been carried out at night, but in the last months of the war daytime raids took over and we watched them setting off and, later, the survivors returning.

D-DAY, 6 June 1944. I stood with my mother for hours gazing into the sky watching the endless stream of aircraft. We tried but lost count of the hundreds of them. Where did they all come from? There were airfields all around us and we watched them gather in the sky, then head off south-east.

We did the same several months later when aircraft went to Arnhem towing the gliders loaded with troops and equipment. Many were towed by the Stirlings dad worked on. He was not up there in one, but he was doing his bit on the ground as a mechanic to make sure they had the best possible chance of getting there and back in one piece. We watched many return with the tow hawsers trailing. Sadly, some didn't come back but the raids had the desired effect and the war eventually came to an end. When I was very young and saw my first aircraft I had asked my mother why they didn't have trailers; maybe someone at the Air Ministry heard me. We were still living at Ebenezer Farm with the Spencers when the Germans surrendered. I remember it well. My mum used to say that when the war ends, "I'll pick up the table cloth by the corners, complete with crockery and all that's on it, and throw the lot into the street." Well, she didn't. "You can't do that when we're in someone else's house," was her excuse.

In the evening of VE (Victory in Europe) Day, 8 May 1945, we drove through Ely. It was packed with people celebrating: airmen, and civilians, young and old, flags flying, banners across the streets, with everyone so happy that the war, at least in Europe, was over. Our car moved at a snail's pace through the town centre but it was all good-humoured; there was a shared sense of relief and a smile on every face. Our car windows were wound down and arms reached in to shake hands. It was early morning when we got home. Even at the age of nearly ten I knew it was very special and can still remember it with absolute clarity.

Two weeks later on my birthday it was my time for a very special surprise. Books were still difficult to get but my mother had been able to buy another for me, entitled *British Birds*. Again, this was from the Waverley Book Company and had been ordered months in advance. I was thrilled! I treasured it then and still do. Inside the cover is written, 'Kenneth Walker, May 1945. West Fen, Coveney, Ely, Cambridgeshire,' in my mother's lovely neat pen-and-ink writing.

Ely was not on the front line but we had been in the war nevertheless, and had served a vital part of the nation's efforts. The Lancaster Bombers that my father worked on had helped bring it all to a close. Many of the aircrew I had met when dad took me on camp were no longer around to celebrate. I had watched them limping along in aircraft with engines, bodywork and crew missing, looking for an airfield to land on. I had seen aircraft half-buried in the ground when they didn't make it. I overheard dad telling mum about one Lancaster he was sent to work on that returned badly damaged. The rear gun turret had been shot away and all that remained of the gunner were bits of skin from his hands, frozen to the gun handles. It had been a serious matter. It wasn't a game. I knew what was going on even at that young age and now, thank God, it was all over and we could live in peace (well for a while anyway).

My dad new in the RAF, back row right

Lancaster Air and Ground Crew, Father back row second left

Lancaster ground crew - bombing up

RAF Mepal football team, Father back row 4th from right 1940's

Dad, Howard, Me, Mother 1942

The Commanding Officer
and All Ranks of the
RAF STATION MEPAL
request the pleasure of the
company of
John Kenneth WHEKER
at a Children's Christmas
Party to be held in the Officer's Mess
from 3.0 pm to 6.0 pm on Saturday
December 16th 1944.

Christmas Party Invitation Mepal 1944

Mepal Airfield 1979

Mother at Ebenezer Farm 1979

Mother at Mepal Airfield 1979

Mepal Memorial

What a difference 30 years makes!
With Beryl at Ebenezer Farm 2009

CHAPTER 3

1945 TO 1950
EARLY TEENAGE YEARS

If my father saw a white horse in a field as we passed he would always wet the tip of his finger on his tongue then make a cross on the toe of his shoe. "That's for good luck," he would say, and we would all do the same. If the horse happened to be pointing the way we were going we were sure to be lucky. I didn't ask him how this superstition started, but to this day I remember his habit and occasionally do the same myself when I see a white horse. Has it brought me luck? I don't know, but there has been much for which I can be thankful, so perhaps things have turned out for the best.

After the war we hung around in Cambridgeshire with my father being called upon to continue looking after the RAF's aircraft engines through towards the end of the year. Initially, Mepal Airfield was used to prepare bombers going out to the Far East for the continuing war effort against Japan. But being married with children meant my father was offered one of the first chances for being demobbed and this was an opportunity he wasn't going to miss. So it was that in the latter part of 1945 we were on the move back to Masham.

Dad had a car, one from all those he had found laid-up that he and I had brought back to running order. It was a little Austin 7 and it was in this that we travelled up the then single-carriageway A1. This Austin 7 was a wonderful car and I remember it well. The seats had rubber tubes in them which had to be pumped up to just the right pressure for comfort. I still remember that the distance home-to-home from Ebenezer Farm, West Fen, to Red Lane, Masham, was 183 miles, and I recall also that it took us all day. The Austin had a top speed of only 50 miles an hour and though we had a few picnic stops at the side of the road and there was very little traffic, progress was really slow.

Round the Dales in Winter
We soon settled back into life in the little cottage in Red Lane. My father took a job driving a milk lorry for Express Dairies, collecting full churns from the farms and taking them to the dairy depot at Leyburn. Sometimes I went with him. That winter of 1945-46 was mild but there was still snow and ice in the Dales. The farmers would put their milk churns on a stand at the side of the road and on cold days we'd often find ourselves skidding past such stops if they were on an icy hill, continuing down to the bottom.

When that happened, dad would get out of the lorry, walk back up the hill and pick up the heavy churns and carry them down to the lorry. I've seen him carrying a churn on his back with the milk leaking out of the top onto his hat and running down his face. He didn't like to miss a collection; the farmer needed the milk churn picked up and had to have the empties for the milk next day. For all his unreliability at other times, my father was conscientious and determined not to let down the people of the Dales.

I started back at Masham School just as the eleven-plus exams were due. It was great to catch up with all those friends from my early years, such as Edwin Sturdy, Wilf Jackson and John Todd. We had lots of scrapes and adventures still ahead of us! Our teacher, Mr Young, told me, "Your name is not on the list of examination papers. If we get a spare set you can sit the eleven-plus. Don't worry though, if you don't sit it this year you'll get another chance next year." As it happened he did get a spare set of papers and I was able to sit the exam. However, I wasn't well prepared and had no opportunity to revise as had the rest of the class. Above all, I had missed so much school during my time in the Fens that I knew I wasn't ready. I thought to myself, "Next year I will be better prepared." But when it came around, I was told that I was now too old. So that was that! There was to be no chance of a Grammar School education for me.

After attending so many different primary schools I found it difficult to fit in with the school authorities and was always in trouble, often getting the cane. Mr Young was a little unbalanced and would go wild over any small thing. After being caned, my fingers would burn and tingle as if on fire. I would go back to my desk keeping as straight a face as I could although I felt like crying, and gripped the iron part of the desk frame to cool my hand.

Our next teacher, Mr Jones was more reasonable and we got along a lot better. He always had a line of white along his lips as if he had been drinking from a milk bottle and hadn't wiped his mouth. Why he never dried it with a handkerchief I'll never know. I wanted to tell him but I knew this could be taken badly. By then I'd had enough of the cane.

In 1946 we moved from Red Lane to a brand new, three-bedroomed council house at No 4 Leyburn Road, Masham. Ex-servicemen like my father were given priority on rehousing and we were one of the first families to move to the new development built after the war. I had my own bedroom as did Howard, though his was very small.

I helped mother with the garden, part of which had been a field and another part was where the cement mixer stood when they were building. This should have been left for a rockery! It was hard work to make a garden of it but after strenuous effort over many months the concrete and stones were removed and we finally succeeded in getting things to grow. I remember my mother sending off for daffodil bulbs and parrot tulips that eventually grew along the edge of the path. The closest my father got to the garden was when he walked down this path.

Dad had a friend who was a farmer at Sutton Penn just outside Masham on Leyburn Road. I think it was where my father later bought meal for our pigs. This farmer had two German POWs working for him on the farm and my father made friends with them, inviting them back to our new house. We'd only just stopped fighting the Germans and my dad had helped prepare the aircraft to bomb them, but now the war was over father didn't bear them bad feeling, as many still did. Gustav and Herman were welcomed into our house to play cards, chat and drink the English tea that by now they were used to (TV was still a few years away). Very occasionally I saw beer bottles on the table. When the war ended some Axis POWs had to wait a long time for repatriation and they spent many evenings with us before returning to their homeland in 1947.

The Pigswill Boiler

My granddad still kept pigs so father decided that it would be a good idea for him to do the same: one to kill, and the other to sell to pay for the keep. Well, who do you suppose was to be the Pig Man? Yes, you're right - Kenneth. I think the only time my father came near them was when he threw an apple over the sty door. I don't know what frightened him most, the pigs or the thought of mucking them out!

I started collecting household waste, peelings, leftover food from all the houses nearby. I boiled this in an old copper boiler at the bottom of our garden, something that inevitably caused problems with those same neighbours. I learned what looked like a very clever and cheap way to create heat to power the boiler from a man called Frank Young. He wore an old ginger wig that was not a good fit and which, while not going grey, had become very tatty. I always watched him carefully, hoping it would blow off in the wind or slip as he worked, but it never did.

Frank's good idea was to use waste engine oil that you could get free from any garage as fuel for his pig food boiler. This oil would not burn on its own, and he had devised an apparently ingenious system. He put a metal tray under the boiler then put sand in it and an old rag soaked in paraffin to get a fire going. The engine oil was then fed into the tray dripping very slowly from a metal pipe with another pipe feeding in water, again dripping very slowly. Each droplet of water made the fire flare up. It had to be hot for this system to work, with the oil/water ratio carefully adjusted. Though it took a long time, the pigswill did eventually boil.

I was impressed and installed a similar system for my boiler. But there was one big difference. Mr Young's boiler was in a small garden allotment, far away from anyone's home, while mine was in the garden at the back of a row of council houses. My new idea lasted only until the first washing day when it was banned by the neighbours. To avoid complaints I turned to night-time boiling, but came unstuck when one of the neighbours left her washing line out overnight and next day found her whites covered in soot. My boiler had to be moved.

The 'Gallowa'

My grandparents' fish and chip shop was still the main provider of cooked meals in the Masham Market Place. The shop had a huge bay window facing out onto the Square on the sill of which were laid out my grandfather's fish knives and mallet. The window was decked out with fresh flowers in vases shaped like fishes standing on their tails, with their mouths wide open. My granny loved them and thought them appropriate for a fish shop. Similar vases were all over the house, some with fresh flowers in and others, unfortunately, with those awful artificial ones made by shaving pieces of wood and sold by the Gypsies. My gran always had some as they brought good luck, she said.

On one particular Sunday I joined gran in the front of the shop, looking out from the spot in the bay window where she liked to watch what was going on in the Market Place. From there you could see the church at the far side with people leaving after the service. An old man named Dr Cockcroft, who sang in the choir, had just left the church. He walked along the pavement then disappeared into the front door of the King's Head public house. She was aghast, "Did you see that? He has been in the house of God, then gone straight into the pub. What a hypocrite." My gran didn't visit either place, though very occasionally she would go to the Wesleyan Chapel.

In those years, I had many interesting talks with my granddad. He sometimes told me about the 1914-1918 war, and his experiences in France and Belgium. After the war, my grandparents had come to Masham from the Darlington/Stockton area, renting premises in the yard of the Bruce Arms pub where they set up their first fish and chip shop. Granddad would hawk fish around the town selling door-to-door with a hand cart. Later, he bought a pony or as he called it a 'Gallowa' (referring to a breed larger than a normal pony but smaller than a horse). In the 1920s he bought a van but my grandfather was an awful driver. During the First World War he had been in charge of the mules and horse transport in the trenches, which he made a good job of handling, but he was not as useful with anything mechanical.

Times were especially hard as they struggled to set up the business and my gran had to take in washing. When he was young my dad often had no shoes to wear and the poor diet of that period caused rickets, which made him bow-legged. He could still run fast however, especially after a football or sometimes when chasing me!

During the Second World War my granddad worked hard at his business and made a lot of money. I believe this was a justified reward for his service in the trenches. Troops stationed at Masham liked his fish and chips and there was always a queue outside the shop. Eventually, the soldiers were demobbed and left Masham. The Town Hall and other buildings which had been commandeered were handed back and peacetime life returned.

I called at my gran's house most days and she usually found me a job to earn some cash. I don't remember ever getting regular pocket money but my granny and granddad made me realise at a very young age that wages were not often given, but were earned by effort. I did odd jobs for granddad and ran errands for gran, but what I really wanted was regular work.

Tommy's Special Sausages

Miss Thistlewaite was the lady who owned the newsagents shop at the bottom of our street. My friend Edwin Sturdy worked there, and she took me on as a paper boy delivering in the mornings before school. But the pay was poor and I soon found a better job working for George Purvis as a butcher's boy, delivering orders on the shop bike. When I started I was barely eleven and could hardly reach the pedals even when the seat was lowered. Orders would be packed in the basket on the front of the bike and I would set off wobbling round the town.

The butcher and his right hand man, Tommy Beaver were more interested in racehorses than selling meat. Tommy had thick black hair always slicked down neatly with Brylcreem. In the back of the shop out of sight of customers, the *Sporting Pink* newspaper would be spread out on one of the chopping blocks. I think Tommy acted as an unofficial bookie; I don't think it was legal for him to take bets but I often saw money and slips of paper discreetly change hands.

When not delivering orders I helped with other jobs. One of them was assisting Tommy with making sausages. He liked to think his sausage recipe was special to him and was a secret that he tried to hide from me, but I watched him carefully and the only mystery was 'where was the meat?' During the day when serving customers he would trim any scraggy or bloodstained dark ends of meat or fat from a joint he was preparing. These he would throw into a bowl under the counter. Beef, mutton, pork, the whole lot would go into the same pot. The customer would think, "What a nice man. He trims off all the nasty bits and I get a lovely joint. Oh, I almost forgot, I'll take a pound of your lovely sausages, too."

Tommy would smile the sort of grin which to me always looked more like a smirk. He'd wrap up the sausages and hand them to the customer. Later, he would empty the bowl of offcuts into the mincer for his 'special recipe', bulking it up with rusks, some biscuit-coloured and a smaller amount pink. To finish them off he'd throw in a handful of spices and there you had it: 'Tommy's Special Sausages'. When there were any left he would generously give me some to take home. I would smile and say thank you, but they never made it to our frying pan. Instead, I gave them to a particularly large family who lived close by: the pigeons and crows of North Yorkshire!

Mr Purvis also delivered meat to the racing stables at Middleham and sometimes picked up a racing tip or two. I knew when he had something hot as he would send Tommy to another bookie in town and pass on all his bets. I listened for information to tell my granddad, who occasionally sent me with a wager to yet another bookie. I sometimes put on a small bet myself. The first one I can still remember, probably because it won. I had 6d each-way on *What no Sun*, a Middleham horse.

George Purvis was an old-style country butcher who had his own slaughterhouse and each week killed the animals for his shop. I kept well out of the way of this; I didn't like to see or hear what went on there. I did help at Christmas though, plucking chickens and turkeys till my finger ends were red raw. Mr Purvis lived in a house across the road from the shop and one of my jobs was to go down to the cellar to chop wood and fill the coal buckets. His wife was seldom without a cigarette in a mouth that was brown at one side from all the nicotine. Mrs Purvis had a lovely big dog and walked miles with it. Wet or fine you would see her striding out with the dog by her side, which was the only time she was without a cigarette and the long walks probably cleared a little of the nicotine from her lungs!

Home Guard Potatoes

Edwin Sturdy of the famous fishing family mentioned in Chapter One, was a good friend and lived close by. Together, we shared many adventures and seldom disagreed over anything, though one day we did fall out. I have to say, though, I cannot recall what it was about nor can I remember who was chasing whom, but we ended up in Fleetham's garden wrestling in the vegetable patch. Our house in Red Lane was just over the wall and my mother must have heard the fracas. Suddenly her head appeared over the wall and she shouted at us, "Stop fighting!" But things had gone too far and we were locked in mortal combat. Though the gate into the garden was not far away it was too distant for my mother who scrambled over the wall and separated us, then gave us a telling off, followed by a dusting down as we were covered in soil. It must have been serious as there was no handshake. Edwin slunk away home and my mother escorted me to our house. She was annoyed and showed me her precious silk stockings ruined with holes and ladders from climbing over the wall. I was amazed at how she managed to do this as the wall was at least a foot higher than she was. Perhaps it was a combination of anger and the thought of her little boy getting hurt that had motivated her!

During the war there had been a campaign known as 'Dig for Victory' to encourage people to grow their own vegetables. The need continued into peacetime as food rationing still blighted lives. So, in the late 1940s, Edwin Sturdy and I, by now reconciled after the fight, took on an allotment together. We grew 'Home Guard' potatoes, 'Little Wonder' peas, 'Ailsa Craig' onions and tomatoes, along with cabbages, cauliflowers, sprouts and other produce. It was hard work but good exercise and very rewarding. However fresh you buy your vegetables there is nothing to compare with the home-grown variety. Peas only made it to the pot in small quantities as I couldn't resist eating them as I fast as I picked them. Our vegetable crops could be dug up and in the pot in less than an hour; Bird's Eye couldn't beat that. We continued with our allotment until my job of potato peeling for my father took over from potato growing.

After the war there were a lot of ex-War Department surplus goods around. The Army and Navy store in Ripon had many items of clothing and equipment including parachutes. My mother would buy parachutes for the silk and cotton material they were made from, carefully unpicking the big triangular panels and using them to machine up new garments such as shirts and blouses.

Edwin and I had decided to try our own parachute jump and I cycled to Ripon and bought one from the Army and Navy store. We took it to Fleetham's fields to the tallest elm tree we could find, intending to hoist it up as high as we could climb and then jump. But when we spread it on the ground we realised that it was impossible because it was so big. The jump was cancelled. Instead, I took it to my mum and helped her unpick the stitching on the panels for her to make clothes on her sewing machine. Looking back, I have to say this was one of my better decisions in life. My first jump would turn out to be fifty years later with a paraglider off a ridge on Whernside.

Dad's Chippy

Following in his father's footsteps, my dad decided to open his own fish and chip shop in the small village of Wath, seven miles from Masham. During 1946 he had finished working for the dairy and started a fresh fish service, delivering to the North Yorkshire villages within a twelve to fifteen mile range of Masham. But now he wanted to expand and open a chippy. There had been one in Wath before the war but it had closed when hostilities broke out. My father rented the shop and we used the van from which he hawked fish during the day to take the fish, potatoes and fuel out to Wath on Wednesday and Friday evenings and Saturday lunchtimes. The fish and potatoes for dad's chippy were prepared in my granddad's shed, which he himself had used for decades for the same work. My dad would cut up the fish and prepare the batter, and I helped peel the potatoes. Though he would later pass most of the other jobs on to my mum and me, batter-making was something that he always did. I chopped the wood and filled the coal buckets which were loaded into the van, and off we would go to the little lock-up shop in Wath.

The fryer was on an old coal-fired range. This had a little metal plate on the front reading, 'Maker: Frank Ford, Halifax'. There were two pans with a fire under each end. It was a slow job getting the pans heated, using paper and wood as kindling to which we added coal. Slowly the fat would melt as it heated up. Sometimes there would be a little soot from the fire floating round the shop. My mother set out the wrapping paper; white paper was still in short supply and expensive at the time and that which we used was cut into small squares. Occasionally you would see a particle of soot land on the paper and my mother quickly moved to blow it off. Chip bags were threaded on a string and hung on a nail, ready to be filled for customers. We all wore white coats - mine a short one! My mother was as proud of her whites as she was of the cleanliness of the shop, and took great pride in washing and ironing them.

Many customers brought us their old newspapers for outer wrappings. These were checked, torn into single sheets and laid out in a neat pile. While this was going on I would chop the first bucket of chips. My dad wouldn't put them in until he could see a slight blue haze rising from the hot fat, occasionally throwing a chip into the fat to test it. If it came straight back to the top frothing the fat was hot enough. My father was the fryer; mother would wrap them up and sell them: 4d for a fish; 3d for chips. My job was to chop the chips. I had to stand on a box to reach the handle of a little square grill with criss-cross knives in it. I placed the spuds on one at a time, endways for longer chips and pulled down the handle at the same time letting go of the spud at the last minute to avoid chopping myself. The chips would fall into the bucket. Customers queuing to be served were amused at watching me trying to look good, chop fast and still keep my fingers!

As always, my father was very critical of us. To be truthful, he was critical of most people. If my poor mother dropped a chip when filling the bag he would kick it away and then glare or swear, embarrassing her. I don't think it was a good arrangement to live, work and be together twenty-four hours a day. They didn't have many disagreements as my mother usually kept quiet, "to keep the peace" as she would say.

I recall the occasional row with my mother's screams coming from the bedroom trying to calm him down, though I don't think he ever actually hit her. He had a short fuse with everyone and would quickly retaliate verbally if he was upset.

There were quite a number of regular customers. One evening when a woman who I suppose was trying to be amusing said loudly, "There's a right smell of fish in here," a few people laughed but my dad was not one of them. He turned round and shot back, "Well, there's two things that smell of fish." The place went quiet and the woman turned red. The joke had misfired and I never saw her in the shop again.

The Stamp Lady
One of our regular customers was Mrs Rand, a lovely old lady. She was only tiny but very polite, well spoken and friendly. If there was no one else in the shop at the time, she would hang back and enjoy a chat. I think she lived on her own as she always bought just a single fish.

Sometimes I would speak to her. I had just started collecting stamps and when I told her she said she had some I could have. The following week I kept an eye on the customers coming in and was pleased to see her at her usual time. When the other customers had left she handed me an envelope saying, "You will take care of it and keep it in your collection won't you." I first looked at the envelope and then at her face. Her eyes were moist as she told us that her only son had been killed in Burma during the war, and this envelope carried the letter with the tragic news from the War Graves Commission. I was only very young but understood clearly what this meant to her. She was close to tears as I looked into her eyes and promised that it would always stay in my collection. By now, Mrs Rand will be long gone to join her dear son, but I have kept my promise and still treasure that envelope with the stamps on after more than sixty years.

It was about this time that at school my name was changed from Ken Walker to 'Fishy Walker'. I hated the name and punched a few noses before realising I was stuck with it. What made things worse was that I knew I smelled of fish and chips. My clothes and hair smelled and I couldn't escape it. School had never been a happy place for me but this only made it worse.

The Winter of 1946-47
Unlike the year before, the winter of 1946-47 was particularly harsh and it snowed for weeks covering all the roads in the Dales with hard, packed-down snow and ice over six inches thick. Extreme cold snaps in December and January saw the temperature in England and Wales fall to minus 21 degrees. The weather brought large snowdrifts to the countryside, blocking roads and railways. February was one of the coldest months ever recorded and further heavy snow in early March made problems even worse. In the middle of the month, a quick thaw saw floods add to the misery. Farming areas such as the Dales were particularly hard hit with as many as a quarter of all sheep dying amid poor harvests of grain and potatoes.

There was no choice for people like us but to make the best of the conditions, get out and earn some money. My father had to travel very carefully on roads that were not at all suitable for driving. We still had to get out to Wath. But he was a very determined character and wouldn't let the snow stop him. In the event, it didn't prevent him getting to Wath and back, though it did cause many problems and upset my mother.

Three days a week we went to Wath as usual, and he also visited the other villages hawking his fresh fish. Driving back after closing the shop in the evenings was the hardest time. We would fill a bucket with ash from the fire so that if we became stuck we could throw it under the skidding wheels for grip. On the way back there is a steep hill down into Masham and during the bad weather my mother was so nervous she would get out and walk while I sat in with my dad. He would start down the hill with the van sliding sideways till we came to a stop. I think he enjoyed it - I certainly did! Fortunately he was a good driver and fearless. We would wait at the bottom of the hill for my mother and had a good laugh as she scrambled back into the van. On one occasion she fell on her backside in the snow much to my father's amusement!

One night, however, we came very close to grief when the van spun round on the ice as we passed over Masham Bridge with only the parapet wall preventing us going into the icy, fast-flowing river. The steel bumper bar on the van scraped along the wall leaving a deep groove that was a visible reminder for many years of how close we had come to disaster.

The shop had been open for about a year when my dad decided to operate a mobile fish and chip van instead. This meant he could visit several villages in a single evening rather than waiting for customers in a small village shop. Dad bought a large Bedford van that had started life as a furniture lorry I believe, and fitted it out with a gas-fired two-pan fryer, a chip chopper and all the other equipment. Then he cut a hole in the side and made a hinged flap from which he could serve customers. We all got roped in to help. My mother, my sister, and me took turns going out with my dad, to chop the chips and serve customers. We would travel round four or five villages every night, stopping between thirty and forty minutes in each. He would blow the horn as we drove into the village then stop at the regular place, in the centre where there were usually a few customers already waiting. The last stop of the evening always would be close to a pub!

On one of the nights when it was my turn to help, the last village we visited was Tanfield. Around 10 pm when the last customer had been served, my father slipped across to the Black Bull for a pint, leaving me to finish off and clean up ready for home. Some of the last customers had been local lads on their motorbikes who were still sitting around. I gazed at them with more than a little envy as motorbikes by now were heavily on my mind. One of them had a Norton and another a BSA. How I longed for one! I always gave the bikers a few extra chips when I served them.

Bush Beating

Another job I took when I wasn't helping my father or spending the occasional day at school, was 'bush beating' when Lord Swinton had a shooting day. The shooters were mainly after pheasants but they would shoot anything that moved, including rabbits, pigeons and hares. Our job was to walk under the gamekeepers' instructions in a line through the woods, driving the birds to the end where the guns were waiting. We also had to collect any birds that were 'winged' and wring their necks if they were not dead. Some of the beaters, I noticed, would hide one and go back for it later!

One of the school holidays coincided with potato-picking time. I think it was arranged this way in country areas, so school children could help bring in the harvest. One of my school friends was Roland Stillborn whose father, Arthur, would get a contract from a local farmer then put his gang of pickers together. I was one of them. Arthur would collect us each day in his Rolls Royce! Don't get too excited - it was an ancient thing with large narrow wire wheels. It had formerly seen service as a hearse but now the rear part of the body had been sawn off and wooden sides fitted, making the whole thing into a pickup truck. We all sat crowded in the back. Nevertheless, how many workers can say they were taken to and from work in a 'Roller'? Arthur was a hard taskmaster. His instructions were, "Heads down, arses up, that's the way to pick 'em up."

Every year the Sunderland Scouts came to Masham for their summer camp in a field near the bridge alongside the River Ure. We played and occasionally fought with them, and we always had a cricket match. I was the Masham team's opening bat, though I never scored many runs. Once, I stonewalled my way through an entire innings while others piled on the runs. Because I couldn't bowl I was the team's wicketkeeper.

I was keen on sport and always looked for something I could play well. I played football for the local Hunters' Quarry team. Hunters had a small quarry at Gebdykes, producing agricultural lime for spreading on the land. They also had a football side that played local village teams on Saturday afternoons, and I started to go with them as by now my father had closed down the fish and chip shop in Wath. An ex-Army or maybe ex-RAF lorry picked us up in Masham Market Place to take us to matches. It was a dull blue-grey Austin with a canvas hood over the back and two rows of wooden bench seats liberally sprinkled with lime dust from the quarry. I always needed a dusting down after riding to and from games.

When I first started going with them they called me their mascot but it wasn't long before I was being called on to play as I entered my teenage years. They were always short of players. After all who would want to run round a field chasing a ball after working all week, including Saturday mornings, in a quarry? This was when I got my first new football boots. I was thrilled with them and rubbed in so much dubbing that I made them heavier.

I remember playing one winter's day when it was snowing on the sharply sloped pitch in the village of Snape. I was playing on the wing, running for the ball as fast as my legs would carry me, up the hill and into the driving snow. One of the opposing team was doing the same but he was running downhill with a following wind, and he was much bigger than me. We crashed! I bounced off him and landed on the ground but managed to pass the ball before falling. I scrambled back to my feet as the other players came to my rescue. I had cut my lip in the collision but had butted the other player in the stomach, and he was winded and a bit unsteady on his feet. Both sides gave me a cheer for having a go against a full-grown man more than twice my size. They took a plaster from the first aid box and stuck it on my lip. We continued playing but not for long as the snow came down heavier and heavier, and the game was eventually called off. Both teams of players gave me a lot of attention and I felt like a hero.

Driving the Van
By this time I was about fourteen and had been driving since I was a little lad in the Black Fenlands during the war. But I hadn't tried anything like the huge Bedford ex-furniture fish and chip van. My father was keen to advance my driving skills and when he thought I could manage it I started to drive the fish van home from the outlying villages each night. Normally I liked driving and was keen to learn, but I hated that journey back from Tanfield in the dark. I had difficulty reaching the controls, especially the fierce clutch, and dreaded having to change down through the gears in a hurry on a hill.

When you leave Tanfield going towards Masham there's a long straight road. Along this I could just manage to get into top gear, but then the trouble started. There's a sharp right-hand bend as you turn up onto the steep hill. What made it more difficult was the fat splashing about in the pans for, although the lids were closed, it would slop out if you went too fast round a corner. So I couldn't get a run at the hill and often had to change gear just as I turned the corner. Then, as the hill became steeper, I would have to go down another gear into second. The gearbox was stiff making second gear difficult to engage, and what was worse was that by this time my father would be shouting and telling me how useless I was. Occasionally I would miss second and grind to a halt in the middle of the hill with the fat swishing about in the back. It would then be a matter of practising my hill starts with my father shouting instructions and me trying to remain calm while close to panic. The first time I made a mess of it he told me to get out, shouting, "You're useless and will never make a driver." He slid over into the driving seat and confidently took over the controls, setting off as I ran round to the passenger side and I just managed to scramble in as he accelerated up the hill.

Sadly for both of us, my father didn't live long enough for me to prove how wrong he was when I became a successful racing car driver. Dad was a hard taskmaster that's for sure, but I did learn from him and maybe my later achievements were due to his teaching. At the time, though, I was often terrified!
If peeling potatoes and bush beating were not enough, my father eased me into even more work. He had never given me pocket money but presented plenty of chances for me to earn money. I didn't mind the work when there was a reward as it meant I could save for future plans.

Before he had his own premises, all the preparatory work for the fish and chips business was done at my granddad's. The potatoes were stored in a narrow stone building adjoining the wooden shed. There was no light and occasionally you would find a potato that a rat had nibbled. Quite frankly, I didn't like going in there and always made a noise by rattling an empty bucket first to scare the rats away - before they could scare me. I don't suppose the occasional rat would bother my granddad after his experiences in the trenches on the Somme, but as a young teenager they could unnerve me.

At first I would fill the buckets for my father to put in the peeler, then he would cut out the eyes and bruised areas. Soon I was doing the lot while he drank tea and smoked with his friend Jack Musgrave. I tried to coax my younger brother Howard to help me fill the buckets, but he was not enthusiastic and deliberately picked only the big ones that jammed the machine when too many were put in together. I tried to encourage him with money and other inducements but that didn't work either. He didn't like the job and made it obvious by being as awkward as possible. I eventually gave up with Howard, as it was more trouble than doing all the work myself. This proved only a temporary respite for him as a few years later when I had escaped from home, he had to take up my roles of peeler and wet fish seller.

Around this time there was another arrival in the Walker household. In 1948 my parents had a baby daughter, Connie, a rather late arrival born sixteen years after Freda, their first. But there was to be no repeat of the treatment meted out to Howard and me, as Connie quickly became the apple of my father's eye. She had the cuddles he never had time to share with us.

The potatoes were bought from Stanley Alton, a local farmer who grew many acres of them. If the previous load had been harvested when it was wet, there would be a lot of soil among them left on the floor of the shed. My grandfather would shovel this into sacks and give it back to Stanley for a refund! Mr Alton had many workers on his farms but always delivered the spuds in a lorry in three-ton loads himself. It looked like a great personal service but I quickly learned there was another reason! After the potatoes had been unloaded, money would change hands. When my grandfather counted out a wad of cash, the farmer's greedy eyes lit up as his big, weathered hands closed round the bundle! He didn't trust anyone else and that was why he made all of the deliveries himself!

Just after potato-picking time, there were times when there was a glut and many were condemned for cattle feed and sold off cheaply. My father bought some for our pigs. When we got them home we found there was nothing wrong with the vast majority, they were just the result of overproduction. They had been sprayed with purple dye to identify them as animal feed, but the dye had been used sparingly and many were not coloured at all. I put some through the potato peeler and they came out looking as good as any other, so we used the best ones for chipping and gave the rest to the pigs. Once my father found how good they were, he went back for more. It was risky as legally they had been declared unfit for human consumption but I ate them myself and they were perfectly good potatoes. Our pigs provided good cover.

Filleting Fish
At the start of his frying enterprise, the fish for my father's shop came from a Hull merchant via rail, but after a while dad decided it would be a good idea if we went to the docks ourselves. We could make our own selection and we'd pay far less.

As you may have guessed, I was involved again which meant more time off school. It also involved an early morning start: very early as dad wanted to be on the West Hartlepool dock for the 6 am auction. This meant leaving Masham at 4 am. For me it was most interesting and one of those rare occasions when I was happier with my dad than being at school.

The fishermen unloaded their catches from small boats moored at the quayside, and the fish were laid out in boxes, mostly cod, haddock and plaice. These were the most popular, but there were lots of other kinds including some slimy and ugly-looking catfish and dogfish. The catch was displayed in ten-stone kits, long rows of boxes with many different kinds of fish.

You had to bid in the auction. The auctioneer went so fast I couldn't keep up with him. My dad would look at him and nod when he wanted to bid, and I would later discover he had bought three lots, one haddock and two cod. Fried cod was the most popular fish with the good people of the Dales villages.

Following the auction, father would go to a wholesaler to buy smaller amounts of plaice, halibut and lemon sole. We loaded the van, with the fish covered in ice from the ice store, then pop into a café for a mug of tea before setting off home.

We didn't have a fridge in those days so the fish was kept covered in ice in a cool part of granddad's shed. Now, the real work would start. Fish bought from the Hull merchant came ready filleted for frying, but this was a 'different kettle of fish' (excuse the pun)! Whole cod complete with their heads were much cheaper but entailed a lot more work. Some of the catch from Iceland was huge deep-sea cod, as it was called, and came almost a metre in length. My job was to cut off the head with the dull grey, flat eyes staring blankly at me, all the time taking care not to take any of the flesh. The gills would be removed and put to one side as there was flesh on them from which my mother would make fish cakes. Then my dad would take over and do the filleting.

After a while he discovered that buying this way involved much extra work that he couldn't pass on to my mother and me, so he lost interest and returned to buying ready-filleted fish from RW Hildred, fish merchant of Hull.

The Kid Catcher
When I wasn't on the docks, in the fields, driving a converted furniture van or chopping chips, I should have been at school. Inevitably, my attendance was dropping fast as dad kept me away to work for him and this was heading me towards trouble. The attendance officer, or as we called him the 'kid catcher', called at our house to speak to my father.

"Come in, sit down, have a cup of tea," said father in his friendliest manner. "Kath, put the kettle on." They would then sit and chat, my dad offering his cigarettes and doing all he could to make friends. The officer would write something acceptable to his superiors, my dad would sign it, and off went the kid catcher for another few months.

This worked for a while when I attended Masham School, but when I moved to Ripon Secondary Modern things changed. After about six weeks my form teacher called me to his desk and pointed to the red line showing that I had been absent every Wednesday.

"Why can't you come to school on a Wednesday like everyone else? Why are you so different?" he asked. He was angry and there was no point in making excuses, so I decided to tell him the truth. "Well Sir, Wednesday is my mother's day off from helping my father fish hawking." (My mother washed all our white overalls on a Wednesday.) "I have to help my father with his business." "Your business is to come to school," he snarled. "Take this register and go to the headmaster." I did as instructed and still remember that long walk along the corridor with the register tucked under my arm, dreading the coming confrontation with Mr Ward.

The Headmaster asked the same question and I gave the same answer. "Well, that's no excuse," he said reaching for his cane. "Hold out your hand." Whack! "Now the other." Whack it went again as he caned me on both hands.

It wasn't my fault but I had paid the penalty. "Now tell your father you must come to school." I thought: "Tell him yourself, you bastard, he will probably punch your nose." I felt aggrieved. That was one of the worst injustices I have suffered in my whole life. The headmaster and the form teacher were fools: I wanted to go to school but had no choice in the matter.

My father was not a great believer in education. He used to say, "They will educate everyone then nobody will want to do the work." One thing he was determined about was that I should remain 'a worker'!

Pop Ryder

The pressure continued to mount. The leaving age then was fourteen years and school attendance was compulsory until you reached this age. Parents and their children would be in trouble if they continued to avoid the law. It was not long before my father had another idea how to get around the kid catchers. As mentioned previously, my sister Freda lived with my grandparents and went to a private school with granny paying the fees. It was only a small school with about twenty pupils and was run by a lovely old man named Pop Ryder. He had earlier retired from one of the universities, Oxford or Cambridge I cannot remember which, and ran the school more as a hobby. Pop Ryder was a wonderful man and very clever.

I envied my sister having the benefit of his teaching for most of her school life, so you can imagine how pleased I was when dad said I could go there too. The downside was that I would have to pay the school fees myself, and the money would come out of my wages for peeling potatoes! Still, I could live with that; I was happy to go and have the chance to learn. What I didn't know until much later was that my dad knew there would be no attendance officer at Pop Ryder's to worry about. It was a small private school that the authorities didn't check. My mother's day off was safe.

Ironically, I was going to the best school possible to spend even less time there. You cannot have everything in life. Had I gone to school more often, perhaps I wouldn't have as much to write about.

I loved Pop Ryder's school and he was a true gentleman. My main misfortune is that I went there for less than a year before the school closed. My sister was Pop's favourite pupil. She was bright but 'cocky' with it and truly thought that she was the brightest star in our family. She never seemed to realise that she was the only one who had the chance to be bright.

Pop's school building was rundown with paint peeling off the walls, and had antique desks and only a very small open fire at the front for winter warmth. There were no school dinners; those who didn't live locally brought sandwiches in a lunch box. Despite all this though, it was a wonderful place for learning.

My short time at Pop's made a huge impression on me. He himself taught many different subjects including English, arithmetic, algebra, geometry, trigonometry, and poetry. Though I cannot recite many poems now, I can still recall my favourites: *I Remember, I Remember; Lucy Grey; The Village Blacksmith; The Sands of Dee; Inchcape Rock, Grey's Elegy in a Churchyard*; and one of Pop's favourites, *Daffodils.* All these were remembered from less than a year with him.

If only I had been able to go to his school regularly, how different my life could have been. Instead, I have gained most of what knowledge I have from the 'University of Life,' working my way through with short spells at a host of different schools. Einstein said knowledge comes from experience but in Pop Ryder's case it can also come from a good teacher. When Pop's school closed down I had to return to Ripon Secondary Modern for the last period before I could no longer be kept in education.

At this time, I had few close friends as they all went off to play together after school, while I went to the yard behind granddad's fish shop. During the days when dad hawked fish around the villages, it was here that he parked his van when he finished. While he would take 'afternoon tea' with a friend, it was my job to unload the vehicle and scrub it out ready for the next load of fish.

As my fourteenth birthday neared with an end to schooling looming, I had to think about my future. Before leaving school I approached Norman Chapman, a local plumber. I did this with the words of my grandfather in my ears, "Learn a trade," he said. This was something I was keen to do and Norman agreed to take me on as an apprentice, subject to my father's approval. But when dad heard he exploded. He marched around to Norman's and got me fired even before I had started. Any agreement with Norman was cancelled, leaving him in no doubt as to who made the decisions in the Walker household. All that was left for me was to join the family firm and what a prospect that was going to be.

This was a period of my early life when I was often unhappy. After doing all my chores, I would sit alone in my bedroom, gazing out of the window at the moon and wondering what was up there ... and what was in store for me down here.

Riding About
I had outgrown my little Hercules bike and wanted a better one. New was out of the question so I decided to build one from spare parts, some new and some second-hand. My sister's misfortune became my good fortune. One day, she parked her bike by the back door of our granny's house. It must have fallen down and my father fell

over it in the dark. In a rage he picked it up and threw it down the yard where it landed in a buckled state.

I did them all a favour and removed the scrap. I took it apart and saved the best bits for my new project. The wheels were buckled so I took them to Leslie Hall's cycle shop and he re-laced them using the centre hubs, fitting new spokes and alloy rims. I watched him fit the spokes, spin the wheel in a special jig and then tighten them so the wheel was true. I bought aluminium handlebars, a new seat and pedals. Soon I had a racer, or as near as I was likely to get. And it was all home-made mainly from spare parts.

I was quite well off due to peeling all those spuds for both my grandfather and my father's mobile chippy. I was paid one shilling (today, 5p) per tub and I peeled on average twenty tubs a week - about a ton of spuds! The potatoes went through a peeler with a carborundum stone spinning around and water washing through it. When the potatoes came out, my job was to cut out all the eyes and bruises with a short pointed kitchen knife. If you let them run longer in the peeler there was less to cut off, but my granddad was alive to this and would creep up and open the machine door before they were ground down. I didn't mind the work. The money gave me independence. I felt good with it in my pocket and I saved for the one thing I had identified as my major future project: a motorbike.

60 MPH

Joe Hodgon had a lovely new Sunbeam S7 motorbike, admired by all us would-be bikers. He offered me a ride on the pillion where his wife normally sat. "Yes please, I'd love a ride," was my quick reply. I climbed on, taking great care not to scratch the gleaming chrome and paintwork, and held on to his coat belt as he accelerated up Leyburn Road. In no time at all we were at Mile House where he turned round. I kept tucked in behind him out of the wind but as we speeded up I couldn't resist peeping over his shoulder. The wind was nearly blowing my head off, but through watering eyes I could see the speedometer with the needle pointing at 60 mph! With the wind in my face and tugging at my hair (I had plenty then!) it was the fastest I had ever travelled. It felt as if we were doing 100 mph. The fuse had been lit: I simply must have my own motorbike, though I would have to wait a while.

For the time being, it had to remain pedal power. But motorbikes were not the only thing starting to catch my eye: girls, too, came on the horizon. Along with a few school friends I would cycle over to Grewelthorpe to visit a few. At that time, the musical star Donald Peers was very popular with the young ladies, with songs like '*In a Shady Nook by a Babbling Brook*' and '*Powder your Face with Sunshine*'. So on the nights he was on the radio we had to leave early as they all rushed indoors to listen.

We often cycled the nine miles each way to Ripon to go to the pictures. Popular films at this time were Harry Lime in *The Third Man* and Alec Guinness in *Kind Hearts and Coronets*. Another was *Once a Jolly Swagman*, which was my favourite as it was about speedway riders. On one rare occasion my father took me to see the film *Stagecoach* starring John Wayne. He loved cowboy films and kept nudging me in the ribs with his elbow when he got excited.

I once rode to Ripon with Wilf Jackson especially to buy a 78 record from the shop Music For All. Wilf bought '12th Street Rag' and I purchased 'Ghost Riders in the Sky' by Burl Ives. Despite being fragile the 78s arrived home safely and I played mine on my wind-up gramophone (bought from the Sale Room, of course). Or I did until everyone was sick of it!

I cycled to Ripon to the dentist many times. Maybe it was the diet during the war that was partly responsible, but I didn't have good teeth and they needed a lot of work. Looking back I have to ask whether they needed as much treatment as they received, or if the dentist just needed the money. Week after week I rode down to Ripon for treatment. Some teeth were taken out and many more were filled. I would sit back in the dentist's chair, trying to relax and avoiding looking up his nose through his ginger moustache. Or I would watch the belt run round the wheels on the bends of the drill arm up to the electric motor, then back to the drill in his hand, going round and round and sometimes skidding when he pressed too hard on my tooth. He seemed to enjoy it, though I don't know whether this was because he was hurting me or reckoning up how much he was taking from the National Health Service. Dentists have never been my favourite people!

Now that I had a bike good enough, I joined the Masham Cycling Club, run by Mr Hunter who also managed the Co-op store that had been taken over from Watkinson's. On Sundays, eight or ten of us would go off for a sixty or seventy mile run through the Dales. This was how I first discovered the old passes between the Dales, unsurfaced tracks, often steep and rutted, that had been used years ago by peddlers, packmen and packhorses. On the steeper parts we had to push or even carry our bikes, but it was great to discover the area. Later, I was to revisit these parts on my motorbike and more recently I flew over them on a paraglider. I have seen a bit of the world but have always felt closest to the Dales - my neck of the woods, my roots! I love the area and always feel most comfortable there.

However on one of our cycle runs I felt most uncomfortable and unpopular. Along the main roads we rode in pairs in a little convoy close together, the front pair breaking the wind for the rest. I was in the second row when I touched the rear wheel of the bike in front making me wobble then lose control. I fell off and the riders behind were too close to take evasive action and piled into me. It was mayhem as about seven bikes and riders ended in a heap with me, the cause of it all, at the bottom. Fortunately no one was badly hurt, we untangled ourselves, stuck plasters on the grazed bits, straightened our bikes and went on our way. For the rest of the day I stayed at the back of the pack nursing a bruised thigh and knee from where I had hit the road. And it was much later towards evening before they were all speaking to me.

I also went on bike rides with my aunt Doreen who by now had married her soldier, my uncle Jig. They bought a tandem and fitted a sidecar so their little daughter Elizabeth could go along too. Her tiny ginger head would bob about as we rode through the country lanes.

We kept our bikes in a little wooden shed on Chapman Lane that had once been a shop. Jig would give me the key so that I could go round to clean my bike. The shed was heated by two old electric radiators, but it wasn't easy to know when they were on or off as they were so slow to heat up. Jig called in one day to find the little wooden shed as hot as an oven! I had been in two or three days previously and had left the radiators turned on. The timbers of the old shed had dried out as the wheel on the meter had spun round, clocking up a huge bill. He threatened me with having to pay but was too good-natured to carry it through.

Jig's Old Pipe

I have uncle Jig to thank for my being a non-smoker. When some of my school friends were trying their first Woodbine cigarettes I thought the time had come for me to try a smoke. I liked the smell of Jig's pipe, and thought this would be best for me.

Without him knowing I borrowed one of his pipes. He smoked Erinmore tobacco, so I bought an ounce of that and a box of matches at the same shop where he sometimes sent me. I wanted to be alone when I tried my first puff so went round to the disused Army washhouse behind the Women's Institute. I took some tobacco from the packet, rubbed it in my hands as I had seen him do, and loaded the pipe, pressing the mixture down tight. The pipe went in my mouth for a practice pull before I struck a match, held it to the tobacco and took a deep draw, followed by another and another. The tobacco glowed, a cloud of smoke rose, and suddenly I felt dizzy and sick. My head was spinning and I felt dreadful so I sat down pleased, at least, that I was on my own. The pipe was quite hot so I put it down and sat still for a few minutes. Eventually my dizziness passed but I still felt ill. I emptied the pipe down the drain and took a drink of water.

I sprinted home hoping the wind would blow away the smell of tobacco, but my head throbbed with every step. After the pipe had cooled down I slipped it back to where I had borrowed it from. I placed the tobacco discreetly into uncle Jig's pouch a bit at a time over the next few days to make sure he wouldn't notice.

So began and ended my smoking career - though I confess to having the occasional King Edward cigar when I felt affluent in later years.

When he was first demobbed, uncle Jig took a job working for ENSA Entertainment. The title letters were often jokingly referred to as 'Every Night Something Awful'. Film shows were very popular in the late 1940s and he went round village halls or institutes where there was no cinema with a mobile outfit, a van loaded with a projector and equipment. Occasionally, I went with him; for me it was a real treat and I loved it. He was the projectionist, my aunt Doreen sat by the door and took the money, and I would rewind the reels ready for the next show. It meant I could watch the film for nothing, sometimes twice-over when there were two houses. It was nice to have a break from wrapping fish and chips!

My sister and I did not always get along and one day this led to a fight. Freda was a fiery and tough girl, and being a couple of years older than me she was often more than my match. During the struggle I fell and trapped my arm against the shed door. I felt something snap and an awful jolt of pain went up my wrist as my arm went limp. I had to surrender! The next day my wrist was swollen and painful so I went to the doctor. He inspected my arm and gave me a bottle of a strong-smelling liniment to rub on it. But this didn't work and I was having great difficulty peeling spuds as I could hardly manage to hold the potato while I cut out the eyes with my good hand (there were no light duties at our firm). I tried to struggle on. It was not easy but there was no point complaining.

After a week my arm was still swollen and painful so I went back, this time seeing a different doctor. He suggested I had an x-ray which meant a trip to Harrogate Hospital, twenty miles away. I caught the bus to Ripon, then another to Harrogate, and then a third to the hospital just off Knaresborough Road. They x-rayed the arm and found it was broken! It was set in plaster with my arm held in a sling hung round my neck and I returned to Masham.

There were still no light duties for me as dad thought the plaster would support the break and make it easier for me to do my work. The cast came down to the wrist and wrapped around the middle of the hand I held the potato in when cutting out the eyes. The plaster soon became soggy and I had to return to hospital to have the arm re-plastered. The doctors and nurses were annoyed and told me that I wasn't to use that arm under any circumstances, and it had to stay in the sling until the break mended. I told them, "Yes, I'll do as you say," while thinking, "You try telling my dad!"

Dad in Austin 7 in 1947

Posing with my ukulele
Gran bought from the
sale room ..... early 40's

First suit with
long trousers 1949

Fish van 1948

Me, Freda, Howard and Connie at
Leyburn Road, Masham late 40's

CHAPTER 4
1950 TO 1953
MY FIRST MOTORBIKE

Maybe it was the local gymkhana that first sparked my interest. In the 1950s, many country towns and villages in Yorkshire held an annual sports day, often called a gymkhana, which would feature as a special attraction a motorcycle grass track race. Straw bales were put out to mark the circuit for the riders. Most were local novices, though occasionally someone would turn up with a speedway JAP bike and clean up, winning all the prizes on offer. He might be a top rider or perhaps just a hack speedway racer, but he would shine among the local lads.

The first grass track race I watched was at Masham in the late 1940s, and I found it riveting. The bikes drifted around corners on the greasy grass the same way as they did on cinder speedway tracks. One of the riders at this event was a local farmer and agricultural engineer, Raymond Chapman from Dallowgill. He had an old four-valve Rudge-engined bike that he built himself. This was lightning quick, despite the handicap of dragging the rider's huge bulk around the track. But the farmer was a bit special, too.

I chatted to him and asked a few questions, "What's the compression ratio of your engine?" "Don't know," was his reply. "I started with a standard piston and just kept welding bits on until it seemed right." It seemed right to me as it was he who collected the top prize.

The racing, the homespun practicalities, the speed and the risks: the bug bit deep. I became a passionate fan, addicted to the smell of exhaust fumes laced with Castrol R (an expensive vegetable oil then used in racing engines). My ears became attuned to the exhaust notes. Mozart came second with his 'Clarinet Concerto', but for now this was *my* music, played with a twist grip. Later, when I bought my first motorbike I bought a pint of Castrol R and put a small amount in the petrol tank to make it smell like a racer.

The bug had been growing for years. By the time I was fourteen, I started spending most of my free time looking at and reading about motorbikes. I would have my head buried in a copy of *Motor Cycle Weekly* or *Speedway* magazine, or a host of books on the subject such as *Tuning for Speed* by Phil Irving. My heroes at the time were Geoff Duke and Les Graham, both of whom were champion International Isle of Man TT (Tourist Trophy) racers. First run in 1907, the Isle of Man TT was the most famous motorbike race in Britain and enjoyed its heyday from 1947 through the 1950s as a generation of boys were able to afford a motorcycle of their own.

My passion for motorcycling dominated all my teenage years.

Joe's BSA

As I guessed he would, my father was opposed to me having a motorbike at first. He had ridden one himself when courting my mum and I had heard talk of his wild ways racing up and down the Masham-to-Healy road with my mother clinging on behind. I had to find a way to get a motorbike. Pleading with my father would never work, but then I had a brilliant idea. I had seen an old 250cc hand-change BSA in Joe Brownless' yard. It was hardly a grass tracker, but was good for a start. I waited to catch my father in a good mood. After much dithering, mainly caused by fear, I blurted out, "Dad, I've seen an old motorbike in Joe's yard. I know I'm only fifteen and can't ride yet, but I think there is profit to be made if we do it up. I'll strip it down if you'll paint it." My father was never one to be gullible, far from it, but he fell for the idea hook, line and sinker! What caught his attention was the profit motive, buying and selling had passed down from his father to him, and now to me. He had bought a new paint spray gun that he used for painting cars and loved working with it. For me, my trump card, profit, while appealing as a motive further down the line, was buried beneath my first great desire: I just wanted to ride this BSA, licence or no licence.

"How much does Joe want for it?" asked my dad. "I don't know," I lied.

"Find out, but don't give him what he asks." My heart raced! "Have you got the money?"

"Yes," I said. Peeling a ton of spuds a week had put money into my pocket, and my motorbike project was why I had saved so hard. I couldn't believe my luck! The first opportunity I was off to see Joe.

Joe Brownless came from Darlington. After leaving the Army he set up a small garage and repair business in Masham. He had a new piece of engineering equipment called a 'welder', and was very good at using it to repair cars and agricultural equipment. Joe had the fastest Jowett van in the area … in fact in any area. He would fly around Masham looking for work (and girls). It was bright green and you kept out of the way. You always knew when it was about to come into sight as the engine had a sound of its own: the twin cylinder throb! We all believed it was painted green so as not to be seen parked in country lanes with one of his girlfriends, or later with Dorothy who he eventually married.

I went to his yard. "Does your dad know you're here?" he asked. Joe knew my father well. In fact, most of Masham knew him and all understood he was not a man to cross.

"How much do you want for that old BSA and will it go?" I asked.

"It's a good bike and only needs some petrol and a clean. I'll take seven quid for it."

"Seven pounds!" I replied. "I haven't that much money. I'll give you five pounds."

"I'll make it six as I know your dad." I dared not haggle any more; I didn't want to risk losing out. I would even have given him the seven pounds to get it. I was almost bursting with excitement which I was finding difficult to hold back. My potato money was in my pocket, waiting. "Ok, I'll give you six pounds, but if the bike won't go my dad will be round to see you." I paid him. He gave me the green registration documents. At the top of the page in large letters was the registration number: HL5682. I looked at the previous owners then at the new owner space where my name would go. I had it!

In its day, BSA was a leader and an innovator in the manufacturing of motorcycles, spearheading Britain's leadership all around the world. At the height of its popularity in 1951, BSA was the biggest manufacturer of motorbikes in the world with one in four bikes in the UK a 'Beezer' (as they were called).

My father rented a large hut that had been the NAAFI when troops were stationed at Masham in the Second World War, and part of this was to become our workshop for renovating the BSA. I pushed it there going the long way round so that as many of my school friends could see me as possible. I almost dropped it with excitement. I think my dad was a little taken aback when he saw me with the bike, not expecting me to close the deal so fast. He looked at the petrol tank with its paint peeling and the chrome corroding. "I'll spray the tank a nice bright green," he said. My plan had worked. Now that I had a motorbike I was certain things would start to improve.

Father took charge of starting it, setting the points at 12 thou and the spark plugs to 25 thou, then kick-starting it. Eventually, it fired into life, smoke pouring from the exhaust with a few rattles coming from the engine till the oil passed round. I turned the twist grip to open the throttle. I was so excited that I don't know if the bike shook me or I shook the bike.

I stripped it down for the paint job and gave it a thorough check. I went as far as to take off the cylinder head, something I didn't need to do but I wanted to look inside to see how it worked. The bike was put back together, now with shiny black mudguards and framework. My dad had taken a lot of care spraying the petrol tank bright green and it looked like new. "Ready for sale now!" he said. No chance, I told myself. He told me to put an advert in the paper which I did, setting such a high price I knew it would put off potential buyers.

Passing the Test

The two nights a week my elder sister Freda worked with my dad in the fish and chip van were also my nights off. So, while they were working miles away I felt safe to take my Beezer out on the roads for a ride. The NAAFI hut was on the edge of town so it was easy to sneak off up the back lane out of Masham. The exhilaration of winding the throttle around to the stop position, doing all of 60 mph, was breathtaking.

As my sixteenth birthday approached I applied for a driving licence. By this time I had ridden quite a lot and had made a thorough study of the Highway Code. I thought why not be clever and put in for the motorcycle test as soon as my birthday arrived. The date of my test was arranged just a few days after I was sixteen and off I went to Harrogate with my L-plates (learner) on, fully confident that I'd be able to throw them over a hedge on the way back. Well it didn't go quite like that.

When I arrived at the examination office in Harrogate I looked for somewhere to park as the bike didn't have a stand. The pavement was wide so I wheeled the bike onto it and leaned it against the wall. I then went inside, up the stairs to the office and signed in. A few minutes later we came down the steps, the examiner first. When he got to the bottom he couldn't see the bike. "Where is it?" he asked. "Just round to the left by the wall," I replied.

"Get it off the pavement; it's an offence," he said.

Then he spotted a pool of oil underneath as I wheeled the bike back to the road. "You'll have to clean that up before you leave," he told me. This was not exactly the best of beginnings. I tried to start the bike, kicking and kicking it over, but it wouldn't start. I felt embarrassed. Passers-by were staring as was the examiner.

"I'll have to change the plug." "Well go home and change it, then come back when your bike is fixed, and clean up that oil before you leave." I made a good job of soaking up most of the oil with a rag and changed the plug before heading home, leaving another small patch that had dripped out while I cleaned up the first one. My L-plates were still intact, regretfully. I had failed the test, or should I say the bike had. A victorious return had been planned but instead I sneaked in the back way.

Straight away, I applied for a re-test, this time it was in Northallerton. I set off with the bike well-tuned and fitted with a new plug. All went well and I passed. That was fifty-nine years ago. I threw away the L-plates and rode back triumphantly into Masham through the main streets - twice, in fact, to make sure everyone had a chance to see!

You might expect the two petrol garages in Masham to be at opposite ends of town but they stood side by side, not much more than a car's width apart at the bottom of Leyburn Road, next to where the White Bear pub had stood before it was flattened by a German bomb. Both garages were made from wood with Todd's garage painted brown and green, and Holland's garage grey and black.

They were owned by two quite distinct families and sold different brands of petrol: Todds selling *Power* and *BP*, while Hollands sold *National Benzole*. On weekends, they would both be open for customers to decide which brand they preferred. Mr Holland kept a low profile, observing business from inside his garage. Tommy Todd, on the other hand, would stand in his doorway looking for customers, arms folded, gently rocking to and fro, an anxious smile on his face while squinting sideways to see what Hollands were doing. If two or three cars chose the opposition he would turn and shuffle 'penguin style' back to his office where brother Percy sat behind the desk. He would have a chunter, then return to the doorway, turn on his smile again and try to attract the next customer by sheer willpower.

At this time, petrol was dispensed from an old pump with two glass bowls. You wound a handle to fill one, and then emptied it into the car while filling the other bowl. Todds was where you took your wireless accumulator (battery) to be charged. Tommy and Percy were also agents for Cyclemaster, a motorised wheel that you could fit in place of the rear wheel on a bicycle to enable the cyclist to reduce pedalling. And it was the Todd brothers who were agents for BSA motorcycles. Tommy's son John - who used to trade comics for fishing tackle when we were boys - had a BSA Bantam, but this wasn't powerful enough to keep up with my 250cc when we went out for a run together.

Obstacles at Melmerby

I soon had the measure of my BSA and felt confident riding it, but I was keen to test my mettle against other riders in a competitive race (I use the word loosely). The first opportunity was at the Melmerby village sports day and I entered my BSA in the last event, a motorbike obstacle race. Riders raced around the outside of the running track on the grass for six laps, but you had to stop each time at the start/finish line to negotiate some obstacles on foot. These included a sack race, an obstacle course and something that involved creeping through hoops. As I still didn't have a stand for the bike, I was allowed a helper who held it while I negotiated the obstacles. It was fabulous. At the bends I threw the bike over as far as it would go without depositing me on my backside, drifting around like a speedway rider with the footrests scraping the grass.

Although it was a novice event mainly for locals, my bike looked the most out of place. For a start it was the only one with hand-change gears, road tyres and lights. The rest were stripped down as proper grass track racers. I was the youngest and my bike was probably the oldest one that day. The crowd must have enjoyed my efforts though, as a loud cheer went up when I passed the finishing line. Although I didn't win I was given a special award!

The following week we were in the same village with our chip van. My dad was frying and I was serving customers when a man in the queue called to father, "Your lad did well at our sports day last Saturday." I put a finger to my lips and motioned him quiet but it was too late, dad had heard.

"What did you say?" he asked. The man ignored me and repeated it to my dad, who looked at me with blank silence. He didn't mention it then or ever after. As we drove home in the chip van we kept our thoughts to ourselves. Was he seeing himself in me? Was he proud? I'll never know. He was not a man for compliments; criticism, yes; compliments no! According to him I don't think I ever did anything right. If I dared question his authority he would just say, "Because I said so." Well, that's the most stupid saying I ever heard. I never said it to my children and later, when I had more than forty men working for me, I went to great lengths to explain what I wanted and why.

The Three-Wheeler

Now I had a licence dad must have thought it was 'payback' time. In exchange for allowing me to buy the motorbike I could drive a van and hawk fish for him! He bought a James three-wheeler van that could be driven on a motorcycle licence, providing it didn't have a reverse gear. Well it did have a reverse, so to comply with the law he fixed a metal plate to prevent the gear lever going into reverse. However, I knew a way around this. If I pressed hard against the plate with the lever I could bend both plate and law at the same time as I selected reverse gear. That's how I managed to drive it until I was seventeen, and I was never checked.

The three-wheeler had a wheel at the front and a JAP V twin motorcycle engine, but you drove it with a steering wheel like a car. The van - hardly a van, more of a pickup really - had a hood over the back and it was from this that I hawked fish around the local villages, selling kippers and fishcakes as well as cod, haddock and plaice, door-to-door. I would do this during the day then work two or three evenings a week in the chip van, my mother or sister working the other nights.

One morning the van was loaded with boxes of fish and I was on my way down the main street of Masham. The locals usually waved but today they were waving more avidly than usual. Then I smelled burning. The van had a petrol tank located at the front above the engine and it had started to leak. I was on fire and flames began to appear around my feet. I pulled over to the side of the road and the local ice cream man, Bushy Leathley, stopped to help. There was a gravel heap for gritting the roads and Bushy took off his trilby hat and shovelled gravel with it onto the fire. Then a door opened from one of the houses and a man came out with a bucket of water and threw it over the engine. The fire went out.

My father fixed the leak, but a few weeks later as I was driving along the road to Grewelthorpe I smelled burning again. I looked down at my feet and sure enough flames were coming through. I pulled over onto the grass verge. The flames were getting bigger and higher so I thought, "Bugger this, let it burn; he can always claim on the insurance." Then I thought, "What insurance; maybe we don't have any?" But I'd had enough and let it burn. The fire was on the engine just below the petrol tank. Flames were licking the bottom of the tank and it could explode at any time, so I moved to a safe distance and sat on the grass bank to watch. It didn't explode and the flames died down to just a flicker. I went across, reached under the tank and turned off the brass petrol tap. It was hot, so an explosion couldn't have been far away. I put out the fire, stopped the next car that passed by and had a lift to a phone box, nervously dialling home with the bad news. It was bound to be my fault: it was always my fault. If a tyre was punctured it was because I had been driving with the wheel in the gutter, rather than because he had bought old second-hand tyres.

The next incident with the three-wheeler was much worse. I was out on my round, loaded with boxes of fish and thrashing along a straight stretch of road near Thornborough. When it was pushed the van could do 50-55 mph. Suddenly, there was a loud bang! I lost control as the van swerved off the road onto the grass verge, down into a ditch, then rolled over the hedge and ended back on its wheels in a newly-ploughed field.

I came round lying on my stomach with my face in the soil, burning as if it was on fire. I saw the battery a few inches from my face. In the van the battery's normal place was under my driving seat so it appeared we'd left the van together and landed side by side. As I looked round I saw boxes of fish and kippers scattered around the field. A man with a dog was coming towards me and as they got nearer the dog picked up a kipper in his mouth. I jumped up to give it a boot but fell over and stayed down. When the man reached me he realised the burning was acid from the battery. He gathered ice from the fish boxes and bathed my face and eyes. I smelled even more fishy than normal but it cooled my cheek. When I stood up and looked around through bleary eyes I could see the chaos. My father would go mad. Salvaging what I could, I gathered up the fish, kippers and fish cakes. Some that were beyond recovery I gave to the man who had helped me for his dog. I will not bother to explain my father's reaction but fortunately for me it was only verbal: I could now move fast enough to get away from him. When we inspected the van we found a link on the steering had broken. He maintained the breakage was a result of the accident, not the cause of it and that as usual the whole thing had been my fault!

The van was patched up, but was soon to be made redundant as I would be seventeen and old enough for a car licence. I could then drive a bigger van and lighten my father's load even more. By this time, it seemed the work ethic from my granddad had jumped straight from him to me, bypassing my father. He had lost interest and would do as little as possible, spending more and more time chatting and drinking tea with customers. The scrubbing and cleaning was down to my mum and me.

Doreen Stands Firm

As explained in the first Chapter, my dad's younger sister and my favourite was aunt Doreen. She had married uncle Jig during the war years and after living in temporary accommodation at various places, came to near where we lived in a council house at 4, Leyburn Road. This was handy and I would be a regular visitor. Doreen would also give me refuge when my father was angry and I would always run to her. She would take me in under her protection, standing in the doorway blocking the entrance as my father would shout at me to get home. He was a strong man and even stronger on the frequent occasions when he was angry, but she wasn't afraid of him and would not be intimidated. I can hear her words now, "Our Les, clear off and leave him alone. He is staying with us." He was not used to backing down but she gave him no choice and I stayed safe for a while. Later when he had cooled down, she would take me home.

Aunt Doreen ran a 'Club Book', which is where my new clothes usually came from, including a first suit with long trousers. Unfortunately, shortly after getting the suit the pocket hooked on the seat of my motorbike and tore a great hole. My mother tried to invisibly mend it, but the material was cheap and frayed badly. The suit never looked the same again. There was no complaint from my father on this occasion: he hadn't paid for it! These club books as they were called, were ways of people buying household items and clothes while paying by weekly instalments. They were issued by companies such as Littlewoods, Freemans, Gratton Warehouses and Kays among others. Doreen would take the orders and collect the money which she would send off less her commission.

Without being greatly surprised, I discovered that while it was all right for me to drive my dad's van for *work,* he wouldn't let me use it for social purposes. "Use your motorbike," he would say. I couldn't get on a motorbike dressed up to meet a girl or go dancing. But again, my aunt Doreen came to my rescue. "You can borrow our car," she told me. Uncle Jig didn't like dancing but Doreen was a big fan, so we decided we could start going together, and loved it.

When I first went to the Town Hall at Masham I couldn't dance and girls didn't want to drag a non-dancer around standing on their toes. I'd managed to learn the St Bernard's Waltz and would line up a partner when it was due to be played. If I didn't move fast I'd miss out, as it only came on two or three times an evening. I was very shy, but I still wanted to chat to the girls and dancing in those days was the answer. I had to do something to improve my chances so my aunt and I decided we would go to dancing classes. It was good to go together as we always had a partner and she had no grumbles if I tripped over her feet ten times a night. We learned and together became quite proficient.

Later on, when I started to have girlfriends I was able to borrow uncle Jig's car once a week to take my girl to the pictures or a dance. I remember sitting in the back row at Northallerton cinema with a girl called Gwen to see *Singing in the Rain*. Gwen Abbott was my first real romance. After school-day crushes she was the 'real thing'. I was still shy but with Gwen I felt comfortable and she was the first girl I got close to. It was a thrill to hold her in my arms. She lived and worked at a farm on the outskirts of Northallerton looking after the farmer's children.

On our first date I called for her in Jig's car. When I pulled into the drive she was waiting by the gate in a long pink summer dress made from seersucker material that was very popular then. She was a tall, slim girl and always smiled. On this evening she looked gorgeous and my heart missed a beat as I opened the car door for her. At dances other boys always chased her, but one night in Thirsk it was me who ended up being pursued by a gang, as their leader had taken a liking to Gwen. They chased me around the town. I managed to give them the slip but couldn't get back to the car where she was waiting anxiously for me – as the gang was waiting too. Eventually they gave up and went off, leaving me to dash to the car and whisk Gwen into the night. We lost contact when I joined the RAF but I often think of her.

It was great to have the use of uncle Jig's car but one night it all went horribly wrong! I crashed on the way home from a late dance, falling asleep at the wheel and hitting a huge elm tree. Luckily, I wasn't speeding or I wouldn't be writing this now, and I was alone. It was a quiet road, especially at 2 am. The last thing I could remember was a close-up of the huge elm tree, grooves in the bark, shattering glass momentarily lit up by the headlights, then darkness. But I was fortunate. John Jackson, the brother of my school friend Wilf, also had a late night with his girlfriend and came along soon after, finding me lying at the side of the road. He took me home. The car was a complete write-off. I could hear my dad say, "I told you so!" But my aunt did not throw a wobbler, as he would have done. She was just pleased that I was ok. After a day in bed (no hospital or doctor), I was back at work. Third party insurance meant I had to pay my aunt. The car was sold for scrap and I made up the difference of the £27 she had paid my dad when she bought it from him.

Before the car was taken away I looked at it and couldn't believe I had escaped so lightly. The chassis was bent and the engine was pushed back into the car. I had smashed the steering wheel with my hands and face and one of the spokes struck me in the chest, winding me. I remembered staggering about in the road gasping for breath, then nothing until along came John Jackson and saved the day/night/early morning!

This was a lesson I would never forget. Years later when I was struggling to get my haulage business established I would work long hours day and night, often much more than the legal limit. I'd leave home at 5 or 6 am and return late in the evening. When I felt drowsy I'd often have a flashback of the elm tree looming up in front of me. This would shake me and I'd open the window and turn off the heater, even in the middle of winter, shivering against the cold but at least awake. If this didn't work I would stop and have a walk for a few minutes in the cool night air. If all else failed I'd pull into a lay-by, stretch across the front seats and go to sleep for twenty or thirty minutes, waking up refreshed for the rest of the journey home.

Doreen soon bought another car and we went back to our dance routine once or twice a week in Masham or Northallerton. They were happy times. With aunt Doreen I could relax and be myself. We never drank alcohol; a cup of tea at the interval was enough. Drink came later in my life.

Four Valves and Fred's Help
I had ridden the BSA across North Yorkshire and I had learned a lot from the experience. But what I really wanted was a competition bike. Although most of the money I earned from working for my dad had been saved for this new project, I was still far short. I would have to build a motorbike from spare parts, as I had done a few years earlier with my bicycle. Instead of a Beezer, this would become known as a 'Bitza', made from bits and pieces of other motorbikes.

I talked to Fred Jackson who was the older brother to John who rescued me in the accident and my school friend Wilf. Fred had served in the RAF during World War Two as a wireless operator and gunner, and now ran a repair shop for motorbikes, cars and agricultural machinery in a workshop not far from our garage. Fred was passionate about motorcycling and had already helped his younger brother Wilf buy his first bike. I liked Fred and he gave me lots of encouragement in developing my plans for getting a competition racer.

"You need one that is much shorter than the BSA you have now," he said. So I searched around and found a New Imperial, registration AUM16. It had a unit construction engine and gearbox which made it short. I could use the frame, though the engine wasn't suitable. I would have to find something more powerful then tune it up.

At this time, my uncle Jig was driving a lorry for I'ansons, a local cattle feed merchant, which involved him collecting imported feed from the docks. I located a motorbike scrapyard in Gateshead that he passed close by on his way to the Tyneside ports, so I started going with him. He would drop me on his way in and pick me up on the way back, leaving me enough time to scavenge through the scrap. Blakelock's Yard was like Aladdin's Cave to me: bits from old JAP, Excelsior, Levis, Norton and Velocete bikes from makers that had won TT races before the war. Eventually I came across a Rudge 250cc four-valve motorcycle. The bike had been in an accident but the engine was still good and extremely powerful, so I bought it for my Bitza. An engine with four valves per cylinder was well ahead of its time and did not become widely used in cars until the 1970/80s. After removing the engine I put it into a sack and struggled with it onto the trolley bus back to the traffic lights at the bottom of the hill to meet my uncle. How I got on and off the bus I don't know. When my uncle pulled up in his Albion lorry loaded with cattle feed he said, "What the hell have you got in that sack?" "Wait and see," I said. "Something special!" He helped me lift it into the cab and we set off for Masham. The old Albion was slow when it was loaded like this with seven tons of cattle feed and it took a long time to get home. This was fine by me as it gave me plenty of time to plan my next move. I was excited now I'd made a start with such a special engine. I went back the following week to buy the gearbox, a lighter load this time.

I told Fred what I had done and he was pleased. "Just right to learn with," he told me. "A good little 250cc; we'll make it fly."

Fred's garage was close to ours so it was handy to enlist his help. But it was perhaps too handy, my dad thought, as I couldn't resist calling there before I started each day's potato peeling. Dad would go wild if he caught me. I would have to run fast to avoid the toe of his shoe. Fortunately I managed this, which was just as well as he had played football for the Masham team, so he could run and kick with some accuracy.

This reminds me of an occasion when I was much younger and helping him with a car repair. He was under the car and I was passing him the tools. I gave him a 5/16" instead of 3/8"spanner. He got to his feet cursing. I knew what was coming and moved fast dashing out of the garage. But I wasn't quite fast enough: he threw the spanner and as I turned the corner it dug into my elbow by the funny bone and temporarily paralysed my arm. I still have the scar.

Fred had an old Matchless motorbike and sidecar for his run-around. After work one day he was getting ready to go and visit his parents at their Spelderbanks farm. "Do you want to come along for a ride in the sidecar?" he asked.

"Yes please." This would give me the opportunity of seeing Wilf so I clambered into the sidecar. Fred closed the hood and fastened it down, nipped out his fag, put on his gloves, kicked the bike into life and we were off. After a mile I looked across at Fred and noticed a small red patch glowing on his ex-RAF greatcoat pocket. I banged on the side of the hood to attract his attention but he just gazed ahead, the bike throbbing away and the noise deafening. After a while the patch grew bigger, fanned by the wind as we rode along. I hammered on the hood but to no avail. I could only sit and watch him slowly going up in flames. Well smouldering anyway!

When we arrived at the farm he pulled into the yard and stopped by the house. As he swung his leg over to dismount his coat burst into flames and fell apart, with spanners, nuts and bolts falling from his pocket to the ground, much to the amusement of his two brothers, John and Wilf, who stood watching as he stamped out the flames.

Kenneth's Training Ground
Now was the opportunity to start building my racing motorbike. The New Imperial short frame was ideal for the project. First, I stripped it down to discard and sell the engine, then with Fred's help I fitted swinging-arm rear suspension, cutting tubes and plates, then waited patiently, sometimes for hours, for Fred to light his welding torch. He had many more jobs to do that he was being paid for, so my bike was not a priority. Slowly, very slowly as far as I was concerned, it all came together. In the

meantime I tuned the engine and read from cover to cover yet again, my book *Tuning for Speed.*

My father let me use a little shed that had originally been a pigsty when we had kept pigs. It still smelled of pigs until I sweetened it up with oil, petrol and exhaust fumes. I stripped down the engine, had it re-bored, fitted a new piston, and shaved the bottom off the barrel to increase compression ratio, to what I'll never know! I fitted new valves and guides, and spent hours polishing the ports with little files and emery paper. Then I carefully lapped in the new piston and rings with Shinio metal polish, working the piston up and down by hand before re-assembling. The engine was bolted into the frame and the job completed. New knobbly tyres were fitted, as with all that power I was going to need grip.

The first time I started it up, the engine fired into life and ran smoothly. I was so excited; it was music to my ears. I kept it at low revs to ease the 'running-in'. It worked, though not perfectly. The engine was noisy and the rockers on the four-valve system always chattered. They had grease nipples but as soon as the engine got hot the grease would melt and run onto the cylinder head, going up in smoke. I started practising racing up and down the hills of Fleetham's Farm. There was a little stone bridge on Swinney Lane which I would ride over as fast as I dare, actually taking off in the process. I would check the marks where my rear wheel had landed to see how far I had travelled in the air. A local man, Eddy Jameson, often sat on the bridge, looking out for traffic and applauding me. The bike was wonderful. Soon I would join a club to enter competitions but for the moment the focus was on more practice. I felt confident and fearless.

My next practice area was Roomer Common just outside Masham, an area of rough bracken-covered moorland that had been used by the Army as an infantry training area during WW1 and more recently in WW2 as a tank training ground. The tank tracks were still there on the steeper slopes. From now, this was Kenneth's training ground in preparation for an entry to the world of motorbike racing.

What I would do was to take a good run on the flat to build up speed then race up the hill. I had built the bike very short, which meant it was good to handle but could easily flip over when I came to the steepest part. I soon found a way to cope with that. At the last moment as the front wheel reared up, I would step off to my right and let go of the bike. It would somersault, landing on the handlebars and seat lower down the hill. At first it bent the handlebars, but to avoid this I slackened the securing bolts allowing the bars to move when the whole weight of the bike came down on them. I only needed to pull them back up for the next run … no damage.   I spent hours on the moor enjoying myself. Fred helped straighten out the bike when it buckled a little. I had a few knocks but I was young and strong enough to take it.

Shortly after, I joined Thirsk and District Motor Cycle Club and rode with them in a few hill climbs and scramble events. But despite all the effort I had put in, I realised that my bike was not good enough against the bigger and better models costing more than I could afford. With the looming of National Service I decided to put on hold my competitive racing.

No Through Road
For now I just used the bike for touring the countryside, going on longer runs alone through the Dales on the same narrow, little-used country lanes, many of them gated, that I had first experienced on my bicycle. I would wrap a spare plug, a few spanners, screwdriver and tape in a cloth as a toolkit in case of breakdowns, stowed away under the seat.

One of my favourite runs was from Masham through Healy and over to Lofthouse. A sign on the road said, 'No Through Road' which to me was an open invitation. The road was unsurfaced, badly rutted and almost impossible to travel over on the steeper parts. It was a challenge but I loved it. At the top I would lean my bike against the wall to cool off, smoke rising from the engine, while I gazed over the hills. For me at seventeen this was as good as it got. I was at my happiest all alone with my bike on the hills away from work and my father.

The views around the wild beauty of the Dales are breathtaking! I have returned many times over the years just to stand and stare down the valley over Roundhill and Leighton Reservoir, towards Healy and Masham, with over to the left Colsterdale, where my mother spent her early years. There you can see the remains of the tiny school, built in 1787, which she attended. Lower, out of sight on the side of the valley was Hazlelbank, where she lived. The house is still standing but today is sadly neglected and overgrown. The trees are so big now they completely engulf the place. I recently went to look around and couldn't find the house until I was almost upon it. I carried a photograph taken in 1935, the year of my birth. How different it looked then. The big house had a large barn and other outbuildings, kennels for the gamekeeper's dogs, an orchard and a garden with a vegetable patch. All were neatly walled around. The bushes, shrubs and small trees on the photograph now tower above and surround the house after seventy-five years of growth!

How proud my mother's family must have felt when they arrived at this beautiful place from Hexham in the second decade of the twentieth century. There were four of them: my grandfather, grandmother and their two young girls, Kathleen my mum, and her younger sister Peggy. Obviously, being head gamekeeper for Lord Swinton was an important position to warrant a home like this as part of the job.

Masham Moor is on the right where grandpa would tend the grouse so the 'toffs' from London could come north to shoot on the 'Glorious Twelfth'!

One hillside still shows the foundations of the temporary accommodation erected for workmen building the reservoir. My uncle Jack, aunt Peggy's husband, worked there on the pipeline that takes the water all the way to Leeds. He worked for the Water Board for almost fifty years, before retiring with a watch and long service certificate. After he died, I helped sort out his hundreds of old black-and-white photos taken at work, clearly showing the various sizes of pipes and trenches. There were many shots of him inspecting joints, along with ancient tractors, excavators and cranes lowering in the pipes.

Jack's life had been waterworks, reservoirs, pumping stations and pipelines ... it was all he knew. If I said, "Jack, I was in Otley last week," he would reply, "Oh yes, we did a twenty-four inch pipeline there in 19-whatever!" They were the milestone markers of his life. He had known little else. He had married aunt Peggy late in life. Colsterdale is also the place where the 'Leeds Pals' trained before going to France in the First World War. They came to Masham by train then marched five miles to the camp that at one time held 1,000 troops. Many would spend their last days there before leaving such a heavenly peace to go to the hell of the Somme, and be blown to smithereens on the order of some bungling four-star general.

Brake Failure
Another of my favourite runs was from Masham over to Kettlewell via East Witton, Coverdale, Woodale, and Great Whernside. It was over these same moors years later I would fly in my paraglider. But riding those narrow, windy lanes and steep hills as a seventeen year-old on a home-built bike, I wonder now whether I was brave, foolhardy or just adventurous. There were few telephones then and the roads often had no habitation for miles. It was exciting, but one day I almost come to grief.

Having checked the petrol and oil, stowed a toolkit, spare plug, chain link wire and roll of tape I set out for what I expected to be just another tour exploring the Yorkshire countryside. I rode through East Witton, along the twisty roads through Coverdale to Woodale, then along past Whernside and over towards Kettlewell. The exhaust note was like music as I wound the throttle. It was such pleasure to feel the wind on my face and blowing through my hair - I wore no crash helmet - breathing in the country smells of freshly-cut grass, new mown hay, the hawthorn blossom and, of course, the muck spreader and occasional whiff of a dead sheep. Freedom! A few miles from Kettlewell on the steepest part where the gradient is one-in-three, is a very sharp hairpin bend. The hill is called Park Rash and was where motor club hill climbs were held during the 1920s. It was also the route taken by the London-to-Newcastle car endurance drivers in the same decade. I have seen a picture where the vehicles are being towed up the steepest part by horses.

There is a long straight leading down to the hairpin. I was going quite fast when I tried my brakes. Surprisingly, they didn't work. Nothing!

I raced on towards the bend changing gears, down one and then two, to slow up, but I was still going far too fast to get round the bend. The road dipped to the left and disappeared. I could see three huge rocks painted black and white, and marking the edge. Beyond them in the distance was the other side of the valley. I pressed the foot brake and squeezed the front brake, but there was no response.

I had to think fast so I threw the bike on its side, let go of it and rolled down the road. The bike shot along on its handlebars and footrest, sparks flying everywhere, before smashing into one of the black and white rocks and bouncing back into the road. I was dazed. I had neither helmet nor protective clothing. My jacket and trousers were now badly torn with newly-made ventilation holes. I stood up to lick my wounds. I didn't fall over or feel severe pains, so I thought I must be ok. I had a few knocks and scrapes mainly to my knees and elbows ... but what about the bike! It was laid in the road with smoke rising from it. Here I was, miles from anywhere!

I limped over to look at the wreckage. Luckily the bike had hit the painted rocks with its most solid part: the top of the forks and the steering head. One rock had moved six inches but it served the purpose for which it was set there. I looked over the edge! One hundred feet below was the road where I would have landed had I gone over. I was in trouble but I managed to think positively: it could have been so much worse.

Few people used this road other than local farmers, so there was little chance of any help. I would have to help myself. I now realised why my brakes had failed: they were only good enough to slow me down when dry but I had ridden through deep water where a stream crossed the road and had forgotten to dry them out.

I inspected the damage. Half an inch had been worn off the footrest and handlebars. They were no problem. The twist grip was torn off and the throttle cable was broken ... big problem! Brake lever broken ... what difference would that make? The lights, too, were smashed so I had to try to get home before dark. The bike was still in one piece and the wheels and tyres were ok, the wheels turned freely and thankfully were not buckled. Now ... how to get home? The AA certainly would not be coming out for me! Petrol had leaked but there was still enough in the tank to make the journey. The kick-start was broken, but that didn't matter as the bike would push-start.

I disconnected the remains of the throttle cable from the handlebars and fastened the shortened end to the front of the seat in a loop between my legs. I then straightened the mudguards and handlebars and looked back up the hill towards home; it was going to be a long way back!

I ran the bike down the hill and felt a great sense of relief when it started. "Maybe I will get home tonight, after all." I gathered my tools and the broken bits of the bike, and packed them under the seat. The clutch was on the left-hand side so I could steer with one hand, reaching down with the other to pull the throttle cable between my legs to accelerate. The bike felt a bit lopsided with one handlebar and one footrest both a bit higher than the other. It didn't feel as if the bike wanted to go in a straight line and I had to lean all the time to keep balance. But I had the road to myself, and I would need all the spare room I could get!

There were over twenty-five miles to go, complete with a water splash and three gates to open and close. But while both bike and I were a bit bent, neither of us was broken.

After a tortuous ride which felt more like seventy-five miles I finally made it, riding down Leyburn Road and into Masham with one handlebar up and one down. By now it was dark and with no lights I was creeping along peering ahead of me. Fortunately, there was no one around to notice. I put the bike out of sight in the shed and went indoors, very weary and more than a little sore, but happy to be home. Luckily, my dad was out with the chip van so I told half the story just to my mother; no doubt she later halved the story again to tell to my father long after I was soundly asleep.

God Save the Queen
The year 1952 was when King George VI died. I remember it well for when I heard I was with my dad hawking fish door-to-door in Melmerby. I walked up a path opposite the Hall with my hand raised ready to knock on the big green door.

Before I had chance to open my mouth and say, "Anything today?" the door opened and a sad-faced woman stood there in a blue overall coat. I was expecting her to say, "A pound of cod fillet and a pair of kippers." Instead what I heard was, "The King has died; I've just heard on the radio." I stopped in my tracks. True, his death would not make any difference to my life or cancel my National Service which was becoming due, but it was sad news as he was not an old man.

A year later, Queen Elizabeth II was crowned. Not many homes had television before, but this was the occasion that hundreds of thousands of people bought their first set, my father among them. On Coronation Day our house was packed with family, friends, and neighbours, along with one or two who had invited themselves. The Walkers were there in large numbers: granddad, granny, my mother and father, aunts and uncles, sisters Freda and Connie, brother Howard, plus assorted neighbours and friends. All sat around the little black and white console, with the picture frequently being interrupted by a 'snow shower' or a 'Venetian blind' as the reception was none too good.

One family member, however, was missing! While the Queen was being crowned in front of an adoring nation, I was outside making the most of the time working on my bike. It was one of the last opportunities I'd have before I took up my new appointment, working for the Queen on my National Service. It wasn't long now before I would have to park up the one thing that gave me much pleasure, my motorbike, and set off on a new adventure. The grainy pictures coming from Westminster Abbey held for me no interest.

Masham cycling club 1949-50

My BSA with Howard and Connie 1951

Wilf Jackson and me 1952

Motorbike I built myself 1953

Home on first leave with Connie at the side of the chip van 1954

CHAPTER 5
1953 TO 1956
NATIONAL SERVICE

This was to be my escape! The first obstacle was the medical. To take this meant travelling to Middlesbrough where I met twenty other would-be soldiers awaiting the same thing. After sitting around for a while we were ushered into a large room with rows of benches along one side, the other half screened off. We were called in turn and told to, "Strip off!" The MO (medical officer) quickly checked me over and placed a little wooden spatula under my balls. "Cough!" he said, and I duly obliged. I learned later that if they moved up and down you were well connected. This was followed by a quick look down my throat, after which we were given a small glass for a urine sample.

The lad in front of me was given his glass and motioned to go behind a curtain to do the deed. He returned almost immediately with the glass full to the top and dripping. The medic looked at him in amazement, as many couldn't pee on command and took a while to perform. In fact, what had happened was he had filled his sample bottle from the overspill bucket. He was given a fresh bottle and sent to try again, this time with an orderly peeping round the curtain! He was just one of many who wanted to fail their medical, getting up to all sorts of different tricks to avoid doing National Service. One way I heard of was to chew nutmeg; apparently this caused an increase in the heart rate. Another was to pollute the water sample, as this lad had attempted.

The medical was not stringent and was soon over. You went home to wait for the letter that would tell you if you had passed. I was fit, felt good and was confident I would be off soon to wherever I was posted.

All this happened a little while after I passed my eighteenth birthday, the signal in those days for a boy's orders to sign-up for what was called National Service. My father suggested I apply for deferment. I said, "No dad, let me go and get it over with," but that statement was not entirely accurate. The true response would have been, "Let me get away from here as quickly as I can. I want to see the world or at least another part of it. And I don't want to spend any more time peeling spuds or selling fish."

I had never been happy working for my father and for many years longed to break away from his control, as I'm sure by now will be clear. In fact, I hadn't wanted to work for him when I first left school, and tried to get that plumbing apprenticeship with Norman Chapman. Dad had put a stop to that which meant it had been the fish business for me.

Now I was eighteen, things would change. Many young men when reaching that age dreaded the thought of National Service, but not me - I was looking forward to it. I was eager to be off and away from my father's control, with poor Howard, my brother, left to take on my role. Like me, Howard was not to have much chance of picking up an education.

It took a few weeks for the official letter with my medical report to arrive. I was sure I had passed, but there was just a small doubt lingering in the back of my mind that my great hope of escape might fail. At last the OHMS (On Her Majesty's Service) brown envelope arrived, telling me that I had passed A1, and would be contacted shortly for enlistment. There was no stopping me now.

As you will recall, my father had served in the RAF during the Second World War and suggested I try to get in that branch. Though many National Servicemen were drafted into the RAF, the only way to be sure was to sign on for an extra year. In that way, you then became a regular serviceman with more benefits, better pay and a choice of trades. If you just waited to be enlisted you served two instead of three years, but you had no say in the matter of what you did or where you were sent.

My number one choice was Sea Rescue, but I didn't have an earthly chance of getting in as they were all long-term servicemen. I would have needed a better education than the meagre effort I had cobbled together in-between times of picking and peeling potatoes. There was a better chance of a driving job in the RAF Regiment, so I signed on the dotted line to serve for three years as a gunner/driver. What I didn't know then was that the only *guarantee* was of me being in the RAF Regiment for three years; what I would end up doing was still a matter of chance. What you had been doing before joining up meant little unless you were lucky or had a special talent. Sportsmen and musicians always received special privileges and a good chance of promotion, otherwise it was largely Hobson's choice.

Square Bashing and Boxing
Every day I watched avidly for the post to arrive, and a few weeks later a second OHMS brown envelope came through the letterbox with a rail pass and instructions to report to Cardington, Bedfordshire, for 'kitting-out'. I was excited and couldn't wait to be on my way. My dad didn't share my enthusiasm for he knew it would mean more work for him and my overworked mother.

But the day had come and I left my parents for the first time in my life, and headed south. Kitting out was quite entertaining as it was all done in a rush: you entered one end of a building in your civvies, and came out the other end with an arm full of RAF uniform and kit, almost before you realised. When you were back at your billet was the time to see how much of the uniform actually fitted. You would exchange the rest with others who had got your size instead of their own!

The next day was 'swearing-in', better known as giving the Oath of Allegiance to the Queen after which it meant you were truly in Her Majesty's service. To me and for most others the Oath was a serious matter, though I noticed several recruits at the back of the room who didn't utter a word and treated it all very light-heartedly.

We were separated into batches and dispatched to various RAF camps around the country to undergo our obligatory basic training. My destination was Padgate, near Warrington in Lancashire. "Great," I thought. "How lucky can you get?" A girlfriend from Ripon had just gone to Fearnhead College, which was right next door to the camp. As it turned out, it might as well have been in Scotland, as we weren't allowed out of camp during training and I saw her only twice.

How my world changed when I arrived at Padgate. The training was mainly 'square bashing', which involved drill, drill, and lots more drill. Here was I, a village lad entering the real world! Now my life education was about to start.

Reveille was at 6 am when we would be marched down to the cookhouse for breakfast. Often, the moon was still clear in the sky and the stars were twinkling as dawn began to break. I wasn't used to getting out of bed this early. One thing at home that really annoyed me - though I kept it to myself - was why my dad called me in a morning from *his* bed to, "Get my lazy self out of bed and to work". He should have shown a better example by getting up for us to go to work together. Only years later did I realise he wanted me out of the house, and Howard and Connie off to school, so he could get my mother back into bed where they had the house to themselves!

Basic training took a straight eight weeks without a break. However, this was also when the squadron boxing championships were on and anyone who volunteered to take part could get a weekend pass to go home. I had learned to box in the Scouts in 1948. Scouts had been run by the local postman, Mr Stubbs, a keen cyclist with an ancient tandem. He often rode this solo around Masham which was an odd sight, the rear peddles going round with no one on the back seat.

Later, I had become a member of the Boxing Club at Masham after taking a terrible beating in the school playground one afternoon. My father had been very fiery when he was young and ended up in many fights. His philosophy was never to back down and that is what he taught me. On that fateful day at school I became involved in a dispute with an older and bigger boy. I suspect he had called me by the hated name 'Fishy Walker'.

Whether it was due to that or for some other reason, we locked horns but he hammered me and kept asking, "Have you had enough?" to which I refused to reply. So the punishment went on. As is usual, the rest of the boys all enjoyed the fight but after a while I could hardly stand, let alone strike a blow. I should have quit but remembered my father's words, "Never back down." I have never been more pleased to hear the bell ring for the end of playtime, ending the fight without me having to concede. I hid my cuts and bruises, and wet my hanky under the tap as I made my way back to my desk. My eyebrow and nose were cut and bleeding. I kept my head down and pressed the cold handkerchief on my face. I felt dreadful. My head was throbbing and so heavy I had to put my elbows on the desk to prop it up in my hands. It was a long afternoon!

That was the reason for learning to box and now I was a little wiser and had a few fights in Masham Boxing Club under my belt. The Club had been run by a retired amateur boxer, Mr Cudden-Fletcher, who showed all the signs of an ex-boxer: misshapen nose, cauliflower ears and puffy eyebrows. But we learned from him and I felt confident enough to put my name forward for the squadron championships.

The eliminating bouts were held in a huge gymnasium. I donned my PE kit and prepared for my fight. When I climbed into the ring I looked across at my opponent to discover he was about my size but stocky and strong-looking. The bell rang and I walked towards the centre of the ring, taking up the stance I'd been taught: gloves up high for protection, left foot forward. But before I could strike a blow he hit me like a whirlwind, the blows landing so fast I didn't know what was happening. I hit the canvas dazed, and the next thing I remember was being helped back to my corner and propped up on a stool. That was it, the bout was over. As I sat there recovering he came over and apologised, explaining that a few years before he was schoolboy champion of Great Britain. To this day I can't remember his name and only met him once; but that was enough!

"I could see that you were a novice, so rather than drag it out I thought it would be best to get it over quickly," he said. "You're right," I agreed. When our gloves were off we shook hands with a smile. There were no bad feelings though I have to admit my head was buzzing for some time! Still, I had the reward of the promised pass and went home for the weekend. I was keen to show off my new uniform, though not so eager for people to see the bruises I had acquired as the price of my leave ticket.

Naffink and Samfink

Back at Padgate, our training continued. One day as we were herded into a lecture hut all talking at once, an NCO picked on an airman who was still talking, "Stand up, what are you talking about?" he asked. "Naffink corporal," replied the recruit in a broad cockney accent. The NCO decided he would try to make him look small.

"Well, come out here and give us all a lecture on 'naffink'," he ordered. If it had been me who was given that order I would have shrivelled up in front of a roomful of fifty to sixty men, but not my cockney friend. He walked out and stood in front of us all with the NCOs watching and smirking, waiting for him to dry up.

What followed was hilarious. "Naffink is samfink you get on your plate ere at mealtimes. Naffink is what you get on pay day. Naffink is what NCOs av got in their eds," he went on and on. This time they had picked on the wrong man. The room was in an uproar and even the NCOs joined in. When he returned to his seat he was loudly applauded and they didn't pick on him again!

Service life was rarely such fun in those early months, however. The following day was a parade ground inspection and an NCO gave us all a 'dressing down'. This particular corporal came to stand inches from my face telling me what a scruffy, dirty little airman I was, his spit splashing my face. He was an arrogant, snotty creep! I could have reached out and strangled him. I looked straight through him, stood to attention and let it wash over my head (literally). I had been up early that day, cleaned and polished my equipment, pressed my trousers, and believed I was one very smart airman.

This was all part of the training, which was meant to put you down and demoralise you, to make it easier to order you about. It didn't work with me and I learned a few lessons in self-control. Sadly, some couldn't take it. One night, a member of our group climbed on to the water tower and jumped off. We didn't hear if he survived for the incident was never mentioned. Some airmen were so worried about keeping their kit up to standard they stayed up half the night getting it spotless.

Most of our basic training was drill and weapons training, yet more drill and lots of bull. This meant polishing our kit and carrying out floor ablutions, including cleaning the parade ground. We had a few lessons in unarmed combat and bayonet practice: first, fix the bayonet on to the rifle, then practice stabbing a sack stuffed with straw with the outline of a man painted on it. We used the small nine-inch round bayonet, not much thicker than a pencil, which didn't much look like a dangerous weapon compared with the long ones I had seen the Army use in the war. We were told it was easier to push into the enemy's guts and, though it only made a small hole, he would still die from the injury. The powers that be had made it that little bit easier to kill!

We were also given gas training, which included being exposed to a small dose. We were all crammed into a room, a gas pellet was thrown in and the door slammed shut. Fortunately, the door was not kept shut for long, but we all felt the dreadful, suffocating effect, and rushed out with eyes and noses streaming.

Winter Gardens and Hogmanay

After the eight-week basic training was over we were now airmen with the rank, AC2. Along with twenty others I was posted to Weeton near Blackpool for a further eight weeks of driving instruction. I had a licence already along with quite a lot of mechanical knowledge, so I approached the course with confidence and found it easy - that is, until I came unstuck! After four weeks' training both in the classroom and driving Hillman cars around Blackpool, we had a test with two airmen travelling in each car along with a civilian examiner. The first driver drove around the test route then stopped and parked in a side road on a housing estate.

"Your turn now Walker," the instructor said. I climbed into the front seat and settled down behind the wheel.

"Now I want you to turn round and go back to the main road." I did a perfect three-point turn, not touching the kerb once. I carried on around town and completed my test. Next day the results were announced and you can imagine my surprise when I learned I had failed. The reason given was that I should have driven further down into the estate and backed into a side road. When I took over the car we had a clear stretch of road with no junction. It was an ideal spot for a three-point turn which is what I thought he wanted. It was a misunderstanding which led to me being given a further week's training, much to the amusement of those who had started from scratch and passed!

The highlight of the driver training was the skid pan. An oval patch of smooth concrete was covered with oil and water. The idea was to drive across this, get into a skid, then correct the car and get out of the skid. I loved it and would have stayed there all day but the examiner saw my competence and ended the fun.

Once we had passed the car test, we moved on to the big stuff of driving 'three-tonners', big QI Bedfords in fact. I soon got the hang of driving these lorries and there was no repetition of my previous failure. This time I passed the final exam with flying colours.

It was a proud moment in training school when I was asked mechanical questions. I remembered what my dad had taught me and knew most of the answers, as did one other lad whose father owned a garage. On occasions, the instructor would ask the class a question but tell the two of us to keep quiet so that the others had a chance. We sat there feeling smug.

While training at Padgate we weren't allowed out of camp, but the move to Weeton brought with it an easier regime. Blackpool was just down the road, sporting the Tower and the Winter Gardens for dancing. This time, though, there was no aunt Doreen to partner. Nevertheless, now was my opportunity to put into practice what we had learned together at our dancing classes.

Blackpool was a real eye-opener for me after the village hall dances I was used to. To me, the Tower Ballroom felt as big as the whole of Masham Market Place, as did the Winter Gardens. All the big bands of the time such as Joe Loss and Ted Heath played there. It was magic. The atmosphere was electric and the music carried you round with little effort to the accompaniment of Lita Rosa, Ross MacManus and Larry Gretton. At the interval the huge organ would rise out of the floor and the organist played popular music reminding me of home while not actually making me feel homesick. My mother and father loved to listen to radio performances by Sandy MacPherson or Reginald Dixon playing the organ in the Winter Gardens or Blackpool Tower. The big musical hit of the time was *Oh my Papa,* played by Eddie Calvert. I loved the tune but it certainly didn't take me back to my papa, who I was only too pleased to be away from!

I wasn't long at Weeton before being posted to Dumfries for yet more training, this time for my RAF Regimental qualification. By the time I reached Scotland it was winter and the weather was cold. The training was tough but I enjoyed the challenge. Our billets were old, cold and damp single-brick structures. Each night I would leave water in my mug by my bed and often in the morning it would be frozen solid. This reminds me of an incident and I'll jump ahead a few months.

At my next posting at RAF Wunstorf, Germany, a lad called Blake kept a mug of water on his locker. One morning he awoke and reaching for his mug as usual, he took a large swig. Imagine his shock when he saw a dirty brown set of false teeth at the bottom glinting up at him. He threw up first, and then threw the remainder of the water at Russell, the culprit, in the next bed.

"You dirty bastard," he screamed. Russell just grinned. He was an old 'sweat' who had been in the RAF for many years having been promoted and demoted many times. He also drank heavily and smoked about fifty cigarettes a day, as his nicotine-stained false teeth would testify. His bed was next to Blake's. He had come in drunk the night before and dropped his gnashers into Blake's mug. Blake was small and thin. His Adam's apple stuck out from his scrawny neck over a shirt collar that always looked two sizes too big. He was hardly likely to get physical. In fact, it was said that he was the only man ever to get his money back from Charles Atlas, the American bodybuilder!

Back to Scotland. New Year in Dumfries was something special. I'd heard how they celebrated Hogmanay north of the border and wanted to see for myself. Well, it was an experience! I wasn't much of a drinker at that time, but this was a special occasion and the Scots certainly knew how to make it memorable. We were fortunate to be guided by a few natives in our section who hadn't managed to get leave.

In those days Christmas slipped by almost unnoticed in Scotland but New Year was grabbed with both hands. Everyone must have a bottle of drink - the stronger the better. After visiting several pubs we met in Dumfries Square in front of the clock, getting ourselves primed for midnight. When the clock struck twelve the crowd went wild. Bottles were handed backwards and forwards. You took a swig from his and he took a swig from yours, 'he' being everyone there. You could stroll down any street and find every door open, walk in, swap drinks and go on to the next house: you were welcomed everywhere! I had never seen such celebrations as this. Everyone was good-natured and happily getting drunk. This went on until daylight when we all staggered back to camp. Apparently, nothing like it happens now.

We had exams throughout our training, with the final one in the last week. I liked to have fun but when the tests came I worked hard and was always in the top group. I liked mechanical things and I understood guns and weapons, too. I could handle and use them.

I had a close friend called Taffy Evans. When it came to the exams he could not deliver and I couldn't help him. He failed and was put back for another week's training. That was the last time I saw him for almost three years, for shortly afterwards I was posted to Germany. In fact, it was at my demob on leaving the RAF that I saw him next. Demob was when you came to the end of your service and had the choice of £3 or a new civilian suit. I took the money as most did. I looked across to see a tanned face I recognised. I went over to shake hands but he turned on me, "You bastard Walker, you've had a good time in Germany, home every six months, while I've been in Aden, a hot, stinking awful place with home leave only once in three years. It was your fault I failed." There was a second of uncertainty before he grinned from ear to ear. We had a good laugh for old time's sake.

RAF Wunstorf Beckons

After RAF Regiment training at Dumfries, I was posted to Germany, but first I had seven days' leave to spend at home in Masham, and a chance to show off my RAF Regiment uniform and take aunt Doreen to a few dances. It was a special moment marking my independence as an adult, though in those days you technically reached that threshold only at twenty-one.

The week passed quickly and it was time for my adventure to continue with my first trip abroad. I had to make a very early start to get a lift to Ripon from where I would catch a train. My mother and father walked down Red Lane with me, my full kitbag on my back. It was still dark and my boots echoed on the road, reminding me of the brewers' clogs when I was so small. Now it was me in the same street making the same noise, while the rest of Masham slept. There were no hugs and kisses in our family. I don't even remember a handshake. Neither of my parents had been out of the country, but here I was heading off overseas, a one-time village boy embarking on an adventure that would see me return in three years, hopefully a man.

The train took me from Ripon with several changes to Harwich in Essex, where I met more airmen going to Germany. The ferry took us to the Hook of Holland, from where we journeyed on by military train to Hanover, dropping off servicemen at various points on the way. It was strange and very interesting to be in a foreign country. The train sped across Holland, which I noticed was flat just like the Cambridge Fens, and into Germany, with some things similar and a lot more very different. Not many years before I had watched our planes leave Ely to bomb Germany. Now, I could see for myself the damage they had done. Even eight years after the war there were still vast areas totally flattened.

I noticed the railways had been a target. In various sidings were rows of old damaged engines along with rolling stock waiting to be melted down to make Volkswagen Beetles. Germany was recovering fast, but Bomber Command had left a mark that would take a long time to erase.

After the train journey we arrived in Hanover and were driven on to RAF Wunstorf. The squadron had just changed from using armoured cars, relics of WW2, and now had Land Rovers and three-ton trucks. Then I spotted the new motorbikes and my eyes lit up. The squadron had six Triumphs, all the latest models. The Army were not pleased when the RAF had them first, while they were still using old Nortons and BSAs. As you can imagine, my first thoughts on seeing the bikes was whether I could serve the three years as a dispatch rider. As it happened, I had to wait until their current riders were demobbed, but my turn would come eventually and I was thrilled to ride these wonderful bikes. They were good machines except for one fault: the bikes were 500cc vertical twin side valve engines and where the cylinders joined there was a hot spot which caused them to overheat. The damned things were always 'tweeting' with head gaskets blowing, which spoiled what was basically a brilliant bike. I rode thousands of miles over Germany during my posting.

The job of the RAF Regiment is to defend airfields. Since we were no longer in a 'hot' war but had to achieve operational readiness because of the Cold War, we had to pretend. This meant marching, shooting, digging trenches and hiding in the woods from supposed enemies. At basic training my rifle shooting had been poor, but with plenty of practice I soon became a good shot and eventually a marksman. I remember the instructor saying, "Hold your breath when you squeeze the trigger." Today, I still do the same thing when I shoot with a camera, and am able to take good pictures as a result. I came to enjoy weapons training, firing different guns, taking them to pieces and re-assembling them. I have always liked mechanical things. Whenever marksmanship tests were held I was always in the top five, but at the bottom of my report sheet was the comment, "Non-NCO material!"

I didn't take this seriously as the RAF wasn't going to be my career. Actually, I didn't take anything particularly seriously. In any case I always had a friend close by with the same sense of humour and we'd laugh our way through National Service. The best of these pals were Stan Thompson, Tom Paton, Adam Lorimer and Paul Ives, and together we would often have the whole squadron chuckling. This made life easier and relieved the boredom from endless amounts of marching, cleaning, polishing, scrubbing floors, maintaining the squadron's Land Rovers and continuously bulling one's kit. Happily, there was only the Cold War we had to worry about, not actual shooting. In any case, if you wanted promotion you needed to do a bit of creeping and that was not for me.

Selection for the RAF Regiment was not due to any special suitability. They just threw in a 'job lot' from all walks of life, shapes, sizes, religions, trades and professions. For example, Arthur Spindler was a little Jewish boy from Manchester whose civilian job description was raincoat machinist. If I was non-NCO material then, probably, he was not even Regiment grade. One day, we were out on weapons training practising throwing grenades. We had finished with dummies, now it was the real thing. The throwing area was in a hollow eight feet deep, surrounded by earth banking and a wall. Each of us was expected to lob our grenade over the wall. We stood in a queue along a narrow passage. When it was your turn you stepped forward into the arena, the instructor gave you a grenade with the pin in place. You took the grenade in your right hand, placing the forefinger of your left hand through the pin ring. When you pulled the pin nothing happened until you threw it. This would set off the fuse.

Arthur, as it happened, was just in front of me. He pulled the pin with no problem but, instead of lobbing it over the wall, he froze and dropped it at his feet. Fortunately, an instructor moved fast, grabbed the live grenade and hurled it over the wall just as it exploded in mid-air, showering us with tiny fragments. All this happened in the space of a few seconds. Arthur was shaking like a leaf with his bottom lip trembling. It was extremely fortunate we were all wearing tin helmets and had ducked down, so no one was injured. For Arthur, though, that was his first and last live grenade throwing session.

By contrast, the other Jewish lad in our squadron, Pomeroy, was a huge fellow, his body shaped from years of weightlifting. His primary interest was the making of money. All servicemen had a cigarette allowance, but not everyone smoked. Pomeroy would collect the non-smokers' rations from the NAAFI and take all of the cigarettes to Hanover on Saturdays in a large sack. We didn't know where he sold them but that sack was always empty when he returned smiling to camp.

During my National Service I revived my cricketing career. I had played for the Masham school team against the Sunderland Scouts, so when names were being taken for a squadron team I put mine forward. Practice day came and two teams went out to play each other. My side were fielding and I was put out near the boundary. It wasn't long before a big hitter smashed the ball high in the air towards the boundary. I ran to where it was due to land, cupped my hands and reached up to catch it. I was very close but not close enough, and the ball ended up by my feet.

I had chance neither to bat nor bowl, so that was the beginning and end of my cricketing at Wunstorf.

However, I liked sport and thought there must be one I was good at. We were nearing the camp sports day so I started to train. There were several good athletes in our squadron, including one Roger Merryman, an outstanding long distance runner who represented Britain in the Commonwealth Games! I competed in many track events, but failed to shine. I was quite good at cross-country and was placed third in the steeplechase, but the hurdles race was a catastrophe. You are allowed to knock some over, but I wasn't sure how many. As I sped along hitting one after another I just kept going and was first across the line. It was a thrill to break the tape ahead of everyone, until I looked back to see the only hurdle still standing was the first one.

While I'd made an impression at hurdles, it wasn't the right one. Clearly, finding a sport I was good at was not going to be easy. Finding those I couldn't do well was an ever-growing list!

Dancing with the Germans
Once settled into the squadron routine, my thoughts turned to dancing. I missed those weekly nights out with my aunt. Just as luck would have it, there was another member of the squadron, Adam Lorimer, who liked dancing. Adam and I would go to town to look around but were quickly disappointed. The only place seemed to be a dive called the Ratzkeller, where hordes of airmen went to drink, play the jukebox and chat up the few *frauleins* who could be found there, and who were in any case outnumbered ten to one by the airmen. It was a dreadful place. However, one Saturday evening we found a dance in a beer garden around the back of a small hotel. It looked nice and we were excited about the prospect at long last … unfortunately we were in for a shock!

As we soon discovered, Germans don't dance as we do. The *Viennese Waltz* may have started next door in Austria, but the Germans have their own version with a rise and fall on every step! Still, that was something we would have to learn. We paid for a ticket at the entrance and sat at a table near the back to enjoy the music and scene. The music would have been easier to march to than to dance to, but when in Rome!

Everything we saw was so very different to the Ratzkeller, with many smartly dressed people. As we were the only non-Germans we felt a little conspicuous, slowly sipping our beer to make it last. Eventually I plucked up courage to ask a girl for a dance but no luck, *"nein danke"* (no thanks). Adam tried but received the same answer. After several refusals I decided to lower my sights for it was obvious the good-looking girls did not want to dance with *Der Englanders*. I noticed a buxom, not very attractive girl who hadn't been dancing and made my way to her table, smiling as I asked her to dance.

She jumped up eagerly, though I was surprised to see just how big she was - the table had hidden most of her! We made our way between the tables to the dance floor and up some steps to a raised area like a small boxing ring with a rope around.

The music started and she took hold of me. I hung on as we went round and round until I felt dizzy! When the music eventually stopped and one or two dancers left the floor I was about to follow, but she hung on until the music started again. I was waltzed round and round once again, but also up and down like a polka. I was dizzy and had to hold her tight for support. Eventually the music stopped and we moved towards the steps. My head was spinning and as we got to the top step she released her grip as I fell sideways over the rope, and down onto a table, sending bottles and glasses flying in all directions as the table tipped over and I slid to the grass.

There was uproar! I tried to get up but it was a struggle as I was still so dizzy. Fortunately Adam came over and helped me to my feet and back to our table, but we weren't given a chance to settle down. I took a sip of beer and looked up to see a huge man standing by the table dressed like a tailor's dummy. He didn't speak a word, just stretched an arm towards the exit as he stood and watched us leave.

Our first visit had ended in catastrophe. One dance, one small beer, then thrown out like drunks. I'm sure everyone thought we were drunk and we decided to give the place a miss for a while. But it wasn't long before we were itching to go back, as it was the only nice place in the district. When we'd plucked up enough courage we went back. This time my luck was better, for I met a lovely girl and we soon became friends. I had gone to the beer garden thinking I would start off with my sights high again and ask an attractive girl to dance. I almost fell over when she stood up and smiled. We danced, but not at a dizzy pace this time, and I managed to negotiate the steps several times without incident. Her name was Rossel. She came from Hamburg and was currently staying with her brother in Wunstorf. There was an added bonus: she spoke English. She took me to her brother's house and introduced me to his family. A few days later they invited me for a meal. I went but this turned out to be quite an ordeal as I discovered that their table manners and habits were very different to ours. She tried to guide me but I fumbled, and I felt her brother was watching my every move disapprovingly. Rossel was lovely though, and made me feel less foreign for the short time she was in Wunstorf before returning to Hamburg. We wrote for a time but never met again.

Panic in the Dark
We were lucky at Wunstorf as the RAF camp was big and its cinema showed three or four different films each week. We saw them all, but occasionally we would be herded into the cinema during the day for a gruelling propaganda film, usually on subjects such as venereal disease explicitly featuring the sufferings of sufferers. The idea was to put us off going to *Zimmer Strasse,* or 'five mark alley' as the red light areas were known. Many of these films were American-made and showed gruesome scenes of men in advanced stages of VD, some with testicles the size of cricket balls. At the end of each scene the narrator's voice would boom out, "And don't forget guys, a blob on the knob delays demob!" The films made you feel sick. In fact, many airmen were so upset by what they'd seen that they had to leave the cinema, but I doubt if it put them off sex for long!

Each winter, the nearby lake froze over and we were allowed to go skating on sports afternoon. I could skate a little and took the opportunity to practise. As it turned out I had one of the best tutors in a friend named Hal Gardener. He had been a professional skater in London ice shows and was a real expert. I learned a lot from Hal.

One of the Regiment's tasks was to help keep the runways clear as it was an operational airfield and aircraft had to be able to fly at all times due to Cold War tensions with the Soviets. The snowplough went through first, followed by us digging through the piled snow on the edge of the runways to uncover the drains. I was put in charge of one of the teams and we easily found the first drain and then a second. So I paced out the distance between them and put in markers the full length of the runway, which saved a lot of time raking about in the snow. It was what we called 'a job and finish', which meant that as soon as we were done we could go to the NAAFI – the all-purpose canteen, shop and store for servicemen. We were pleased with progress and were nearing the end of the runway when someone shouted they had found another drain in-between the markers! We had only uncovered half of them, so we had to go back and clear the missed ones. I was not very popular as our NAAFI trip was delayed somewhat.

Mention of the NAAFI reminds me of a particular incident. There were few black men in the British forces at that time, but in our squadron in charge of the stores was a Jamaican sergeant - a good man, mild-mannered and polite. We were in the store waiting to be served at the kiosk when there was some pushing and shoving. We made our way to the front. Sergeant James was next to me when a German girl who worked in the NAAFI poked her head out of the window, looked straight at him and said in a loud voice, "Do not behave like zat, you are not in ze jungle now!" Though we called each other awful names at times we would never say anything like that. She was out of order and there were many nasty things he could have said in reply, but he just smiled and let it pass.

Much of our time in Wunstorf was spent training, often on assault courses. I didn't mind at all. In fact I enjoyed the challenge as I was young and fit. In athletics and cross-country running I was usually not far off the front runners, the ones who got back first and enjoyed the hot water in the showers before it ran out. My RAF training had been good for me and, though you are by no means overfed, I had put on weight since joining up. I was fitter than I had ever been and the way of life was healthier than late nights at work and a mainly fish and chip diet.

One day on the assault course as we were being harassed by the NCOs in an underground tunnel, there was a lot of noise of thunderflashes and explosions. We were pushed into the darkness in single file with the tunnel becoming very narrow and pitch-black. We found ourselves creeping along on hands and knees as the tunnel became low. I was pushed from behind so I pushed the man in front who had lost contact with the man in front of him. Suddenly he stopped and we were jammed in what appeared to be a dead end. At this point, he panicked and started crying, groping about for a way out. Behind us men were pushing and shouting. I felt uneasy but stayed calm and kept my head: there had to be a way out but this man had already given up and could do nothing. It was so narrow but with difficulty I managed to reach past him and groped about the tunnel walls in the dark.

It seemed like a dead end and appeared to be boarded across, but as I ran my hands up the front I reached a ledge and realised the tunnel continued at a higher level. I helped the airman to his feet and pushed him up the next level, but all the time the buggers behind were pushing and above ground the NCOs were stamping and letting off explosions to add to the chaos. It was a pretend war situation, though at the time it seemed real enough to me. Eventually, he scrambled up to the next level and crawled along to where there was a little light. From here we found the exit. I followed as did the others and was never so pleased to see daylight. The airman who had panicked was even more pleased. "Thanks mate," he said as he dried his tears. It can be very moving to see a grown man in tears brought on by fear and panic.

That was one exercise I never looked forward to again, but another I did enjoy was night orienteering. We'd climb blindfolded in to the back of a lorry at night and be driven out into the countryside where we were dropped off with brief instructions on finding our way back to camp. All we had was a compass and a map and our money had been confiscated. It was good fun to see who got back first, though when we found that someone hadn't handed in all his cash we might find ourselves unavoidably delayed by a visit to a bar en route to the camp.

There were training areas on the coast we made use of to fire our Bofors anti-aircraft guns out to sea, travelling there in a convoy of forty to fifty vehicles. The commanding officer led the way with a blue flag on his Land Rover with the vehicle bringing up the rear displaying a green flag. By now I was a dispatch rider and would be tucked in following the CO's vehicle. When we came to a crossroads or junction one of the dispatch riders would park his motorcycle, stopping any civilian traffic till the convoy was clear. Then the fun started as we had to catch up and overtake the vehicles and get back to the CO's Land Rover before the next junction. I had to ride like a lunatic and fell off many times on the smooth granite sets, lethal when wet, from which many German roads were made.

On our way back from one exercise the squadron visited the Bergen-Belsen concentration camp, the liberation of which I had watched with my mother on newsreel at the cinema in Ely back in 1945. The camp had been landscaped and surrounded by trees to make it look more like parkland. It was said the people in the village didn't know about the camp during the war, but whether they knew or not I speculated that present-day Germans wanted to disguise it and forget it was ever there. It was eerie: there was complete silence with no birds or indeed any other signs of life. The huge burial mounds had notices saying, "Here lie the bodies of X thousand". The gas chambers and furnace had been partly demolished but the remains were a chilling reminder of what had gone on. It was a sombre and moving experience that affected the whole squadron and few words were spoken.

The next training exercise was held near Cologne and we were given time off to look around the city. It had been badly damaged by bombing and was slowly being rebuilt, though like most of the big cities I visited there were many bomb sites still to be seen. I climbed to the top of the twin spire cathedral that survived the raids almost undamaged, but as I looked out across the Rhine I saw the railway bridge still had only a single track.

Another area we used for operations was Luneburg Heath, a vast area of scrubland where Germany had surrendered in 1945. We slept in tents and I remember the ground being frozen so hard we couldn't hammer in the pegs - this was before we were issued with camp beds leaving us to sleep just on groundsheets with a tot of rum to keep us warm! Previously, I thought that rum was only a naval custom but we always had a large, closely guarded, stone jar with us, the treacly contents of which were watered down to drink. One of our officers was an alcoholic and the jar was kept well away from him! He was ex-aircrew and had been decorated in the war for his bravery. He was an odd character but who knows, perhaps it was what he went through in the war that made him this way?

Out on the Triumph

I couldn't have been happier riding the Triumph motorbike delivering dispatches all over the British Zone of West Germany. In those days, the autobahns were rarely busy though they did carry huge lorries pulling big trailers, something I had seldom seen back home. I fixed my bike so the throttle would stay open; normally when you let go of the twist grip the throttle would close. With my camera hung around my neck I could speed at 60 mph, then sit with arms folded, watching other traffic go by or take photographs of the German countryside. I might add, this was often to the amazement and amusement of other road users, and I still have some of the pictures to prove it!

As a dispatch rider I had authority to stop overnight at any military establishment. Whenever I did I carried my overnight kit, which included a razor. A few years after I left the RAF I discarded this and never used a razor again. Once, when travelling along the autobahn, I saw a sign for Hamelin, which reminded me of the Pied Piper tale, so I turned off and rode through the town centre, before rejoining the autobahn. Later, when on leave in Yorkshire, I told my friends and family I had been to the town from where the Pied Piper had come!

Squadron convoys regularly used the autobahns to get around, which meant that when we travelled to Berlin we had to pass through the Russian Zone at Helmstedt. Inevitably, the Russians made a big job of checking our vehicles and scrutinising our documents.

Berlin is an interesting city, and while there we visited the Olympic Stadium where the Nazis had staged the Games in 1936, and caught a glimpse of a film festival on the Kerfurstendamm (Main Street), packed with people trying to see the stars. At this time there was no wall dividing the city and East Germans had not yet felt the grip of Communism or realised how rotten it would become. We knew the boundaries however, and made sure to keep out of the Russian sector. Incidentally, there was a tower, known as the *Funkturm*, which was like the one at Blackpool. My pal Tom and I went to the top for a magnificent view across Berlin.

We served as guards for a time at the Spandau Prison in Berlin, which housed notorious Nazi war criminals such as Rudolf Hess and Albert Speer. Hess stayed there as the last prisoner until he died in 1987.

Firing our heavy Bofors guns now moved to a range on the Baltic coast where we went often in winter. On one particular trip it was exceptionally cold. As we stood by the sea we could see a band of white ice floes in the distance slowly drifting past the harbour mouth. Some large chunks broke off and drifted towards land, eventually gathering in the shallower water in front of us like mini icebergs. A friend called Paul Ives and I decided to have some fun jumping from one to another as they bobbed around. It was great fun and quite daring but few followed our lead. I was already known as a risk-taker as would come up again many times in the years ahead.

On the way there we had passed through Hamburg, driving round the outskirts and through the dock area. I was amazed at the extent of the damage that remained almost a decade after the end of the war. The docks had large ruined areas, with the shells of buildings stripped bare by bomb blasts, and rusting hulks of ships and submarines half-submerged in the water. These sights were a continuous reminder of what had been inflicted by Bomber Command. I'd seen films and pictures of the damage in Germany, but to stand there on one of the sites is beyond description. Sometimes the ruins extended as far as the eye could see. It was the same when we passed through Kiel where the U-boats had been based and where much of the harbour was still useless.

Nevertheless, by the early 1950s the Germans were recovering fast, and we passed many construction sites with tower cranes reaching into the sky. A full return was still long off, but the reconstruction gave an important economic boost and full employment.

Wherever I went in the British Zone I found that Germans were rarely very friendly, though I did notice they became friendlier the nearer we were to the border with the Russian Zone!

Watches for Home
Periods of home leave were few and far between, and usually lasted for just seven days at a time. I had been in Germany for six months before getting my first chance to go home.

Wristwatches could be bought quite cheaply in Germany and I decided to take some home for gifts and to sell. But how was I to avoid paying customs duty? I could wear only one on my wrist, so I bought a spare pair of underpants and stitched three watches into them. The journey was a repeat of how we had travelled to RAF Wunstorf: by train from Hanover to the Hook of Holland then on the ferry to Harwich. Before disembarking, I slipped on the spare pair of underpants and walked straight through Customs. No problem!

Three ferries were used on that route, namely the *Parkston*, the *Wansbeck* and the *Vienna*. Hard luck if you got the *Vienna* for I was told it was flat-bottomed and rolled about in rough weather. I don't know how true it was but I was once on one of the others during an especially rough crossing and almost everyone was seasick. The place was awash with stinking spew and it was difficult to get to the toilets without sliding on your backside.

After that first trip home I brought watches every time I was on leave and on the last occasion I took a portable radio and a camera, too. The radio battery was big so I removed it and hid the camera inside. German cameras were the best; the Finettas were the ones I used and my hobby of photography was now well-established. I bought the very best I could afford (a good move as was proved later when I needed money for an organist in a hurry).

I was never homesick, though I used to feel sorry for my mother and brother shouldering the burden of work for the fish and chip shop. After I'd been in Germany almost a year I heard that my granny in Masham had died. There was no question of getting compassionate leave for a grandparent, so I was left in Wunstorf on my own with my tears. She had been a big part of my growing up.

I don't know if it was caused by all the marching and drill, but I was having trouble with ingrowing toenails. These were painful as we spent so much time on our feet. I reported sick and the Medical Officer told me to cut the nails straight across, which would make them grow towards the middle. It made no difference at all, so after a few weeks I reported sick again. When it was my turn I was shown into the MO's office where he sat behind a large desk. "My toenails are no better sir," I told him. "Well, put your foot on the desk," he instructed me. He picked up a pair of scissors, held my toe with his other hand and jabbed the scissors down. Blood spurted out and I thought, "Am I squeamish or is he mad?" He cut down the side of my toe nail, then back to the top and removed a strip of nail a quarter of an inch wide. By now blood was all over his desk. "Now the other foot," he ordered, and did the same to that. By now, I was pouring sweat as well as bleeding. "Now go next door and get a dressing on them," he said. Operation over, I hobbled out leaving a trail of blood behind. I limped around the camp for the next few days but instead of getting better my toes simply became worse. I reported sick again, but luckily saw a different MO who said my toes had turned septic and sent me straight to the RAF hospital at Wegberg. I was operated on immediately and remember lying on a trolley being given injections and coming round, but nothing thank goodness in-between!

While I was in hospital I talked to the airman in the next bed. He was an airframe fitter and had been working on the wing of a jet aircraft when he dropped one of his tools. As he jumped down off the wing to pick it up, a ring he was wearing caught a rivet head and sliced through the finger. This put me off wearing rings for many years.

One of my first and best friends in the RAF was Stan Thompson, from Whitehaven in Cumberland. We shared the same room and the same sense of humour, and we're still buddies more than fifty years on. Stan had a serious girlfriend from whom he received regular letters. He would lie on his bed at night reading and re-reading with me increasingly envious as I seldom got a letter from home.

We both liked music and the radio was always on. One of the highlights of our week was listening to the Top 20 on Radio Luxembourg on Sunday evenings from 11 pm to midnight. We would lie in bed listening, often falling asleep before the 20th record, only to be wakened in the early hours by a horrible whistling noise when the station closed down.

The RAF Regiment were always training, drilling or marching. It didn't take long to get sick of it. Sometimes we would stand on the parade ground for so long your feet would go numb as they lost circulation. You then tried to rock gently to relieve them without moving too much to be noticed or you'd be bawled at by one of the NCOs. I don't know which was worst, summer or winter. If it was hot and we'd been standing still for a long time you'd occasionally hear the clatter of a rifle hitting the tarmac as an airman collapsed. When he revived he would receive a bollocking for dropping his rifle! In winter we'd almost freeze to the spot.

Before a big parade the Padre would say a few words of prayer. First the instruction would be given for Roman Catholics and Jews to, "Fall out to the rear." After prayers they'd return to their places for the parade.

Even though I criticise the RAF Regiment, I'm proud to have been a member. We were smart, good at drill and often won competitions with other regiments, including the best that could be offered by the Army. It still gives me pleasure to see them at Remembrance Day parades.

We were also very loyal to one another. If an airman was in trouble when we were out in town, the first thing to find out was whether he was from the Regiment. If he was, we would all wade in to rescue him. Now I think about it, if he was in the Regiment he was more likely to be in a fight in the first place. Most other RAF servicemen kept a lower profile.

A Contribution Mostly Visual
Stan was a musician and had played the cornet in the Workington Brass Band. He quickly became a member of the RAF Wunstorf Band. Often, while the rest of us were drilling, the bandsmen were away in a hut practising. They would join our parade at the final drill having missed most of the endless hours of parade-ground bashing. Stan asked me, "Ken, why you don't join the band?"
From the time I had been little I had tried many musical instruments brought from the Ripon Sale Room by my gran. These included a ukulele, mouth organ, bugle, and guitar, but I hadn't managed to master a single one. "I can't play a note, Stan," I said. "That doesn't matter. Our bandmaster is easy-going and we're short of bandsmen. I'll get you in; you'll be ok."

"All right Stan, I'll do it!"

So I joined. Stan told them I hadn't played for a long time and needed practice – how true that was! The trouble was I did practice but never got any better. I was issued with white webbing for ceremonial parades and given a brass harp badge to go on my sleeve above the crossed rifles for marksman. I couldn't play, but the badge would look good when I went home on leave. Still, the main compensation was that while the rest of the squadron were marching about, I and my fellow bandsmen sat around relaxing in the band hut.

Before we went on parade the bandmaster, Flying Officer Jeffries, would key us in. We had to blow the same note he blew. Fortunately, I could manage this. Out on parade, I would march along holding the bugle to my lips but only blowing the occasional note. One day, we were playing a very stirring march. I felt good and blew a few notes more than I should have, then a few more. To me, they mingled with the sounds all around and sounded good. I thought, "At last I've got it and can blow the bugle." I was thrilled. However, marching in front of me was Sergeant Burrows, a big man banging a huge drum and he was getting my notes directly in his ear. Suddenly, he turned his head sideways and out of the corner of his mouth said, "Walker, if you play one more note out of that f*****g bugle I'll come round and push it right up your a**e." I was devastated. I thought I'd made it. I survived in the band and continued to dodge drill, but after that my contribution was purely visual.

The top brass came for their annual visit, which meant more parades, rehearsals for the band, and lots of bull, spit and polishing of kit, barracks and vehicles. Mostly, these items were spotless anyway, but to get us to do it over again was a way to occupy servicemen. In those days, being in a peacetime Army or Air Force meant hanging around forever on standby. Hair had to be cut short, especially at the back of the neck. We didn't like it and looked like convicts. If you gave the German barber a couple of cigs he wouldn't scalp you completely. Four days after having my hair trimmed, I was on parade rehearsing for the visit of Air Officer Commanding Second Tactical Air Force Germany (the biggest of the bigwigs as far as we were concerned). The inspecting officer walked down the ranks and, as he passed, tapped me on the shoulder as he'd already done with many others.

"Haircut Walker," he ordered. I was surprised and annoyed. We had to pay for the trim *and* the cigarettes. After the parade my room-mate, Stan said, "You don't need a haircut. It's only a few short hairs on your neck. I can trim them for you with my electric razor."

"Good idea," I replied. It saved me a shilling, at which I was most pleased. As a serviceman I earned just ten shillings a day, so it was welcome.

The next day was the AOC visit. We lined up on the edge of the parade ground for inspection with our boots polished like glass, uniforms pressed, brasses sparkling, white ceremonial webbing spotless and instruments gleaming. It was the same officer inspecting us who had found fault with my hair. I felt confident that I had done as ordered, well sort of. As he neared I was still unworried, all the way right up to when he stood directly behind me. Then things changed suddenly! He went berserk shouting, "I thought I told you to get a haircut, Walker." "Yes Sir, I did."

"Well who did that bloody mess?" he shouted. I stammered but nothing came out that made any sense. "Sergeant, put this man under arrest. Take him to the guardroom, charge him with disobeying orders and coming on parade in a disorderly manner." I was marched off and charged, getting fourteen days 'fatigues'.

When I returned to the barracks some of my mates were standing around tittering. They were obviously amused at something, and it was only when I looked in a couple of mirrors that I saw the scale of the mess. My mate had trimmed my hair all right, but hadn't known where to stop. He'd left a line across the back of my neck which made it look like I was wearing a wig. They called it the Boston cut. Maybe it was ok in Boston but it wouldn't do for Wunstorf. The next day I was marched to the barbers with Sergeant Phipps standing over me, instructing the barber. "Higher,

higher, more off," he kept saying. The poor barber was trying to please both sides but I ended up with a scalping.

"Now give him your shilling and let it be a lesson." It was that all right. In trying to save a shilling, I had paid the money in any case. In addition, I was stuck with fourteen day 'jankers' involving visits to the guardroom in full kit from first thing in the morning until last thing at night. As well as this I had to work in the cookhouse washing greasy tins in warm water with only vinegar for detergent. What made it worse was my mates watching my trips to the guardroom and cheering me on my way.

Bulldog's Rage

It was not long before I was in trouble once more and again found myself in the guardroom. Wunstorf was an operational camp and other aircraft came to visit, often staying overnight and calling on the RAF Regiment for guard duties. A huge American B47 landed one day to stay overnight with a 24-hour guard. The aircraft had secret radar equipment on board so the guards were issued with live rounds for our rifles. When it was my turn to patrol round the aircraft, I marched backwards and forwards as dusk closed in. I wanted to look inside and the gloom would help me do it without being noticed. The door was open, the steps in place and no one was in sight. So I laid my rifle by the bottom step and climbed up. This plane was enormous and towering above me there must have been at least twelve stairs. I reached the top and peered inside. I was tempted to enter but decided to settle for just a quick look. There were masses of wires, panels and switches on either side of the long body. I was savouring the moment when I heard a voice below shout, "Walker!" I turned around to see Corporal Wilson, the guard commander, at the bottom of the steps holding my rifle. I was in trouble as this was a serious offence and he would savour this moment, the bastard.

I didn't like him and, in fact, not many others did either. And he didn't like me, so he made a meal of it. I was marched to the guardroom with him holding my rifle. I was put in a cell under close arrest to await my fate, which came next day. I was up before the commanding officer and the charges were read out, "Being absent from duty while on active service and endangering RAF secret equipment." I had no defence so I told the truth: I was in the RAF and had never even seen inside an aeroplane let alone flown in one. I was simply curious. "No excuse," was the response.

"Fourteen days detention and leave cancelled. March him out Corporal Wilson." What a smart NCO he was. I would get my revenge later!

I didn't have long to wait and a few weeks later my opportunity came. Bulldog, Corporal Wilson's nickname, gave Paul Ives, a London lad and close mate, and me some extra drill. His nickname was fitting for his fat squashed nose was spread over a large area of his face, and along with puffy eyebrows and lips always open he was the image of the breed.

"Walker and Ives will be outside the billet at 7 pm with full kit and rifles for extra drill training," he ordered. It's a pity there isn't a film clip of what followed as it was hilarious.

Bulldog was trying to punish us but we made him look silly. Every command he gave we did the opposite: "Right turn," we turned left or one went left and the other right. We pretended not to hear and marched off the road in among the trees, about turned, face-to-face with each other, marking time. By now the squadron were watching and applauding. It was chaos and he eventually gave up. He forced a laugh but I know he was closer to tears – of rage! Later, I felt a little sympathy for him. He took his work far too seriously and he made life as difficult for himself as he did for others. Unlike us, he didn't have the safety valve of a good laugh.

Demob Nears
For the most part, National Service did me a lot of good. I have to say though, it was not an entirely positive experience. Before I joined up I'd been a regular churchgoer and member of the choir. Very few of the new friends I made at Wunstorf went to church. In those first few months on Sunday evenings I would walk alone across to the church, as my mates went to the NAAFI or out of camp for a drink. After a few months I stopped going to church, spending the time with my friends instead but drinking very little as I wanted to save money for the future. Occasionally I would 'let go' and have a night on the town with friends. We'd buy a bottle of whisky or rum from the sergeants' mess, procured by a friendly NCO. The cost would be 7/6- or about 36 pence in today's money. We would find a table in a bar close to a window, behind the curtain of which would be hidden our bottle. We'd buy the establishment's cheapest drinks, mixing them with our own supply and enjoy a pleasant, inexpensive night out.

I always had money in my pocket. In fact, I was the squadron banker and lent money every week to friends though I never charged interest. However, if anyone missed a payment the book was closed to them. Some would pay me back on payday, then borrow again the next day.

Another special friend, Tom from Glasgow, showed me how to break a bottle to defend myself in a pub brawl. "Dinna smash it on the table," he said. "It'll shatter in your hand. Just bring it up and catch the table edge close to the base of the bottle; that way the bottom comes off." He also demonstrated how to break a windowpane without even scratching his hand. You hit it hard just at the extent of your reach and draw back your fist immediately. "Strike it that way and your fist does nae go through the pane," he said. He taught me a few lines of an Orange Man's song from Glasgow, but told me never to sing it outside our room. "You could get your throat cut for singing it in certain parts of Glasgae," he said. In later years I visited Glasgow several times and have never had occasion to sing the song nor needed to break a bottle, I'm glad to say. Though I had been in a few fights as a lad, never backing down as I was taught by my father, I have now learned when to back down, when to show self-restraint, and when to punch a nose as a last resort!

As 'demob day' approached, time began to drag. Many of us made it worse by ticking off each day on the calendar. Closer to the end re-settlement courses were made available. These might include a refresher for the trade you had left or preparation for something new you wanted to try. I was anxious to get on a course but there was nothing for fish fryers! There was one I thought would suit me - a typing course at a camp near Cologne.

When I went for the interview I told them I would be returning to an expanding family business. One of my responsibilities would be to look after the bookkeeping and accounts, and it would be a great advantage if I could type. I was delighted to be accepted and off I went to Cologne. The teacher, a lovely officer's wife I think, was both patient and friendly. It was all very strange; I'd never even looked closely at a typewriter. "You must learn to touch-type," she said. After a good look at where the keys were she gave us a wooden box to put over them. I struggled through, finally achieving twenty-five words per minute. She told me that was quite good from scratch. I only wish I could do that now. After leaving the RAF I didn't type for many years and almost completely lost touch, only starting a few years ago when I bought my first PC.

The course had the added bonus of plenty of time off, and I was able to have another look round Cologne and a closer look at the old cathedral. I spent a day on an interesting boat trip down the Rhine to Koblenz.

But three weeks after it started I was back at Wunstorf to await my demob date. Close to leaving the service all airmen were interviewed and asked if they would like to stay on and make a career in the RAF. My service record was on the table at my interview with the CO. When he asked if I would like to continue it came as a big surprise, as I thought they would be pleased to be rid of me. He said, "You have all the qualifications necessary for immediate promotion and would make a very good NCO. All you need is to take the job seriously and stop fooling around."

At last, I had received a compliment! I knew my trade and understood the various weapons we used including rifles, sten guns, bren guns, rocket launchers, two-inch and three-inch mortars, hand grenades and Bofors light ack-ack guns. I could and did drive every vehicle on the squadron, in particular the Triumph motorbikes. But the CO had said something that struck home: I didn't take service life seriously enough. My answer was, "Thank you, Sir, but no thanks." I had other plans.

Eventually the day came. There was always a demob party in the NAAFI the night before airmen left. I still wasn't a big drinker, but as it was a big party night my mates worked on me and put whisky in my beer which, foolishly, I drank! Was I ill? I couldn't stand even the smell of whisky for years.

The magic day that had been marked on the calendar months before arrived and next day I left Wunstorf along with several other airmen. There was no sadness, quite the contrary: we were in high spirits despite the fact that we were all suffering hangovers. Our National Service had expired and we were on our way home to a grateful nation (some chance!). If there was one thing I regretted from living abroad it is that I didn't learn a foreign language. I can get by, as they say, but it was an opportunity missed.

I took a last look at the camp where I had spent two-and-a-half years of my life. Though much of the time had been boring and dragged by, there had been plenty of good times too. I'd met and made good friends and, most importantly, laughed with them, often when there was nothing much to laugh about. But it had made some of the worst times bearable. There is something special about the friends I made then; pals like Stan Thompson, Tom Paton, Paul Ives and Adam Lorimer, I will never forget.

Here we were, demobbed servicemen in our early twenties, travelling by train across Germany to the Hook of Holland for the last time, and across the North Sea back to Harwich. It was then on to RAF Cardington to hand in my kit, change back into 'civvies' and head home to Masham. I came back feeling far more worldly and maybe just a little wiser. I had left a boy and come back a man.

Padgate 1953, back row 3rd from left

Weeton 1954

*Sat on a camouflaged
Austin truck bonnet 1954*

1953 Wunstorf

Wunstorf 1954

Wunstorf 1955

Wunstorf in front centre 1955

Wunstorf with Stan Thompson 1955

Baltic coast Germany 1955

1955 on Jankers

1956 with new German trucks

CHAPTER 6
1956 TO 1960
BUILDING FOR THE FUTURE

As an eleven year-old I had avoided going anywhere near George Purvis's slaughterhouse when I worked for him as a butcher's boy. Now, demobbed and twenty-one nothing much had changed, I still didn't want to know about the work of an abattoir. So it was with something of a heavy heart that I took up my first job back in civilian life after leaving the RAF: driving for the Wensleydale Meat Company based at the firm's slaughterhouse at Bedale, seven miles north of Masham. Once again, my main aim was to keep as far away from the sounds, sights and smells – the cattle bellowing and the pigs screaming their last breaths. Although I got a bit harder after the first few weeks, recalling one of the slaughtermen in action makes me shudder to this day.

I arrived home from Germany in 1956 with savings from three years in the RAF in my pocket. I didn't want to fritter this away and set about looking for a job at the first opportunity. That meant working for someone other than my father, of course. My parents were still running the mobile fish and chip business but I wasn't going back to peeling spuds and delivering wet fish to customers in the Dales. My father realised this without a word being said, and the subject never came up. From now on the only way I was ever going to eat fish and chips was when someone else was doing the frying.

I had learned a lot in the RAF though nothing that would help me find suitable work in North Yorkshire. I thought about joining the Police Force and this would have met with my granddad's approval, but I was a fraction below the minimum height requirement at the time.

All I could do was look for a driving job, but in the autumn of 1956 a serious fuel shortage followed the invasion of Egypt by British and Allied troops in what became known as the Suez Crisis. Day after day, I looked through newspaper advertisements and called in at yards and warehouses, but there was nothing doing: no employer was going to run the risk of hiring a new driver while petrol was so scarce. At last, just as winter started, an opportunity came up, probably because it was not a popular choice – driving for Wensleydale Meat in Bedale. I swallowed my distaste and took the job.

It was just as well, as I'd been out and bought myself a motorbike, this time a competition model intended for off-road use. It didn't have lights, but it was needed to get me to and from Bedale which meant making it roadworthy 1950s-style. I clipped on two bicycle lamps, not much help to the rider in the dark but at least other drivers could see me, and they made the motorbike legal. Fortunately, in those days in the Dales there was still not much traffic.

Work began at 7 am and with winter now underway the daily ride was cold and the roads icy. My mother insisted on getting up early each day to make breakfast and see me off. Often on those cold, dark mornings she made my tea with a spoonful of whisky. "That'll keep out the cold," she would say.

One exceptionally icy morning I arrived at work frozen stiff, leaned my bike against the wall and dismounted. But when my numbed feet touched the ground I immediately fell flat on my back. The ground was a sheet of sheer ice. I checked the road I'd just ridden over and found it was the same. How I rode to work without falling off was unbelievable. Had I known how bad it was I would have stayed in bed; sometimes it is better not to know the danger.

This driving job involved me delivering meat from the Wensleydale Meat slaughterhouse to butchers in the area. Loading the vans brought me into proximity with where the killing was done, and in the first few days I tried to ignore what was happening. There were three large vehicles to load and the drivers helped each other, though I quickly found myself doing most of the heavy work. One of the drivers was old and I always stepped forward to spare him carrying the weightiest quarters of beef, which came in at around twelve to fourteen stone, or sixty-five to eighty kilograms. The other driver was a cockney and a lazy sod who always stood back when there was a 'big one'. I was young and strong and didn't mind the overload. There are many jobs that require a strong back: a meat porter, or 'humper' as they're known, is certainly one of them. Wensleydale Meat Company was ahead of its time in some ways and was one of the first in the country to sell pre-packed meat to shops.

To get to the firm's canteen we had to walk through the area where the animals were slaughtered. I usually passed through quickly, avoiding looking at what was going on by keeping my eyes on the ground. But the day came when I did look up and what I saw shocked and sickened me.

Sheep came into the building in single file along a narrow passage. There was a gate at the end where the slaughtermen worked. They would open the gate with one hand and grab a sheep by the horn with the other, before closing the gate. The next move should have been to put a set of tongs over the sheep's head, the handles of which looked like a pair of garden shears. When the circuit closed on these, an electric current went through the head of the sheep, stunning the animal before its throat was cut. This was unpleasant enough, but it wasn't the way one particular slaughterman went about his trade.

He was a big, strong young man who I could picture as the school bully with more brawn than brains. He grabbed the sheep by the horn and instead of reaching for the tongs, an act that required two hands, he picked up a length of heavy duty plastic waterpipe and gave the animal a great whack at the back of its head. It immediately slumped to the floor, legs twitching. He took a knife from the pouch hung round his waist and slashed the throat of the animal. Blood gushed on the floor as he thrust a cormarell between the sheep's rear legs and pressed a button on the electric hoist to pull up the animal. It hung there, suspended in front of him in less than a minute, still dripping blood, ready to be gutted and skinned. I had seen enough and disappeared into the canteen.

I felt quite disturbed by this and over the next few days glanced in to see if that was the way he always dealt with sheep. To my dismay, it was. He was the only one of the four slaughtermen that used the cosh method; the others employed the proper, humane way with the tongs. I didn't know what to do. I hadn't liked what I had seen; it was wrong. The other workers weren't at all bothered. It would be pointless to confront him, so I waited for an opportunity to mention it more diplomatically. A few days later it came when I was next to him in the canteen. "Don't you think it's a bit cruel the way you stun the sheep?"

"Cruel?" he bawled out. "The f*****g things are going to die anyway. What difference does it make? And I'm on bonus. It saves time." End of conversation! Now I was the one who was stunned. I thought him an ignorant brute, but nothing I could say would persuade him to change his ways. In fact, he acted as if he thought his method was especially clever.

Other practices at the slaughterhouse were pretty awful too, even though they broke no laws. When a cow was killed, it was hoisted up by the back legs and gutted. Then the slaughterman stripped off the hide. As he tore it from the fatty carcase there was a warm sickly smell that stuck in your throat, making me feel sick and putting me off eating meat for a long while.

At the back of the slaughterhouse was a stinking yard with stacks of cow hides ready to go for tanning, and sheepskins to be made into rugs. In a corner was the midden and next to that a little shed. Inside, worked a man named Tim whose job was to empty the contents of the animals guts and intestines into the midden. I thought this must have been one of the worst jobs in the world, but Tim seemed happy enough for he worked away not at all bothered by the s**t and stink, never missing a day off work. He would cut open a cow's stomach; wash, cut and trim it, then put the stomach onto a tray marked tripe.

Even worse was the way he stripped and cut up the intestines, selecting lengths of uniform size then drawing them through his fingers – there were no plastic gloves in those days. After stripping out the intestines, he ran water through them and folded them neatly onto a second tray. And there you had sausage skins! He wore a long oilskin apron that hung down over his - three sizes too big - Wellington boots, reaching almost to the ground. When he came into the canteen he would have the place to himself in no time at all!

More for the Birds

Many of the butchers I delivered to were quite generous and gave me a tip or a pork pie. One day I made a delivery to a large shop, the owner telling me to go to the back for my free pie. They were just coming out of the oven and smelled delicious. I watched men rushing about with trays of meat and sausages, among them one individual who carried a large tray of old stale pies. These he tipped into the top of a great mincer followed by a bowl of chopped pork. I watched this mixture go through the mincer into a tray ready to be made into the next batch of pies! When I was given my pie I said, "Thank you, I'll eat it later."

On the way home I threw the pie over the hedge for the birds – probably the descendants of those who had my kind offerings of Tommy's sausages all those years before. I never ate a single pie from that butcher, but one day my dad asked if I had any pies as he fancied one. Well, it just so happened that my free pie had not yet made it to the birds so I said, "Yes, I have one. Take it." He later told me, "That's one of the best pies I've ever tasted. If you get any more from the same place save them for me."

"I will, dad," I replied. I smiled to myself but didn't tell him how they were made and actually made sure I never passed over another from that particular butcher.

Another shop I delivered to was in Harrogate. The front was very smart, painted black and white with a sign across the front in gold letters reading, 'Oliver Bros Quality Pork Butchers'. On my first visit as I walked in via the front door, the owner grabbed my arm, spun me around and hustled me back into the street. His first words were, "I can see you're a new boy so I'm going to tell you something. Never, ever come into the front of my shop again." He took me up a side street and into an alley that led to the scruffy back entrance. "This is where you come, and don't forget it," he said, strutting off back to his shop.

I did as he said and as the weeks went by it became obvious why he didn't want anyone to see his deliveries. He bought the cheapest meat available from the slaughterhouse, consisting of cow beef and pork from old sows and boars. Meat from a boar is strong and tainted, and has to be used in something highly seasoned like Haslet meatloaf to hide the taste. He was up to all the tricks. The shop front gave the impression of quality but in reality it was quite the opposite. The prosperous, well turned-out folk of Harrogate queuing in the shop had no idea what they were eating - though like them it was smartly dressed!

Every week I delivered to a butcher in Richmond, an old man who ran a little shop on the corner of the market. His weekly delivery was only a single lamb, half a pig and a hind quarter of beef. He was too old for the heavy carrying, which I did for him. When I arrived the first thing was to go to the back of his shop and carry last week's beef to the front, hanging it near the counter where it could be cut. Then I'd bring in the current week's delivery and put it in the back. He always hung meat for a week and many say that's the best way. Nowadays, meat has to be fresh with a sell-by date; years ago we simply used our noses!

The delivery vans didn't have tail lifts. You climbed into the back, lifted the meat off the hook and placed it against the rear doorpost. Heavy work indeed with a quarter of beef weighing as much as a man. After setting it up I would get out of the van and lower the beef onto my shoulders, being careful to get the point of balance just right. On one particular day I didn't get it properly balanced and it shot over my shoulder, falling in the street outside the shop. The old butcher usually shuffled slowly, but on this occasion he was like lightning. In fact, I'd never seen him dart so quickly as he appeared from nowhere.

"Oh dear, what will my customers think if they see the meat laid in the street?" he said, close to tears. It was impossible for me to pick up the beef from the ground, as you can only carry such heavy weights when lowered on to your shoulders. He had no strength and was of little help, so all I could do was to drag it across the cobbles into his shop. Fortunately, no one noticed. In fact there was little chance of being seen by any of his customers as he only had about a dozen! I left him in the back scraping grit off the beef. There was no tip that week!

Farewell to Masham

After being in Germany and travelling through Europe, Masham seemed such a very small part of the world. Apart from some new council houses, Masham was just as I had left it and I was unsettled. It had been a great place in which to grow up, but opportunities were few and I felt a larger environment would suit me better as a young man with ambition. I wanted to get on, though I didn't know what form it would take. I saw many of my old friends standing around on street corners, smoking and waiting for the pubs to open. This wasn't for me and I hatched a scheme for the family to move.

What had changed while I was away made me even more unsettled. My grandparents had sold their shop in Masham and retired to a cottage in Ripon. Sadly after only a year in retirement my gran had died. Granddad had bought two bungalows in Ripon for his daughters, my aunts Doreen and Madie. Madie's husband Jack got a job with ICI at Redcar so they moved, taking granddad with them and not long afterwards Doreen and Jig followed. Jig had been told by the doctor that sea air would be good for the dermatitis he caught when diesel had infected a cut. My sister, Freda, had married as a teenager in 1950 and moved with her husband first to Ripon, then to a council house in the village of West Tanfield.

So, the clan had dispersed and there wasn't much to hold us in Masham any longer. After my experiences at the slaughterhouse, a new job would be very welcome to me, while a change of location would suit the rest of my family too, I believed. Driving around the Dales villages with a mobile fish and chip van was a hard way to earn money, and my mother and brother Howard - my dad too - deserved better. My parents were getting older and this was not an easy route to retirement. I thought a good idea would be for them to buy a shop instead of operating the van. It was a straightforward matter to plant the seeds by dropping hints at every opportunity. However, when the decision was finally made it was all my father's idea, which, of course, he had been planning for some time!

The search started. First stop was the shops-for-sale ads in the *Yorkshire Post*, and eventually found the ideal business: a fish and chip shop on Main Street in Burley-in-Wharfedale, a village half-way between Ilkley and Otley. The setting was still rural within easy reach of the moors, but it also offered close proximity to the big cities of Leeds and Bradford.

So it was that we said goodbye to our council house at 4, Leyburn Road, Masham, and relocated the forty miles to Main Street, Burley-in-Wharfedale. The fish and chip shop was in a terrace house with the chippy in one front room and a café in the other. It had a sign saying, 'The Oldest Fish and Chip Shop in Burley' which was something I suppose. It was a good business. The previous couple who sold to my father had made some decent savings, which they took with them to a new life in Australia – a wise move in my opinion.

We lived in the kitchen at the back, and our bedrooms were upstairs: mother, father, Howard, Connie and me made for a crowded existence. Our social life would become centred on the café when it was closed to customers. At the first opportunity Howard took a job with Dewhurst the Butchers, but still helped peel potatoes after work, sometimes helped by his new friend Eddie Thorne.

If there was any sadness in moving from Masham – and there wasn't much on my part – there was none at all when I quit my job at the Wensleydale Meat Company. I now set out to find a new employer. Again, I took a driving job, the first in fact that came along, as the repercussions of the Suez Crisis were still being felt. It meant working for farmer/contractor Arnold Groves in the nearby village of Pool-in-Wharfedale. Another early start, but I had become hardened to such things. Just as my father had done when he first came out of the RAF in 1945, my job was to collect milk churns from the farms in the area. These I delivered to the Co-op dairy in Leeds. As I rolled off the churns from the back of the lorry, a girl would take random samples to check the quality as some farmers had a habit of watering down the milk. If caught out they would say that the cooler was leaking!

Then it was back to Arnold Groves' farm to fill in the rest of the day with haulage work, delivering cattle feed from the local corn mill to farms, or collecting a load of waste shoddy from a mill in Dewsbury to spread on the land. Having started at six in the morning, I rarely finished before six at night.

I didn't see Arnold for the first two or three days, and when I did he asked how I was getting on. I could have said that the old 1940s Maudslay lorry he had given me to drive was ready for the scrapyard, but I didn't. Instead, I said I was fine and mentioned I was even getting in some overtime. "Overtime!" he gasped. "We don't pay overtime here. Some days you'll finish early and sometimes late; you have to take the rough with the smooth." I said nothing, but planned a bit more smooth! Next day after I finished the milk delivery to the Co-op, I went home at 2 pm, and the day after at 2.30. When I saw him next he asked why I hadn't done the afternoon haulage work. "Well Arnold, I've now worked the forty hours you pay me for," (my wage had been agreed based on a forty-hour week).

"This will never do. We can't go on like this," he shouted, getting quite angry. I responded, "I won't ask you to pay me for work I haven't carried out, but you must pay me for work I have done, otherwise I cannot work for you." Soon after that we parted company. Later I learned he had chased someone off his farm with a shotgun after a similar dispute!

Failure on the Hill
Now that I'd bought a very good AJS racing motorbike I started thinking about entering competitions again. This time I hoped things would be different as this bike

was much more sleek and powerful than the old Rudge I had ridden before National Service. I joined Guiseley Motorclub and after some unofficial practice on Ilkley Moor entered my first race at Post Hill, Leeds. Hill climbs had been held there for many years and the scramble circuit included a steep gradient, which would make the race quite tough. I arrived early, did my practice laps and felt good despite the long spell I had been away from competitive riding.

About twenty of us lined up for the race. The start was on a flat area about a hundred yards from the bottom of the hill. When the flag dropped we all shot off towards the hill. I had made a good start and was about fifth as we climbed the hill. Here, the track narrowed and there was much elbowing. Near the top it narrowed further to a point where only one or two bikes could pass at the same time, so we all had to slow down. Unfortunately, the bike in front of me almost stopped as he tangled with another rider. I piled into him and others crashed into me, ending up with eight bikes all in a big heap. Quickly, we untangled ourselves, made hasty adjustments to the many bent bits, and those that could rode off to catch up with the leaders. I had a great rip in my riding breeches, a bruised leg and my shoulder throbbed ... otherwise I felt great! My bike fired into life with no problem, but the forks and mudguard were out of line and the handlebars were twisted, There was no way I could continue so I rode slowly back to the paddock and retired, somewhat disillusioned and very sore. My first race after three years had ended just a few seconds from the start!

I had ridden to the meeting on the AJS which meant somehow riding it home. It was a big effort to make it roadworthy as there were still bent and broken bits, but it seemed just like old times sneaking home. I couldn't let my father see me in this state even though I was now a big boy, and I hid the bike out of sight when I arrived at Burley.

The next day I took stock of the damage and the cost to put it right. Overall, it had been an expensive day with little pleasure. During my National Service I had been careful with the cash, with no smoking and not much spent on alcohol. I couldn't spend like this if I wanted some day to work for myself, so motorbike competitions would have to be put on hold.

On the Buses

In the early part of 1957, my father suggested I get a Public Service Vehicle – or PSV – licence, enabling me to drive passenger-carrying buses and coaches. So I applied for one with Samuel Ledgard, a local private bus company which operated services across Leeds. They had depots in Otley and Ilkley, which were both within easy reach of our home in Burley. When it was time for my test I went to the Ledgard HQ in Armley, a suburb of Leeds.

For reasons that are understandable, the PSV test was stiff but I was confident of my driving ability and by now had driven many different types of vehicles going all the way back to when I was eight. The buses were garaged in a depot basement off the busy Leeds-Bradford A647 road. Coming out of the depot you had to drive up a steep slope, now called Ledgard Way, and met the main road on a sharp bend, making it a highly difficult manoeuvre. To make matters worse, they gave you the oldest Leyland double-decker bus for the test, a vehicle kept specially for this purpose and complete with a push-on hand brake. You eased this back towards you for the hill start. This test was not going to be easy.

I was told that if you were able to get out of that garage and into the traffic flow on the main road without incident, you had passed. I took a deep breath, then drove onto the A647 without a problem, remaining calm and in control. I was so focused I remember listening to the old Leyland engine ticking over so slowly you could count the beats as I eased into the traffic. I was thrilled when I passed and took the job on the buses the firm offered. I was only twenty-one, the minimum age allowed for driving a PSV, and I had become the youngest driver on the Samuel Ledgard fleet, almost younger than many of the buses!

Samuel Ledgard, the famous owner and founder of the firm, had died in 1952 leaving crippling death duties. As a result the executors of the company could afford only second-hand buses bought from other, larger fleets. So nothing was standard. The company painted its buses blue and cream and put them into service, making a motley-looking fleet at best. Many were ex-London Transport Daimlers, but there were also many AECs and Leylands. The oldest was an antique GUY Arab, a relic from before the war that still had wooden seats on the top deck. This would peak at 32 mph and was dreadful when changing gear. In fact, you had to wait for the revs to die down and the engine almost to stall before you engaged the next gear. When I started work at the company no one wanted to drive it and it was always last off the park. But I was confident and determined to get it right so I actually asked for it every day. By the end of the first week I had mastered driving the Arab and could change gear without any crunching noise.

The firm had Leylands of different models and vintages. Some of them were also difficult to drive without grinding the gears, but for me it was all a new challenge and an interesting experience.

Samuel Ledgard was so poor a company they couldn't supply uniforms and the crews were a wild-looking bunch when seen together. Each person wore different clothes in different colours and together were a sight when compared with the firm's opposition, the West Yorkshire Road Car Company, with their smart red buses and pristine black uniforms. However, we were tougher, man and bus! When the snow began to fall in winter, it was the smart red buses and black-uniformed staff who quickly disappeared back to their depots, while Ledgard's hotchpotch collection of men and vehicles ploughed on to serve the routes with pride.

(Ledgards continued to limp along, barely profitable with its ragtag fleet of vehicles, until 1967 when it was finally taken over by its West Yorkshire competitor. The company had a special spirit, though, and inspired many people. Today, there is a Ledgards enthusiast society.)

I used my RAF battledress and trousers for work, dyed navy blue by my mother. Some time later the firm managed to issue us with proper coats, light blue with a dark blue collar and trim, long for conductors and short for the drivers.

In the late 1950s, Ledgards ran a service on visiting days from Ilkley to the TB sanatorium at Middleton Hospital. This was housed in wooden huts close to the moor on the hillside above Ilkley, and was where patients were given the 'fresh air' treatment. I didn't know at the time but Pete, the eldest brother of my school friend Wilf Jackson, was there for a number of years having caught TB in the Navy during the war.

There was an early morning bus service to the AVRO factory at Yeadon. The bus was rarely full as the factory workforce numbers had declined severely. During the war this was a very important aircraft plant producing more than 5,000 planes, including the most famous bomber of them all, the Lancaster, which my father had helped maintain at Mepal Airfield in the Fens. It was said to have been the largest factory in Europe housed under a single roof. The outside was camouflaged to blend in with the surrounding countryside, and during the war it had been one man's job to climb onto the roof and move around the wooden cows and other animals to guard against aerial photography by the Germans.

By now the wooden cows had long gone. The bus terminus on the opposite side of the road to the factory was the size of a football pitch, with rows of bus stop signs bearing town and place names all over the area, some twenty miles away, from where the thousands of workers had been drawn. But by the late 1950s, the car park and terminus were virtually deserted; grass and weeds were reclaiming the territory. It was sad to see the decline. There was good news later on though, and today the site is the location of the Leeds Bradford Airport and adjoining industrial estate. With the modern era of flight travel what was once the AVRO factory again hums with activity.

As I learned the routes and passengers I would slow down by individual house doors and gates to drop off regular bus users. I liked people-watching; it added a little interest to what was basically a boring job. I noticed that every Tuesday in the early evening, the landlady of a pub in the centre of Burley-in-Wharfedale caught the Leeds bus, getting off at the White Cross, Guiseley. She would walk across the road and get into a waiting car, a Ford V8 Pilot - there weren't many of them about and I noticed that too.

Later, when we came back through Guiseley on the last trip of the evening she would be waiting at the same stop. After giving a quick wave to whoever was in the car, always parked in the same place, she would settle down for the short trip home and get off at the Red Lion in Burley. Whenever I was on that shift I looked out for her and it was clear to me that she was having an affair. I knew her from the village and knew her husband, Eddie, too. The affair went on for a long time but I said nothing, though I often wondered what Eddie did on his night off!

Black Looks from Cyclists
My home base was the Ilkley depot where some of the Samuel Ledgard buses were garaged. The caretaker who cleaned the buses and generally looked after the garage was a man called Joe, who was a bit deaf. One day his wife called at the depot with his sandwiches, but she couldn't find him. She searched, calling out his name, but

Joe was nowhere to be found. Eventually, she found him in one of the coaches enjoying something much tastier than his lunch. He was cuddled up on the back seat with one of the conductresses. I don't know what Joe received when he got home that night: his sandwiches or his just-desserts!

On the longer stretches between Leeds and Otley cyclists would often tuck in behind the bus for a 'tow' in the slipstream or as the Americans say, "draughting". None of us bus drivers liked this any one bit as it was so dangerous. Even though our buses rarely reached much of a speed, if we had to brake suddenly the cyclists could easily run into the back. So we all looked out for ways to shake them off, and I found what I thought would be the ideal method.

When driving one of the Samuel Ledgard buses with an AEC engine, if you lifted your foot off the accelerator for a second then stamped the throttle back down hard to the floor, the engine would blast out a cloud of black smoke and diesel fumes. As we travelled along, the cyclist would keep looking out on the driver's side to see past the bus and check what was in front of us; this was the best position to get them with the smoke. It was an art to time this accurately, but nearly all of the time it worked perfectly and the cyclist would get covered in soot and diesel fumes. He would drop off and think twice about getting a free tow again. But I had to be careful as sometimes I would be in for some abuse if the cyclist caught up with me at the next stop. Once, I was almost dragged out of the cab by a very angry young man. I tried to calm him saying, "You've no idea what it's like driving these old buses, trying to push them along and keep on time." I don't think he was convinced and what made keeping a straight face even harder was the unwitting 'black look' he gave me.

At about this time, my brother Howard started learning to drive, and my father appointed himself as his instructor. I knew this wouldn't be good; the same thing had ended disastrously with my mother. My dad took Howard for a lesson in an old car he had bought from an auction, perhaps thinking that as a first-timer my brother couldn't do much harm to an old banger. I went with them sitting in the back as Howard drove to Bradford to get used to heavy traffic in the town centre. There was a lot of construction work going on in Forster Square and the roads were very congested. Howard was doing well until he stalled at some traffic lights. When he pressed the starter there was only a click and it didn't turn the engine. We were surrounded by other vehicles, many hooting their horns. My dad reached under the seat, pulled out the starting handle and gave it to Howard saying, "You'll have to get out and wind the handle; the battery must be flat."

Embarrassed and red-faced, Howard went around to the front and pulled and pulled on the starting handle until, at last, the engine burst into life. My father found the whole thing very amusing and I confess I didn't help: it made a change to see someone else get the treatment I had had to put up with for years. "That'll teach him not to stall it," my dad said with a laugh.

Howard threw the starting handle into the car boot, climbed back behind the wheel and drove on. My father was still laughing at the incident while Howard drove us home in stony silence. When we reached the fish and chip shop in Burley he parked the car, jumped out and slammed the door while giving the keys to our dad. "That's the last time I will ever go out driving with you," he said. And it was, too. "Good for you," I thought. "Stand up for yourself." Howard booked driving lessons and soon passed his test. What this showed was that yet again the person who had really failed was my dad, who was anything but a decent driving instructor. He failed with Howard who pressed on regardless and he failed with my mother when she tried driving in the Fens, but she never drove again. At times he would be bad-tempered and impatient; at others, he was unhelpful and sarcastic. In our family I was the only one who survived his tutoring and passed my test without driving school or any other instruction.

Wooing Wendy

Driving buses meant working shift hours and left part of some days absolutely free. So, to earn extra money I took a part time job at a garden centre potting chrysanthemums and other plants. It was not interesting but at least it was temporary and a reasonable way of earning extra money. Very soon, though, I found there was another major attraction.

On the other side of the lane from the garden centre was a farm. I noticed – I could hardly have failed to – that one of the farm workers was a strikingly attractive girl. She was tall and slim, and looked a little out of place on a farm. Actually, she looked a lot out of place there! She was helping a friend with the horses.

Although National Service had given me more confidence, I was still shy around girls and try as I might I couldn't get a chance to talk to her. I hadn't been driving long for Samuel Ledgard and I found that occasionally she would catch the bus I was driving between Ilkley and Burley-in-Wharfedale, getting on in Ben Rhydding. I would then stop at the end of the lane that led to the farm where she worked, allowing her to get off there and saving her having to walk from the nearest bus stop. I was convinced this had got me noticed at least!

Saturdays were dance nights at the Ilkley Winter Gardens and by this time I had become a regular patron when I was not driving. One Saturday, who should turn up at the Winter Gardens but the girl from the farm. This was my chance. Our eyes met, as the saying goes, and I walked over and asked her for a dance. She agreed! We quickly made friends and had a good laugh about me stopping the bus for her. A date followed; then another, and another!

Her name was Wendy Threlfell and she was not yet eighteen. She was lovely and we hit it off right away with Wendy becoming my steady girlfriend after that first night. Saturdays at the Ilkley Winter Gardens was our main venue, but it depended on whether I was working or not. If it was my duty night, I could usually arrange it that I would drive the dance bus, taking the dancers home. Wendy would get on with the rest and I'd be waiting in the bus. On this late-night service we didn't have a conductor, so Wendy would sit at the back and ring the bell, one to stop and two to go. When we'd dropped everyone off I turned out the bus lights to drive back to the depot. This was Wendy's opportunity to drive a double-decker bus, even though she was only a learner with a provisional licence! It was a tight squeeze in the small cab for the two of us, but quite pleasant! I sat on the edge of the seat as she held the huge steering wheel. The main problem was the cab only took up half of the bus width. This was hard for her to judge as the nearside wheel was a long way away, and she sometimes caught the kerb or verge until she got used to it. Needless to say if I'd been caught it would have meant the sack!

Chris Youhill
Wendy and I had a friend called Chris Youhill, who had what we called 'a dressed up job' in an insurance office in Leeds. This meant he wore a suit, collar and tie. He hated it and yearned to work on the buses with me. Eventually he left his secure office job and became a bus conductor … much to the dismay of everyone who knew him. "What a waste of a good education to drop down to a bus conductor," they said. And Chris was another like Wendy, who I let have the occasional sneak drive!

Like me, Chris had only recently returned from National Service and coincidentally he also served in the RAF. Once we moved to Burley-in-Wharfedale we met and became friends. After leaving the insurance company and starting with Ledgards he would go out of his way to change shifts with other conductors to be on duty with me. Although he had only a motorbike license I would let him drive when the opportunity arose, especially at night when the bus was not in service and returning to the depot without passengers. Eventually, Chris did qualify as a driver and spent most of his working life on the buses, first with Ledgards, then with West Yorkshire and later for bus companies in South Yorkshire. In time, he became a real authority on buses and bus companies, publishing many articles about his experiences. I liked Chris a lot. He had a good sense of humour and we worked well together, always running our services on time.

Coming out of Leeds we would go like the clappers, only stopping to drop off passengers when we were out of town. At rush hour with a full load of sixty four passengers including eight standing, I would wind up the old double decker as fast as it would go. We'd drive up the long slope to West Park, round the long sweeping right-hand bend, crossing the old tram lines still in the middle of the road, with my foot hard to the floor. The bus would lean over to the left at a sharp angle and I'd glance in my mirror to see how much of the rear tyre was showing as the body leaned away from the wheels.

One morning we were on the route from Leeds to Otley. It was just after the end of the rush hour when hundreds of office workers had been taken into town and it was now much calmer. We could look forward to some time off when we reached the depot in Otley and we didn't want to be late, so my foot was again hard down to the floorboards. As we approached Holt Lane the traffic lights were green and I was close to the car in front. Suddenly, the lights changed to amber just as we were right on them. I decided to go through feeling sure the car in front would do the same. But no; he put on his brakes and a second later I hit him and launched his car straight through the lights. I think the driver must have let go of the steering wheel with the impact, because the car veered to the left and shot onto the pavement, coming to rest in the Barclays Bank doorway. I parked the bus and walked over to see how he was. He was just struggling out of the car, shaking from head to toe.

"The l-l-lights d-d-did ch-ch-ch-change d-d-didn't they?" he stammered. Well, I couldn't argue so I said, "Sorry, I hope you're all right." By this time he'd stopped shaking and was unhurt, though a little unsteady, and a small crowd had gathered. We exchanged names and addresses and someone from the bank rang the nearest garage for a recovery vehicle. As no one was hurt we didn't need the police and I was anxious to get away. As I walked back to the bus I looked at his car. The back was badly damaged: the boot was pushed in about two feet and buckled, and there was a large circular mark where the bus headlight had made contact. When I inspected the bus there was no damage at all, only a small mark where some paint had been scratched revealing the brass of the headlight rim. The glass wasn't even broken!

I was expecting trouble as it was my fault. But when we arrived in Otley my conductress came to me with a piece of paper given to her by someone who had seen what had happened and offered to be a witness. The note said, 'Your driver had no chance of stopping and was not to blame'. I handed the paper into the office with my report and heard no more of the incident. What a thoughtful person!

Lucky Escapes
Even though I could get to the Ilkley Winter Gardens, I didn't like the late shift on Saturdays. It meant I was working while other people were out on the town enjoying themselves, and I couldn't be with Wendy until last thing. One Saturday I was driving the Otley-to-Ilkley service, picking up passengers in Otley Bus Station at around 9.30 pm. A gang of six youths jumped on the bus and went upstairs. They looked as if they'd just come from a pub and were a little worse for wear. They were heading for more beer in Ilkley and then on to the Winter Gardens for a dance.

When we started on our way a dreadful racket began with the lads singing and stamping their feet on the floor just above my head. I wasn't happy anyway with working the Saturday evening, but having to put up with a load of drunks was too much. As I drove I was getting more wound up. When we arrived in Burley-in-Wharfedale I stopped the bus and rushed upstairs where I told them what I thought. "You lads are having a good time drinking and enjoying yourselves while I have to work and drive along listening to the noise and your feet stamping on the floor a few inches above my head. Now cut it out or you'll all have to walk the rest of the way."

One of them put up his hand and there was silence. "Quiet lads, he has to work so let's keep the noise down."

"Thanks," I said, and went back to the cab, continuing on our way without further disturbance.

When we arrived at the terminus in Ilkley the lads gave me a friendly wave as they crossed the road and piled into the Star public house for more beer. I went round to have a word with the conductor (not my good friend Chris on this occasion) and asked him why he hadn't dealt with the problem himself.

"Ken, you're a brave man or mad. There was no way I was going to approach that lot. Do you know who they are?"

"No Idea," I said. "But they were drunk and rowdy, annoying me and no doubt the passengers. They needed sorting out."

"Well, it was Haggis Hargreaves and his gang," said the conductor. "They're notorious for causing trouble and you don't mess with them. You are lucky they reacted as they did." Maybe, I had a lucky escape! I later learned that Haggis and his gang upset many people in the Otley area but eventually he annoyed one too many! One night someone waited for him by the swimming pool and beat him to death. The person was caught and went to jail for the killing.

One time you didn't want to be a bus driver was when it was foggy and during the late 1950s we had some real 'pea-soupers'. This name conjures up the thickness of smog caused by a mixture of natural heavy mists and clouds of smoke at a time when every house had coal and wood burning fires. Buses would leave Leeds in the early evening, taking workers home, struggling through the thick fog and heavy traffic, stop-start all the way to Ilkley, arriving late and with no time for a break. We would turn around, go back to Leeds and do it all over again. By 11.30 pm you'd done three round trips and had enough of driving buses for a lifetime!

On one particularly bad night I left Leeds for Otley in the usual throng of traffic, stopping many times to drop off or pick up passengers. When I stopped at Bramhope Church I heard a tap on my driving door. I opened the window to see a man standing there.

"I just want to say thank you for getting me home. This is where I live and I couldn't have managed without following you." At first I thought he was a grateful passenger but then realised he'd been driving a car that followed close behind me all the way from Leeds. He reached in through the open window and placed two half-crowns in my hand. I said, "Thanks very much. Tomorrow is my day off and I'll have a drink on you."

On the Ilkley-Guiseley-Leeds bus route we passed Kirkstall Forge Engineering works. Thousands of men worked there making axles for commercial vehicles, tractors and excavators. At lunchtime many who lived locally rushed out to catch the bus on its way into Leeds, dropping off along the Kirkstall Road by the rows of back-to-back terraced houses that bordered the road. They would snatch the quickest of meals then catch the bus back. I'd recognise the same men on our bus travelling both ways, returning to the Forge after a twenty-five minute break. Whatever they had for lunch it had to be better than sandwiches!

The Ford Prefect
Just like his mother, my father loved to visit auctions and car auctions in particular. Often, I went with him, picking up hints on buying things along the way. My relationship with Wendy was continuing to strengthen and the time came when I needed a car to drive her around. Usually, you get what you pay for at a car auction and it comes at market price ... though not always.

This particular day I was late arriving at the Leeds auction and the sale had started, with the cheapest cars going first. I pushed through to the sales area just in time to see a little blue Ford Prefect being offered. It was a wet day and buyers had crowded in from the rain. It wasn't easy to inspect the car as the auctioneer was already calling for bids. I gave the car a quick look over: it looked shiny and bright with the rain drops on the cellulose. I walked round and saw the tyres were ok and there were no signs of bumps, accident damage or rust. It looked worth a bid. When bidding began I put my hand up and immediately down came the hammer: sold to the young man with the beard. Mine was only the second bid they had.

"Can we have your name sir?" the auctioneer asked. It had all happened so quickly. I walked nervously to the side of the rostrum, gave my name and address and paid the deposit of £5 then rushed outside for a closer look. The Ford Prefect was parked with the other sold cars. It looked good and a real bargain, but I wondered why it was so cheap. I went to the sales office, paid the full price and set off home. It's always an uneasy time when you drive away from an auction with your 'bargain'. You change gear listening for any growls or noises. The gearbox was ok. I put my foot down hard on the accelerator to see if the clutch was slipping. I tried the brakes and looked in the mirror for clouds of smoke. My new car passed all the tests and, reassured, I drove home.

My father had been unable to come with me and when I arrived back in Burley the first thing I did was to show him what I had bought. He seemed impressed. "Is there a spare wheel?" he asked. There was no key for the boot, usually just a t-bar with a square end. So I used a screwdriver. As it opened I saw something I didn't expect to see: *my feet!* There was no floor to the boot. It had rusted and rotted away, and that was why there was no key and no other bids in the auction.

Later, I learned that it's usually a bad sign when you buy having had to make only one bid. Probably, the guy who owned the car was the one who had made the bid before me, just to get things started. Maybe the auctioneer had begun things at the reserve price, then looked around for someone like me!

I comforted myself with the fact that the rest of the car was good. The boot would have to be repaired but I knew just the man: a Polish chap called Tony Guzdec. He had been in the Polish Air Force during the war and had settled in Burley-in-Wharfedale opening the Hill Top Garage. He'd christened me *brojate*, Polish for man with a beard.

Tony was a good welder, which was exactly what I needed. He agreed to have a go but said it wouldn't be an easy job as there was nothing to weld a new floor onto. He had an apprentice called Jim, a steady lad who plodded around at his own pace while Tony dashed about fussing over his customers. Jim was helpful but he didn't have a spark, despite Tony harassing him. Tony would shout across the garage, "Jim, what you bugging about at?" (The 'er' sound never quite made it to his vocabulary.) "Come and help me!"

Jim wore the same overalls week after week, becoming so thick with oil and dirt I think they became waterproof. When he took them off he didn't hang them but rather stood them up! Tony did a wonderful job of the welding but it cost more than I had expected: £12. I ran the car for a while before selling it for a small profit, then it was back to the auction arriving earlier, on a dry day and a lot wiser.

A Wedding but no Bells

I heard of an allotment going for sale in Burley-in-Wharfedale. The owner had been in trouble with the authorities for neglecting his pigs, and had let the smallholding run down. It needed a lot of effort to put right, but I have never been worried by a little hard work and had the experience of pig-rearing when I was young to fall back on. I bought it and set to work. The allotment consisted of a small plot of land, five brick piggeries, a store shed and a hen house. I bought a pig from which to breed and some day-old chicks to rear into laying hens.

The chicks were fun. A little cardboard box arrived containing a hundred day-old chirping chickens, all crammed together for warmth. Food and heat is what they need to grow. You were always supplied two or three more than the hundred you purchased, and I took up the challenge of raising them all to adulthood, often being successful. They were very fragile and needed constant care. I fixed up one of the sheds to rear them in, made a circle out of cardboard two feet high to cut out any draughts, put wood shavings along the bottom and set up a lamp heater hung on a chain. Little by little, I would turn down the heater as the chicks' yellow fluff turned into feathers and they no longer needed the extra warmth. There was no electricity on the allotment so I used a paraffin heater, which needed pumping up at regular intervals. I had to do this first thing in the morning and last thing at night. The allotment was about half-a-mile from my parents' fish and chip shop up Station Road. Some nights Wendy would come with me. It was warm and cosy in the shed with plenty of straw bales lying around to help make the place feel more snug. After pumping the heater Wendy and I would check for draughts. On occasions, we were unavoidably delayed!

To enter our house we had to walk through the fish and chip shop. One night when we returned from priming the lamp - and after checking our clothes for bits of straw - we walked into the shop past a queue of customers. One of them pointed at my feet and everyone turned to look at my wellies, which were on the wrong feet! How had that happened? My father looked round from stirring the chips. Although he couldn't see my feet, by the look on his face I think he got the message. I rushed into the back part of the house with a face as red as a West Yorkshire bus. Fortunately, Wendy had gone in first and was spared any embarrassment.

Wendy and I began to see more and more of each other and we grew closer. Eventually marriage was mentioned. We were both still young though, and I said it was better to keep on saving hard; by this time I knew I wanted to set up my own business. But Wendy thought differently. She had turned eighteen, an age she thought specially suited to marriage. She made it clear she wanted me and worked on me to change my mind. Gradually I started to come round to her point of view, becoming increasingly pleased at the prospect.

A lot less pleased at the thought of our marrying were our families though. When finally marriage was mentioned, it went down like a lead balloon with both sets of parents.

"You haven't known each other long enough," we were told. "You aren't old enough. You'll have to wait. We won't agree." Wendy's parents, Bill and Edith, had made up their minds. Or Bill had. Like my father, he made the important decisions. Her mother was a wonderful woman with whom I had been friends from day one, and we thought she would have been willing to agree. But, like my mother, she went along with Bill's opposition 'to keep the peace'. As far as they were concerned there were going to be no wedding bells for Wendy and Ken, at least not yet. I was nearing twenty-three, but Wendy was considered by law to be still a minor at eighteen. She needed her parents' consent.

As matters proved though, it was her parents' opposition that drove her further into my arms. But what were we to do? In those days the newspapers were full of young lovers eloping to Scotland where the law of England and Wales didn't apply. North of the border you could wed at sixteen whether you had permission from your parents or not. Young people would elope to Scotland and the first place they came to was the small but famous village of Gretna Green. This had been the place of choice to get married for generations of runaway brides and grooms and now it was our turn.

My Ford Prefect, with the by now-welded boot, was mechanically sound enough to get us there and back. Getting back was equally important for me because I had to return to work. Without breathing a word to anyone but each other (except to my mother who kept the news from dad), we set off in the early hours of the morning. My shift pattern would give us a day to get there, a day to get married and a day to get back before I would find myself once more at Ledgard's depot.

In the Ford with a top speed of 55 mph it was a long drive and almost midnight when we arrived in Gretna Green. The only place open was an all-night transport café, where we had something to eat. The jukebox was playing Pat Boone's *Love Letters in the Sand*, a touching number about young love and highly romantic in the circumstances. We were short of money so we slept in the car, which was a lot less romantic. Next morning we made enquiries about getting married but were shattered to learn that new rules had come into force: you had to be a resident in the village for three weeks before you could apply! There was no way we could be away so long and, in any case, as we hadn't told her parents and my dad we were starting to worry about how they would react. We decided there was no alternative but to go home and make other plans.

How did our parents feel about this attempted elopement? Well, I don't actually recall any further argument; it seems that few words were spoken. Maybe this meant they had accepted the situation, especially Wendy's father. Bill Threlfell worked for an insurance company. There was an older sister, June, who was a school teacher and later married a man called Mike Stocks, a scenic artist with ITV and a keen jazz musician with a great sense of humour. We often shared a laugh. At this time, Wendy's brother, Peter, was studying and, driven on by Bill, eventually qualified as an accountant and went to work for a large firm in London.

Nothing being said about Gretna, we pushed on with arrangements to get married in Ilkley. We still faced opposition but by now it was becoming clear that Wendy's father wouldn't actually stand in our way. We wanted a church wedding but as neither family was going to give us any financial support, we'd have to go it alone and pay for the ceremony ourselves.

Firstly, we went to meet the vicar who gave us a talk on the importance of marriage. Then he told us the cost and advised that it would be extra for an organist. "We'll just have to do without," I said. When Wendy and I talked about it later though, we agreed the ceremony would be a bit cheerless with few guests and without music, so we decided we would find the money for an organist somehow. One of the bus drivers I worked with was keen on photography and admired the German Finetta camera I had brought back from National Service. I caught up with him and sold him the camera, then went back to the vicar and booked the organist.

Nevertheless, it was a very quiet wedding – apart from the music almost silent in fact. Wendy's parents, or I should say Wendy's father, were still in firm opposition which meant they would not attend under any circumstances. My dad was being as dogmatic as Bill and, that meant my mother felt it best not to come either. For me the most unfortunate thing about this whole upset was that my mother would never see me get married. Who says that men in those days didn't rule the roost? Here were two who certainly made the big decisions that everyone else was expected to live by.

The wedding went ahead. The date was 15 March 1958 and the ceremony was held in Ilkley Parish Church. Wendy was eighteen and I was twenty-two. In addition to a dozen friends, the only family members were Howard and Wendy's sister, June. It was a Saturday, and the following day was our one-day honeymoon spent in a little rented flat over a shop on Leeds Road in Ilkley. We didn't have much furniture and only a single bed but we managed! Then it was back to work at Ilkley bus depot on the Monday for me, and Wendy went to her job in a coffee bar on Wells Road. Here was I, a married man!

Thoughts of Australia

In our wedding photos I was clean-shaven but shortly after started to let my beard grow. In those first few weeks I'd drive the bus with one hand and scratch the new growth with my other as it itched like mad when it passed the initial stubble phase. Few men wore beards in those days, mostly only eccentric professors, hobos and beatniks. Our manager at the bus depot, a man named Jack Tapscott, was of the old school and I thought he'd have something to say, so I stayed discreetly out of his way. Nevertheless, I received much attention and many comments, one from a man who asked, "What does your wife think of it?" I replied, "She loves it; it tickles her cleavage!"

Australia was very much on my mind at this time and I'd recently applied for Wendy and myself to receive an assisted passage to emigrate to Australia. It seems strange now with the attractions of lifestyle and weather so well known, but back then there was a real problem getting people to emigrate and the Australian government was doing all it could to get people to go. An assisted passage was provided to selected people, usually those with a skill or trade the Australians needed, and the whole trip out there cost just £10 with the rest being funded by the authorities.

There was a TV programme called *Whiplash* set in Australia in the late 1800s and I didn't miss an episode. Watching the pioneering spirit of the early settlers fuelled my enthusiasm. I was prepared to go out and tackle the toughest of jobs, even cutting cane or sheep sheering. It would mean a new start and a wonderful adventure.

While we were waiting for approval my old RAF mate Stan Thompson came down from Whitehaven to visit. By coincidence, he too was driving buses. We talked about Australia and I asked Stan, "Why don't you come?" But he wasn't enthusiastic. He went home to Cumberland and we lost contact. Months later our approval came through but Wendy developed second-thoughts about leaving her elderly parents - all of fifty years of age! Bill had by now accepted the inevitable and had welcomed Wendy and me back into their lives. So the idea of moving Down Under was abandoned.

It would be forty eight years before I again met Stan and where was it? You guessed - at his home in Australia. He told me that he had gone home, thought about it and decided to go. He also told me that he felt sure I would be there somewhere.

Jonathan Makes Three
For the most part I was willing to make compromises in my marriage. The early date for the ceremony was my way of meeting Wendy's wishes, as she was keen for us to tie the knot while I would have preferred to save for longer. Then soon after she wanted to start a family and, again, I agreed.

So it was that Jonathan Walker arrived on 14 July 1959, born in St Winifred's Nursing Home, Ilkley. He was a bonny baby and appeared healthy with, as we were soon to find out, a healthy set of lungs. But he didn't sleep at night, and this caused much anxiety and loss of sleep for us. Wendy took the brunt of it, so that I could get rest for the long hours I was working with a full-time job and attending to livestock in my spare moments.

She was constantly worried that there could be something wrong with him and became quite depressed. She was only nineteen, I was not much older at twenty-four, but here we were with the responsibility of a young family and me wracking my brain for the big idea that would set me up in business. The early days of our marriage were not easy.

Engineering Turbine Blades
The time came in 1960 when I'd had enough of driving buses and decided to quit. Having made up my mind I was pleased to speak to Jack Tapscott, and hand in my notice. I wasn't so pleased two days later, however, when he asked for me and gave me the sack. In his hand he held a letter. It was from a woman who said I had failed to stop for her. He read, "I put out my hand but he refused to stop, and as he passed he made a rude gesture!"

"Go now," Mr Tapscott said, pointing to the door. "We're not having our service ruined so you should leave right now!" As a result, I didn't get the full week's pay or my holiday money. Clearly he assumed that my decision to leave was accompanied by me abusing the firm's service standards.

What actually happened was this: going into Leeds through Horsforth three different bus services passed that particular bus stop, all going to different stations in Leeds. If you stopped on the off-chance that the waiting passengers wanted your bus, you arrived late in Leeds and had no time for a cup of tea or for the conductor to have a smoke. During that last week when working out my notice period, I'd decided that if there was no hand out requesting the bus to stop I would keep on going. As I approached I saw a woman standing there and I slowed down, but she didn't put out her hand so I put my foot back on the accelerator. As I sped by I did see a hand shoot out, but by then it was too late. Tea time! I waved back and just carried on.

So, that was it: my career on the buses had come to an end.

My next employment was my first working in an engineering shop, Hepworth and Grandage at Yeadon. The firm made turbine blades for jet engines, which required a great deal of skill working to very fine tolerances grinding and polishing. Most of the workforce was East European: Polish, Hungarian or Ukrainian. Some were very hard men. I wondered what they'd done in the war and why they were in Britain. I could picture a few as guards at prisoner of war camps, maybe even Auschwitz or Belsen. At lunch break they would rush down their food, often bread and salami, then crowd around a chessboard until they started work again. They loved chess and the competition was intense.

Our section charge-hand, Dennis, would make sneak visits to the toilet, getting down on one knee and peering under the door to see if the occupant was reading the paper.

One of my best friends, an Italian called Enzo Sacheto, was brilliantly skilled and made a lot of money on piecework.

Another special friend from that time was Kish Imre, known to us all as Jimmy. He left his native Hungary during the 1956 uprising when the country was cruelly crushed by Russian tanks. The Hungarians had shown extraordinary bravery in trying to break free of the Soviet bloc and, sadly, many paid a heavy price. Jimmy was one of those who had fled to England. He spoke little of his experiences but I have since learned what happened. It makes me emotional to think of my friend Jimmy being in the centre of Budapest when the Russian tanks rolled in. The protestors had little more than rocks and petrol bombs to throw at them. I have found a trait among people who have lived for years under an oppressive communist regime: they don't speak much of their experiences. In the past, fear would have closed their mouths, and their newly-found freedom only slowly reopens them. Jimmy lived in Manningham Lane with some of his Hungarian exile friends. I invited him to our house in West Terrace, Burley-in-Wharfedale, where we had moved a few months after our wedding. Jimmy cooked goulash for Wendy and me, and we drank Bulls Blood, the famous Hungarian red wine. Sadly, I lost track of him and wonder if he made it home when the Iron Curtain lifted in 1990. I have been to Hungary many times and find myself scanning the faces looking for him.

Another friend was a Pole named Jan Wysoki. He told me he was leaving to go and work in a woollen mill. "Why don't you come with me; we can earn good money weaving?" "Can you weave?" I asked him.

"Yes," he said. "Well I can't. In fact, the only mill I've been in was a corn mill," I responded.

"I'll show you," he said, becoming persistent. "It's easy. Just tell them you used to weave a long time ago, but on a different loom and you need a little time to get back into it." It sounded a bit like the invitation for me to join the RAF band.

This conversation took place over a pint in the Peacock after work. Jan had ordered two pints of bitter. "I'm surprised you're drinking bitter Jan, I thought you'd prefer vodka."

"Well I did Ken. When I first came to England I thought bitter beer was awful but I made up my mind to get used to it. So every night I went out and drank two or three pints and as you can see, it's worked. Now I like it." He did too!

Weaving a Future
I agreed to give a try to changing jobs again and went with Jan to start work at Booths Mill, weaving cloth for ladies' coats. This led to me working twelve-hour night shifts, five days a week. I had four Northrop looms to tend, and the idea was to keep three running with the fourth spare to cover any major breakdown that couldn't be immediately fixed. This would be left for the day shift fettler to mend. What I didn't realise was that it was all piecework: we were paid for the amount we produced based on the length measure of cloth. I had never even seen a loom before and didn't know where to start. That first night I stood by my loom and thought, "What am I doing here?" The noise was deafening from machinery clattering away all around me, while mine were silent as I hadn't turned them on! I put my hand on the picking stick but dared not launch the shuttle. I didn't know where to start.

I decided to go and watch Jan, who by this time had two looms running and was working on the third. I stayed with him as he got that one in motion, then brought him back with me to help get mine started. The idea was to get three looms running and fill the bobbin magazines. Then you were on standby waiting for one to stop - and you didn't have long to wait. The loom stopped as soon as a thread broke (and there were thousands of them). I had to locate it, mend it and set the loom going again. Sometimes I would be mending a thread on one loom when another would stop. If you weren't quick enough the third loom would break down too. All three would go silent and not earn a penny.

It wasn't hard to become demoralised, though that wasn't the way to be a successful weaver and earn money. All my life I'd been determined not to give in – my father's words again – and I would fight to mend the thread and keep the machinery working. When all three were clattering away, I'd feel a real sense of achievement, filling the magazines with bobbins and waiting for the next break. It was a lovely sound in those rare moments when they ran in harmony, though the noise of the fifty looms in the whole shed was horrendous.

The wool we used was of varying quality. When there was a lot of shoddy in the wool mix the quality was poor and the weft would continuously break, making us rush continuously from one loom to another. When the wool was better quality, they would clatter away while we just stood and watched them: clip clop, clip clop, as the shuttle shot backwards and forwards. That's how you spent twelve hours a night to earn your wages.

That first week I earned what Jan was paid for one night's effort! But whenever Jan's three looms were running he rushed over to my aid. I was a fast learner - I had to be as I needed the money. Soon, I caught up and we were earning the same.

"There you are," he said. "I told you so." It was strange starting work at 7 pm and coming home at 7 am, going to bed in the mornings when Wendy was up and around. I became used to it, though working nights led to a bit of weight loss.

I worked as a weaver for just a few months and picked up a fair bit of savings. During this there was one catastrophe. One night a loom stopped. I found that a wooden bobbin had broken when being changed. I took the broken bits out of the shuttle, replaced it with a new bobbin, mended the threads and set the loom in motion. As the shuttle shot across the warp it cut a strip fifty centimetres long. The loom stopped immediately. What I had done wrong was clear. Where the thread came out of the shuttle there is a little curved piece of metal to guide the thread when leaving the bobbin. This had been pushed up by the broken bobbin and I hadn't noticed when I launched the shuttle. The result was that it cut across the warp and stuck up like a shark's fin slicing through hundreds of threads. I had to leave the loom for the day shift to repair and was told it took six hours to pick up the threads and a large part of the warp was ruined.

I liked many of the foreign workers I met at work and always gave them a little extra time. I had been one myself when I was posted to Germany in the RAF, the first time I had left my native England and I too had been a foreigner in a strange land. I had some understanding of what it felt like to be the odd one out who couldn't speak the language and didn't know the customs. It can be a very lonely feeling. In those days, I always made an effort to make foreigners feel less foreign. I have to say now, though, I am beginning to feel more like a foreigner in my own country!

I had tried my hand at a few different things, driving, engineering and now weaving. But working for others was not going to me my thing. Whether it was my father or Corporal Bulldog Wilson, Headmaster Ward or bus manager Jack Tapscott, I had lived my life until then pretty much under the instruction of others. I was never content with taking orders; now it was time for me to take control of my own destiny.

Ilkley Moor 1957

*Bus Driver and the pre-war Leyland
that I passed my test in*

*A very special motorbike - an
International Norton 1958*

Our Wedding Ilkley

Allotment

Feeding the pigs 1959

The allotment, Laddie and the pigs 1958

Laddie playing with Squeaker 1958

Jonathan feeding the stock at Manor Park 1959-60

Family gathering Otley early 60's

With Jonathan at Bosomworth's Garage Skipton 1959

CHAPTER 7

1961 TO 1969
INTO BUSINESS

The sixties was an important decade. All sorts of things changed forever: attitudes towards love and marriage, views on personal rights and responsibilities, and the way things were done. It was an interesting time to be young and ambitious, and it was when I struck out to make a mark on the world of my own.

When I qualified as a bus driver at twenty-one I had been pleased to be the youngest driver on the Ledgards fleet of double-decker buses, but after two years I had become sick of the job, quite literally ill with stomach trouble. Doctor Green was ex-military and a little abrupt, but we got on well. He checked me over and asked about my work, then told me what was wrong. "It's tension. I believe you don't feel fulfilled as a bus driver, sitting for hours behind a wheel with a stop-start routine. You need more than that to keep your mind and body active; if you can find a way to work for yourself I'm sure you'll be all right."

There it was: even medical opinion said I needed to become my own boss. Instead of driving the bus, racking my brains for ideas, I should just get on with it. I needed to get out of working for others and become my own boss, even if it meant greater effort. At least I should be able to reap the full reward of my labour.

Pigs and Pigmen
Shift work suited me as it left time to spend on the allotment. Right from the start I'd been good at breeding pigs and rearing hens, the legacy of my tending of the family pigs in Masham as a teenager. As the 1960s unfolded I became increasingly successful. I sold the eggs to local shops and my workmates. I took the young pigs to the auction at Otley Market – the well-known Otley Farmers Auction. When I first started I was in a new and strange environment. Though I knew a little about farming, I had to look and learn as I was among men who were livestock experts.

One of these sharp old hands, John Willie Hardcastle, brought along two or three big pigs to sell each week. When he'd unloaded them into a pen he fussed about, brushing and stroking them. I think he brushed linseed oil on their coats to make them shine and look good. When the auctioneer came to one of his pigs John Willie would shout out in a loud voice "She's full of young and due to farrow in't next two weeks. She'll make a good mother." By the size of their bellies they certainly looked like they were carrying large litters.

I put up my hand, bid twice, and the hammer went down. I had bought a pig with two weeks of my bus driver's wage. I took her back to my allotment and put her in a nice clean pen with straw in a corner where she could make a bed ready for the big day. When a pig is due to farrow she will often make a nest ready for her young. The next morning my new pig didn't look so big. Her belly had gone down and the pile in the corner of the sty was the reason - she'd obviously been well fed the day before! About ten days later she showed signs of farrowing and I stayed with her late into the night. Eventually the first one appeared, then a second and a third, up to six, then no more. I placed them where they could suckle and waited for the remainder, expecting a litter of at least ten. But she had no further piglets. That was it; she'd obviously been only half full of young and half full of food when she had looked so promising lying in a pen at the auction.

Later I was told that some breeders give their pigs a special large feed containing sugar beet pulp before bringing them to the auction. Plenty of water would be given to them to drink to swell out their bellies and make the sows look 'full of young'.

I didn't buy any more of Mr Hardcastle's pigs but he was there every week and always sold them. I found another pig breeder who was a lot more trustworthy: Pat Brier of Moss Brook Farm. He was a good man and I used to help him collect swill from factories in the Leeds area. In turn, he sold me good stock at the right price. Later, he sold me his midden when I had no work for my new lorry, but more of that later.

Crossing my Wires
As the allotment didn't have electricity I decided to rear chicks in the cellar of our West Terrace cottage in Burley-in-Wharfedale. I ran an electric cable from the kitchen to the cellar for the infrared lamp keeping the day-old chicks warm. I coupled this into the back of the power point in the kitchen.
When I reached home after work the following evening, Wendy had a large bandage on her hand. "What happened?" I asked.

"You got the wires wrong and the plug exploded, badly burning my hand. And you fused the electricity all along the street! When the Electricity Board inspector came he went mad when he saw the wiring. 'Who did that?' he asked."

She told him, "A friend of my husbands." "Well he's certainly no friend, he could've easily electrocuted you. I want his name. He must never touch anything electric again." He didn't get the name of course - well you don't shop your husband do you! I re-fixed the wiring, properly this time, and prepared the chick-rearing area. The lamp was switched on and I went to my usual supplier, buying 100 day-old chicks. They were very cosy and thrived in the cellar. However, a few weeks later we had a thunderstorm and the cellar took in a lot of water. Fortunately, the chicks didn't drown as their legs had grown but the water soaked into the shavings and droppings. The stink was dreadful, not just in the house but outside in the street, especially if you walked on the pavement past our house where you got it full-blast. You could smell it even on the other side of the road by the bus stop. I was worried that our neighbours would complain but people on either side were used to smells of their own and said nothing.

Most days I took boxes of eggs to work for the staff and once a week took a live hen to Leeds in a cardboard box stowed under the driver's seat. I heard the occasional cluck as it shuffled around in the box. From the terminus in Cookridge Street I would take the hen to the tobacconist's shop on the corner of Great George Street, owned by two Jewish brothers. One would take the box, giving me back last week's empty one and pay me £1. The hen had to be alive and I would select one that had just ceased laying. It was a regular order and went on for many months.

In this way I earned extra money on top of my wages, stowing it away in preparation for starting a business. But what form was this to take? It was on my mind constantly. I looked around, talked to people and scratched my head. It would be easy to follow my parents into the fish and chip business as this was something I knew from A to Z. But I didn't want that; I wanted to make my own way with my own ideas.

Having started on my allotment with one breeding sow, by 1961 I had six and regularly sold eight-week old piglets, or weeners, in the local market. I fed them well and by the time they went to auction they were strong and healthy, and usually made a good price. Unscrupulous buyers and butchers were a problem though, as they organised an unofficial cartel to control prices among themselves. They picked which lot they would buy and agreed not to bid against each other.

At this time I made friends with a man called Rod Parish who had a small farm at Clifton. Like me, he was often disappointed at the price fetched for his weeners. Together, we devised a scheme.

In most businesses the seller puts a price on what he is selling. But for farmers at the Otley Farmers Auction this was often not the case as they had to accept what buyers would pay, even if this was less than the cost of rearing the animals. One day after his pork pigs had been sold, I overheard a farmer say, "Those pigs have taken my money with them," meaning he had sold below cost. The lucky butcher who bought them would make a killing.

One important buyer of young pigs had a large farm where he reared them until they were ready for the bacon factory. His name was Oswald Lister, a gentleman farmer, and he looked smart in his brown tweeds, matching porkpie hat and Veldtschoen brogue shoes. He would give a good price for strong pigs and often bought mine. Like my gran he didn't like to be outbid. Unfortunately, when he was involved other buyers might drop out of the bidding, leaving him with good stock bought cheaply.

When the auction was about to start he would scramble onto the platform above the pens and stand beside Michael the auctioneer, moving along with him to get the best view of the pigs as each pen was offered. He held a small cane and chewed a soggy cigar stub that had gone out some time before. His ruddy face was normally expressionless but when he was bidding and getting anxious he would tap the side of the pen with his cane, at the same time rolling the cigar along his lips with his tongue, his squinty eyes searching to see who was bidding against him.

When Rod's pigs were going under the hammer I would watch Oswald very carefully. If others dropped out of the bidding I would join in easing the price up, but taking care not to go too far and buy them myself. When it was my turn Rod did the same. We knew our man in Oswald. He was determined to buy good stock and wanted our pigs. But we never pushed him too far and our little scheme worked well for a long time.

Squeaker and Laddie

I suffered a setback with my breeding pigs due to following advice I came across in a pig-breeding book. The writer said that pigs like acorns and, by coincidence, the road leading down to my allotment was called Oak Avenue. There were plenty of acorns around and they were all free. I gathered up a large number in the autumn and mixed them in with the feed. Some of my pigs were in the early stages of pregnancy and were due to farrow in two to three months, but as the time drew near their bellies didn't get any bigger. Eventually the due-date for the first one came and passed without sign of young. Then the second and third sows passed their due-dates. I couldn't understand what was happening as they definitely had been pregnant. I asked around and found that while pigs love acorns, too many can cause them to abort and that is obviously what had happened. I'd saved a small amount on my feed bill, but it had cost me dearly when I lost three litters.

At the allotment I kept a guard dog, Laddie, who slept in a kennel just inside the gate. Whenever I was there, he was let off his chain to run free. He would first greet me then go and look for his mate, 'Squeaker', a little pig that never grew and whose squeak never changed into a grunt.

When Squeaker was born he was what you might call a late arrival. His mother had delivered eleven little brothers and sisters and all had found a teat and were taking their first drink of milk when out popped Squeaker. He was a tiny thing half the size of the others, and all white except for a few blue spots on his back. He looked lifeless but I picked him up, cleared the mucus from his mouth and blew gently into it. He gave a twitch and started to breathe, very shallowly at first, his body hardly moving. I took a handful of straw and cleaned him up, then made a space between the others to suckle. They'd all taken up their positions at the long row of teats and objected to being disturbed. But he needed to drink some of the colostrum first milk. As long as I was there Squeaker was able to suckle, though if I turned my back the others would push him away.

Wrecklings or runts are a usual feature of large litters and often die. They can be killed by being rolled on by the mother as they lack the strength to get out of the way quickly enough. I decided that Squeaker should have the same chance as the others, though this involved me in extra work. After a good drink he was able to stand. I stayed with him until he was stronger then went about my work, returning at frequent intervals to see that he was feeding. After a while he was able to run around, keeping out of the way of the more boisterous members of his family. As long as I was there to ensure he had a drink he had a chance.

Somehow Squeaker survived and slowly gained strength. He grew much slower than his brothers and sisters, but he had a big heart and was very agile and full of life. He was 'wick' and deserved to live, and live he did. When the others were eight weeks-old they went to the auction, but Squeaker stayed behind as a pet and Laddie's pal.

After unchaining Laddie I would let Squeaker out of his pen. The little pig didn't try to jump up and lick my face as the dog would, but he was just as pleased to see me, running round squeaking and pushing his nose into my wellies. Then it was feed time and they were given their different food in separate dishes side by side. It was all very orderly and they kept to their own dishes but you could see them eyeing each other, gobbling their grub down as if in a race.

Now it was playtime and Laddie would start to hassle Squeaker, who preferred to follow me looking for spillage as I fed the other pigs. Laddie had been chained up and now wanted exercise. He continued to tease Squeaker until suddenly, without warning the pig would shoot off like a rocket around the allotment as fast as his little legs could carry him, closely followed by Laddie. You might expect it to be no-contest with a dog chasing a pig, but Squeaker was smart. He knew that Laddie had long legs and was quick on the straight, but he also fathomed out that he couldn't twist and turn sharp corners. Laddie seldom caught him. If he was getting too close, Squeaker's trump card was the chicken coop that was so close to the ground the pig could just squeeze underneath. Here he would stay, his little pink snout just peeping out while Laddie paraded around, barking. Eventually, Laddie would lose interest and wander off, and Squeaker would emerge for round two. They often played like this. When they'd had enough they would settle down together on the grass to rest.

Sheepdog Turns Ratter

Laddie was a sheepdog but on one particular day he turned into a very good 'ratter'. I cannot stand rats and became alarmed when I first saw signs of them near the hen battery cages. The problem was that food for the hens was available 24-hours a day in an open trough. As this meant an easy meal for rats, it would draw them into the vicinity, leading them to feed on whatever was around, including eggs. I bought a wire cage trap, baited it with fish from my father's shop and put it by the feeding troughs. On the following day, I was pleased to find a big brown rat frantically running around inside the trap. As I looked at the dirty, horrid creature it reminded me of the most awful torture of the Middle Ages when a cage would be strapped to a prisoner's stomach. Inside, was a starving rat and the only way out was via the prisoner's stomach. It is hard to imagine such cruelty.

Rats give me the creeps, even when they're in a trap. So how should I dispose of it? I could take it to a nearby house whose owner had constantly complained about the smell of my pigs and free it in his garden. The chances were, though, that it would find its way back to my allotment where it had been so well fed. So it had to die. While I pondered this, I put the trap on the ground and Laddie came for a look. He sniffed around with his hackles up. Laddie was a sheepdog cross-breed, not a ratter, but it could do no harm to let him look. He began to snarl and showed his teeth. The rat didn't seem intimidated. I thought it would be a good idea to let him kill it and opened the door. Laddie poked his nose in and like lightning the rat bit him, digging its teeth into the skin at the side of his mouth and locking on. Laddie drew back dragging both rat and cage. He shook his head but the rat held on as the cage fell to the ground. The rat then made a big mistake and let go, but before his feet touched the ground Laddie made his first ever kill. His teeth sank into the back of the rat's neck and he shook it violently. I could see the blood oozing from the bite in Laddie's lip and his eyes were wild. That was the moment he changed from sheepdog to ratter.

I wanted to bury the rat but Laddie didn't want to part with it and snarled at me when I tried to take it from him. Only later was I able to get it when he was distracted at feed time.

It was now all-out war on the rats. Laddie could sniff them out and found where they'd established themselves under the battery cages. I started digging with him beside me, sniffing and scratching. He was so enthusiastic I was getting in his way! He went wild scratching out the stone and soil, working his way forward until all that was visible of him was his wagging tail. Suddenly he backed out with a rat in his mouth, his teeth dug into the back of its neck. He gave it a quick shake, then flung it close to my feet and dove back underneath. It wasn't long before he was back with number two, then three, four and five. He'd keep going back, searching for more and not wanting to quit. At last, I had to coax him away. From now on Laddie was on constant patrol and if there was a rat it would soon disappear.

Quite the Farmer

My next step up from running the allotment, was to rent a field near Manor Park for grazing and I bought three calves. However, it wasn't easy to rear them without cow's milk and they soon died. I was determined not to give up, and bought three more and this time they survived. I was gaining experience. The calves grew stronger as I learned how to feed them on milk substitute.

To start with when they were still young I kept the calves inside a barn. It would be a good idea, I thought, to get a crop of hay from the field. I paid a local contractor, Arthur Hanam, to cut it. Arthur was a bit old-fashioned and still used a little grey Ferguson tractor, but he didn't charge much. A few days later after work I went to check if it was ready to gather. I couldn't believe my eyes when I looked over the gate. Instead of hay the field was just a patch of black charred dust where the hay had been. Apparently, a fire engine had been called by a local resident, but by the time it got there my crop had gone up in smoke. This all happened while I was away and how it started remained a mystery.

When the calves were big enough I put them in the field but had trouble keeping them in. The fences were poor and as I only rented the field, I was reluctant to spend on mending them. The problem was caused by only one of the calves, which was quite wild unlike the docile other two. The wild one liked to roam and the others would follow her. They sometimes broke into the neighbouring field, owned by a not very nice man. He was a wealthy mill owner who farmed for a hobby, though unlike my grandfather's adage I'm sure his hobby didn't pay. The farm was rundown and badly managed, and he couldn't keep farmhands working for him.

I hadn't been home from work long one day when the police called to see me. "We've received a complaint from a Mr Patchet who says your cows have been in his fields again and as this is trespass, he has impounded them. You should go and collect them sooner rather than later and pay the impoundage fee, as it will be charged on a daily basis."

I went to see him at Greystone Manor. Round at the back of the hall was the tradesman's entrance and I knocked timidly on the door. A woman who looked more like a housekeeper than his wife opened it, asked me in, then led the way along a passage to a room where old Patchet sat in a chair by the fireplace. By him was a large desk cluttered with papers. I hadn't offered to take off my shoes and as I looked round the place I thought it was unlikely that I could spoil anything. The whole place was scruffy and for a man with money so was he. Perhaps that was the reason why he was wealthy: certainly, he didn't spend much as his dilapidated, tumbledown farm buildings would testify. He didn't offer his hand, only pointed to a chair and mumbled, "Sit down".

He then started to ask me questions about farming. What experience had I? What kind of animals was I used to dealing with? Was I used to milking cows? What about sheep? And so it went on. Then he asked me where I was working now. I said I was a bus driver and kept cows and pigs in my spare time.

"You're a what?" he said jumping up. "A bus driver," I repeated.

"Well what the hell are you doing here looking for a farming job?" "I'm not here looking for a farming job. I'm here in response to your complaint to the police, and to collect my stock."

That he mistook me for a job applicant upset him. He must have felt a bit silly and his mood changed dramatically. He paced up and down in front of the fireplace on the threadbare carpet, laying down the law. For a man who obviously knew little of farming, as his neglected farm would confirm, he knew even less about how to treat people. I found it hard to take, having to sit there like a little boy. There was much I could have said in retaliation but there was no point as it might increase the impoundage fee. What rankled most was that the fence through which my stock had strayed was his responsibility. I decided it wouldn't help to mention this and biting my lip waited while he cooled down. He walked to his desk, took a piece of paper, scribbled some figures on it and handed it to me.

"That's how much you owe me for feeding your stock and I won't charge you for breaking the fence on condition you mend it and see this doesn't happen again. If they're ever on my land again, I will send them to auction."

What else could I do but pay him the fee? I took my stock back to the field, mended his fence, and then went to feed my pigs. There was no more trouble from him. The cows settled down as they grew bigger. Eventually, I sold them in the auction for beef and the smallest, a little Angus Heifer, won the 'Best in Sale' prize. As a bus driver/part time farmer I was very proud.

False Start

Maybe this was my route towards working for myself. I would have liked a smallholding but didn't have the capital to stock it. Then one day, I had a chat with one of my bus driver colleagues. The previous year he had bought a second-hand tipper lorry and had left Ledgards to work on a motorway building project. Unfortunately, his vehicle had spent more time broken down than working, losing my pal his investment and forcing him to return to bus driving. But the seed had been planted with me. I thought hard about this, especially the bit about the old lorry letting him down. If I was to consider similar work I would need a reliable vehicle.

Time passed. What little spare time I had after working and tending to my livestock, I spent looking for work on motorways or large construction projects. I scrutinised the local paper and *Construction News* for information, and visited worksites where tippers could be needed. A new reservoir was to be built at Thruscross, just a few miles from my home in Burley, and I thought this would be ideal. I made regular visits to the site looking for any sign of the contractors, then one day there was a lot of activity. An area was being cleared and a huge sign read: 'Cubits, Holland and Hammond, Main Contractors'. I spoke to the workmen and they told me the name of the site manager. I was excited. This was great news.

I returned the next week having remembered the name of the manager. There was no need as his name was in large letters on his site office door. I knocked and went in. "I'm looking for work for a tipper lorry. I understand there's a lot of excavation to be done here?"

"There could be," he said. "Do you have a tipper?" "Yes," I lied. "It's only an old one but I'm thinking of buying a new Thames Trader if there's work here, and I'm local." "This project will take three to four years and we're going to need about four tippers all the time." "What about a contract?" I asked. "If we give you the work and you can be depended on then that is the contract. Don't forget we're here for over three years, so there'll be plenty of work and you can earn good money."

"Ok," I said. "If I sort out the tipper, when can I start?"

"You get the lorry and come and see me," he said. We shook hands on what I thought would be the start of my new business. Now I was really excited.

I went to see Tate of Leeds, the Ford Commercial vehicle distributors, and spoke to their salesman, Ron Allanby. He gave me a quote for a brand new Thames Trader tipper; I wasn't going to risk a second-hand lorry. They allowed me £150 on the old Bedford I'd bought in the Leeds auction some time before for £35. So I was already ahead. The new tipper would cost me £1,450 to buy, arrange tax and insurance and have it ready for the road. An order was placed, which I signed with trembling hand. After paying a deposit, the rest would be on hire purchase: that way I could work long hours and get maximum earnings.

I rubbed my hands in anticipation. While I waited for delivery I sold the remainder of my livestock, the allotment and my car. My new life was starting.

The tipper arrived. This was the first time I'd bought a new vehicle of any kind. I'd been brought up on second-hand vehicles by my father and without a car I can remember going to a Chinese restaurant in Otley in the tipper, parking it in a back street, then helping Wendy out of the very high door.

Other haulage vehicles in the area were painted red, blue, black, brown and a mixture of colours. I wanted to be different to make my wagon stand out, so I painted the bodywork bright grass green, the cab white and the mudguards and the chassis black. It looked smart and smelled new inside the cab. I couldn't wait to earn some money. I rushed up to Thruscross and parked as close to the manager's office as I dared in order to show off my new tipper. I knocked confidently on his door and walked in.

"Do you remember me?" I asked. "I came to see you a few weeks ago about work for a tipper."

"Oh yes, I remember," he replied. "Well I don't need you now. Our company at Retford has decided to send up four of our own tippers to work here permanently. So we won't be hiring any locals."

To say I was stunned would be an understatement. I was devastated. Speechless, I didn't even have words to tell him what I thought. I turned and left his office, walking back in a daze to my lovely new wagon with hardly enough strength to climb into the cab. I sat and looked out over the valley where the reservoir was to be built. How my hopes and ambitions had been dashed in those few short minutes. I had signed an HP agreement to pay more per month than my wages had been as a bus driver. What was I to do now?

On the Road

My first thought was, "I'll look for a full reservoir and run my wagon into it." I felt sick as I drove home, racking my brain and thinking, "What next?" Before I arrived I'd recovered a little: after all it wasn't the end of the world. I had a lovely new tipper and a strong back, we would work together somehow. It would be a month before the first HP payment of £42 was due and I needed to get out and earn that cash.

One of the first places I visited looking for work was Menston Station's coal yard. I spoke to the manager, Sid Teal, who was helpful and we soon became friends. His supplies arrived in railway trucks and he was allowed a number of days to empty the coal, then British Rail would charge him daily demurrage rent on the trucks until they were fully emptied.

"I can give you work, emptying the trucks," he said. "You'll have to shovel the coal from the truck to your wagon, then tip it in the yard on top of the existing coal. I'll pay you £1 per ton."

Well, beggars can't be choosers, as the saying goes. I needed the money. In any case I had no carrier's licence to haul goods on the roads. This work was in a yard so no licence was required. The big railway trucks held up to twenty tons and I could empty one in a day. It was very hard work but thank the Lord I had a strong back and have never shied away from manual labour. I'd read about the navvies who built the railways. They had moved the same amount in a day as I was going to do, but all they had to help them was a shovel and a wheelbarrow. They'd wheel each load up a plank out of the cutting, only to have most of their wages stolen back from them in the Railway Company's tuck shop.

Though back-breaking, this work meant good money, £20 a day. I drove the wagon only a 100 yards down the yard, tipped it and then went back again. I hardly used any diesel. It was me who was doing the work not the wagon, but I'd change that later. This little Thames Trader and I were out to make money.

About this time I made friends with Barry Normington. He also lived in Burley-in-Wharfedale and drove his own lorry, hauling coal in the Leeds area from opencast sites to power stations. He liked a pint and had a good sense of humour, though he drove his car very fast and sometimes frightened me. He was a good mechanic and often helped me with repairs on my wagon. One morning when my wagon wouldn't start he coupled a rope to his car and towed me down the road - a four-ton tipper lorry being pulled by a passenger sedan would you believe! Few people would do that.

Some time later when Barry had a huge eight-wheeler tipper, he drove up Bradford Road early one morning with the tipper up and crashed into the railway bridge tearing the body off the chassis. He had been working on it the day before and had forgotten to disengage the tipper pump. It was early morning and dark and as he drove up the road the tipper flipped up. Barry was shocked but unhurt, though the bridge bears the scars to this day.

He played cricket for Menston cricket club and we often went to watch him as there were always fireworks when Barry went in to bat. He could hit the ball so hard it would fly out of the ground, over the main road and into a garden at the other side. Or he'd miss and would be straight back to the pavilion. There were no half measures with Barry.

The next job found me really in the s**t. Pat Brier of Moss Brook Farm, my farmer friend, had an enormous manure heap, which was removed once a year and spread on the land. I could see a way to earn some more money and asked, "How much for the midden Pat?" Being a farmer, he gave nothing away but we had helped each other out in the past, and now it was my turn to benefit.

"£25 to you," he said. "I can get more from my regular man but you're a friend, and you can pay as you go." Normally I would have offered him £20, but the credit would help.

"By the way what will you do with it? "he said.

"Wait and see."

As my farmer friend didn't have a loader the manure would have to be forked onto the wagon by hand. I placed an advert in the *Yorkshire Post*: 'Farmyard manure £1/10 shillings a ton, delivered to the Leeds area, minimum of three tons'. Soon the phone was ringing. Wendy took the orders and I forked the manure onto the lorry. Rose growers and allotment holders bought the lot. It was hard work forking it onto the wagon and the stink hung around. Even after scrubbing my hands I could still smell it and the aroma of 'new' was soon gone from my wagon!

The last load one particular Saturday afternoon was delivered to a rose grower at Eldwick, near Bingley. Since we'd no car at the time Wendy decided to come for a ride and bring our little boy Jonathan. I tipped the load, got paid and set off towards home. Jonathan sat on his mother's knee but he kept reaching over to get hold of the steering wheel. "Pass him over," I said. "I'll let him have a drive."

He sat between my legs, grabbed hold of the steering wheel with both hands and swung it around before I had time to think, taking it completely out of my hands. He was only two and a half but his strength caught me unawares and we ended up with the front wheel in a ditch. It all happened so fast. I felt annoyed with myself. Jonathan of course thought it was great fun and was jumping up and down with excitement. The front wheel had dropped about two feet into the ditch and with no weight on the back wheels I couldn't reverse out. We were stuck. I had to walk two miles to Menston and ask Barry to give me a tow. Jonathan's driving lessons were temporarily put on hold!

It took a month to shift the manure but I earned enough money to live on and pay the HP. There was also plenty of time to think while I stood on the manure heap forking it onto my wagon, after all I didn't want to dwell too deeply on what I was doing at that moment!

Ellerbeck Quarry
I had read in the paper about a new motorway that was to be constructed - what would become the M6 between Preston and Birmingham. I made enquiries and found that the headquarters for one of the main contractors was at Bamber Bridge near Preston. I decided to have a ride over the Pennines. My brother Howard wasn't working and asked if he could come along. I still had no car so we went in the tipper. We found the yard in Bamber Bridge and discovered that Conlon Brothers was the site contractor for all the tipper hire. The excavation work was just starting and tippers were needed urgently. They were pleased to see us.

"When can you start?" "We can come back next week."

"What's wrong with now?" the manager said, peering through the window at our wagon. I glanced at Howard and he looked back at me, both of us not believing our luck. "Ok, what's the deal?" I asked.

He told us the rates of pay, and that we could have a weekly or monthly cheque, then added, "You'll be required to work long hours while the weather is good."
Could not be better I thought, as I reached out to shake his hand. He then took a temporary licence from a folder, wrote in the number of my lorry and handed it to me. "Put that in the window of your tipper, go to Ellerbeck Quarry and haul material to the motorway."

We started then and there. We soon found the quarry at Ellerbeck near Chorley and joined the other wagons queuing to be loaded. When it was my turn, I backed up to the huge excavator where the operator had already filled the bucket, holding it out for me to back under. Before I knew it the wagon bounced and shook as he dropped about four tons of gravel into the back. Then in double quick time it shook again and my lovely new lorry sank to its knees with about eight tons of gravel piled in the back. I selected bottom gear and crept slowly out of the quarry and onto the road. It felt so different from carrying loads of three or four tons but, after all, this was what it was made for and now it must earn those monthly hire purchase payments.

As we drove along I turned to my brother and asked, "How will you get home Howard if I stay?"

"No Ken', he replied. "The question is, how will you get home if I stay?"

I looked at him and said, "You can't stay. You're only twenty and not old enough to have an HGV license." He quickly replied, "That doesn't matter. I'll be twenty-one soon. Why don't you go home, look for another wagon, come back here and we'll work together." That set me thinking. Here I was with a lovely new wagon in which I'd invested my life savings. I wanted to drive it myself, not pass it over to my brother ... but the potential intrigued me.

That first day we made several trips from the quarry to the new motorway. It was great as it was something we could enjoy doing and earn money. After thinking about his proposal for a while I said, "Ok, I'll go home, but I want you to look after my wagon."

"Don't worry," he replied. "Go home and get another tipper, come back here and we'll work together." I sat in the passenger seat while he did two or three trips to get the hang of things. This was the first time he had driven anything bigger than a van, and here he was driving a truck loaded with eight tons of gravel without a licence! I was nervous but he seemed confident and was obviously enjoying it.

After work on that first day we found a place to stay at Euxton where many of the motorway workers were living in huts. This had been part of a huge ammunitions factory during the war and was now temporary accommodation for motorway workers.

Some were Irishmen over for work. You'd occasionally see a tipper lorry parked up on wasteland, the driver having returned to Ireland when the HP payment was due! Howard and I made friends with Joe Furry who was working there with his tipper lorry. He lived in Leeds but was from Ireland originally and was as full of the Blarney as anyone I've ever met.

He always had a tale to tell and make us laugh. He was one of a large family brought up in a small village near Cork in the south of Ireland, and explained the tricks the boys did to amuse themselves. One of them was to hold a lighted match or candle close to their backsides to see who could make the biggest flame when they farted! Next day I went home. On the way I worried about what Howard had said, "Soon I'll be twenty-one." His birthday would be 8 October 1961 - still six months away! I didn't turn back!

When I arrived home, Wendy was surprised. "Where's the wagon?" "I left it with Howard."

"You did what? You must be mad. You know he's only twenty and doesn't have a licence, and anyway he drives faster than you."

"Well," I replied. "That means he'll get more work done and we'll earn more money. Don't worry, he'll be all right. He's a good driver. I'll buy another wagon and go back and join him."

The next question was: "How and with what?"

I'd already asked myself that very same question. "I'll find a way," I said. But to this day I don't remember how I collected enough cash for the deposit. I didn't borrow or steal the money. But I fiddled it somehow and got enough together to buy a second-hand vehicle at auction, once again on finance. This time it was a BMC diesel tipper and I quickly headed back to Preston.

Howard and I were pleased to see each other. As we talked, I wasn't looking at him in the eye; I was scanning my tipper. He could see I was concerned.

"Don't worry," he said. "There's been no bumps and I've done over twenty loads a day; far more than anyone else." He smiled proudly. We had a few drinks in the local pub then I booked in to stay in the workmen's huts at Euxton.

The next day I gave him the bad news. While he had been taking care of my wagon I had wrecked his car. Howard had an old Jaguar and I used it when I reached home to make arrangements for the new wagon. I had checked the oil and water before driving his car and finding the oil level low, I topped it up with the same oil I used for the wagon. This proved a bad mistake. What I didn't know was that diesel engine oil used by my tipper was very different to car oil. It contained a strong detergent to keep the engine clean. Well, the old Jag was quite dirty until the new oil got round. I looked in the mirror on my way to Leeds to see clouds of smoke belching from the exhaust. The detergent had cleaned out the sludge and carbon from inside the old engine and it was ruined, burning oil and issuing smoke from the exhaust. To his credit, Howard wasn't bothered.

"Don't worry about that," he said. "Let's get to work to earn some money, and we'll see to the old Jag when we get back."

I checked my wagon in with Conlon Brothers and entered the rat race at Ellerbeck Quarry. We started at 7 am, joining twenty lorries queuing at the quarry. All were owner-drivers, and all were anxious to be first as we were paid by the load. Howard and I were usually near the front. By midday we'd lapped most of the others and by the end of the day had lapped them again, doing two more loads than anyone else. We only stopped for a pie and a bottle of milk. The weather was good, and we were making money and enjoying it. The only drawback was that my wagon was much older and less powerful than the one my brother was driving, but I couldn't ask him to swap!

Red Shale and Fly Ash
The excavators working in the quarries used red diesel oil which was duty free and a fraction of the price of road fuel, but it was illegal to use in our vehicles. However, that didn't stop me buying some from one of the excavator drivers at just 6d (2.5p) a gallon. This was a great saving but after a few weeks I started to worry as rumours were going about that inspectors were checking vehicles. I ceased buying the red diesel and went back to using normal road fuel.

Two days later I stopped for my bottle of milk and a pie, and as I walked back across the road to my wagon a blue van pulled up behind me. A man in a navy blue uniform jumped out and came across. "We're from HM Customs and Excise and would like to take a sample of your fuel."

His mate appeared with a pump and a long siphon tube, as my heart missed a beat. I hadn't completely emptied the tank of the red diesel, only running it low before topping up with road fuel. What if there was enough left to show on their tester? The Customs man poked the pipe into the tank and sucked up the fuel. I watched it fill the glass with a white filter inside, trying to stay calm. I joked, "What happens now?"

He answered, "If in thirty seconds that white filter changes colour you're in trouble." We gazed at the glass but fortunately it stayed white. They smiled, and one of them said, "You're clear."

I was feeling more confident by now. I looked him in the eye and said, "I could've told you that and saved you the trouble." The pie was in my hand but for those few moments I had lost my appetite. Now it tasted really good!

There were many collieries in the area where the new motorway was being constructed and a way was found to make use of the great slag heaps that for many years had blighted the landscape. When coal is brought to the surface it is put through a screen where any stone or slate is removed then dumped on land nearby, eventually growing into an ugly grey mound. Sometimes a fire would start inside the heap and it would smoulder on for years fed by the combustible material and coal dust. When it finally burned out it would leave red shale. This material was great as a cheap fill for the base of motorways.

Our next job was to haul this material from Ince Moss Colliery. After a few days as the loading shovel worked its way into the centre of the slag heap, we could see that the shale was still smouldering and some of it was quite hot, blistering the paint on some of the tippers. The one I was driving had a wooden body and I didn't want it all to go up in smoke so I asked to be moved to another job. I was sent to a power station where they had found a use for another waste product, fly ash, and for the next few days I hauled this material.

Business was good but I knew it would last only a few months until the motorway was finished. So I started to think of a longer term plan. There was plenty of tipper work nearer home, concentrated on the limestone quarries in the Skipton area, but it was almost impossible to get a haulier's licence. It was a closed shop. There were too many old established companies and British Rail, all of which were protected by the then licensing system and would object to any new applications.

I broke off the motorway work for a few days to go home and make some enquiries about licences. I called at one of the Tarmac quarries and met the owner, a wonderful man by the name of Brian Booth. He said that business was good with all the road building programmes, and he could certainly use extra tippers at peak times - if I had a licence.

"I want to get one. If I apply will you support my application?" I asked.

"Certainly," he said. He clearly liked me. We shook hands and that was the start of a good friendship that would later put thousands of pounds worth of business into my haulage company.

My application was for a license to haul road making materials within fifty miles of Ilkley. I went back to Howard and the motorway to carrying on working while the application was being processed. By now we had more than enough money coming in to pay both HP agreements.

The licence application was to be considered at the Leeds Traffic Court in due course. When the date came through, I phoned Brian Booth. "Alright lad," he said. That was how he talked. "When is it?"

I told him. "I'll pick you up and we'll go in my car," he replied. I remember his car, a Sunbeam Rapier, one of the best saloons available at the time.

The traffic court was similar to any court where you state your case and the powers that be decide either yes or no. British Rail had objected as they always did, but Brian stood up and shot them down in smoke. "There's no railhead at my quarry." He looked directly at the British Rail representatives and asked them, "And how would you handle hot tarmac delivered to roadworks all over the county?" To which they had no reply. In fact, Brian made them look so silly they withdrew their objections. The court granted me my first 'B' licence, allowing me to carry roadmaking materials within a fifty mile radius of home. I was in business!

I was thrilled and felt like hugging him. He enjoyed the moment too, "Come on," he said. "Let's go and have a drink and something to eat." He took me to a smart bar off the Headrow in Leeds and paid for the drinks and food. He was not only doing me a big favour but treating me at the same time. Brian was a wonderful man and one of the first to help me. I later learned he had been an officer in the Army and had suffered badly at the hands of the Japanese, being mentally affected all his life from the ill treatment he received. He later tragically ended his own life. It was a sad end for a very good man.

Lime Spreading

I found a second quarry where they needed transport. This time it involved hauling agricultural lime to spread on the land. I applied for an additional vehicle on my 'B' licence. Just before the licensing hearing Howard came home as the motorway work was nearing completion and took the vehicle that was already licensed to the Tarmac quarry near Skipton. This had good haulage rates set years before for three-to five-ton lorries. We actually overloaded to ten tons and made a better profit. The licence for the additional vehicle was subsequently approved. British Rail certainly couldn't object to agricultural lime being hauled to farms. So I started with the second tipper at Settle Limes working for another good man, Henry Towler. We became friends and he was another to give me a leg-up in business.

Henry ran the spreading department using tractors and a fleet of ex-US Army six-wheel drive vehicles converted to lime spreaders. Some of them had seen service at Normandy as they had been converted from DUKW amphibious landing craft.

Trade was good as there was a big subsidy for farmers. The lime cost the farmer very little and improved his land by reducing the acidity. It was particularly good for hill country. I collected ground-up limestone from a quarry at Threshfield and transported it to each farm, where I would meet the company's tractor driver who then spread it on the grass fields.

Sometimes when we were spreading near a railway line, I would walk along the line and collect lumps of coal that had fallen from the steam engines then coming to the end of their working lives. The coal didn't burn very well on our small open fire though.

One of these tractor drivers was Alan Atkinson. He was keen to get in some overtime as he was saving up to get married, and I was always eager for some overtime to get another lorry. We worked well together. As long as I arrived at the farm with another load before dark he would spread it. Quite often much of the lime spreading was done in the hilly district around Hebden Bridge and Halifax where the land was poor and needed lime. To get orders, the salesmen would go round farms telling the farmers, "We can spread almost anywhere with our new four-wheel drive outfit." Consequently, we found ourselves on some very difficult, steep land to spread lime on, high up valley sides, literally looking down the mill chimneys below.

I was with Alan one day at Mytholmroyd. I tipped a load onto his spreader and off he went up the lane to spread it, a job normally taking only ten to fifteen minutes. After thirty minutes had passed I was getting concerned. By now it was late afternoon and the light was fading. Maybe the farmer had stopped him for a chat, which wouldn't have been unusual. In these lonely places they didn't see many people and when they did they often didn't know when to stop talking.

I walked along the lane following the lime trail that led me into a field and up a very steep slope. I couldn't see him nor could I see the cloud of lime dust that normally followed the spreader. I walked across the hill to where it suddenly dropped away into a hollow. Half way down, the tractor was laid on its side. The spreader had broken away from the tractor and lay upside-down lower down the hill. I ran across as fast as I could to find Alan lying on the grass on the high side of the tractor which had obviously rolled over him. He lay still and appeared unconscious. I didn't waste time and turned and ran like hell to the farm where they phoned for an ambulance. The farmer went to Alan and I went to the bottom of the lane about half a mile away, as it was difficult to find the way up the narrow lane. I waited for what seemed like hours, though it actually arrived in minutes. Alan had come round a bit when they put him into the ambulance but he looked bad and I felt awful too.

How could this have happened to such a careful driver? I just couldn't believe it. He always looked the fields over for the best approach up and down the steep sides and never went crossways. Alan went steady and never rushed around.

The next day the hospital said we could visit. I went with Wendy and Alan's girlfriend, Melinda. Alan was propped up in bed, just able to talk. We were delighted as there was hardly a sign of his ordeal. There was no mention of what happened - that could wait for another day. But the questions remained unanswered, as Alan died the next day. Apparently, a clot of blood had moved. We were devastated!

Alan was buried in the little graveyard at Hubberholme not far from Deepdale where he had lived and grown up. It was a sunny day. The little church looked lovely on such a sad occasion. I don't know how Melinda found the strength and courage to stand in the church beside Alan's coffin, close to the spot where they were to be married. They had been sweethearts from school and had saved and planned for the day when they would get married. The two of them would come to our house at weekends. Alan seldom took a drink and was careful, never spending much, saving every penny to get married. How tragic it was that they should fall short by only a few days.

As they lowered him into the ground, we stood under the trees by the moss-covered wall listening to the preacher. In the background I could hear the ripple of the water in the river. It was so tranquil yet so sad.

The World's Worst Job

I came to know the staff at Threshfield Quarry very well. Gordon Cowling and George Ryder, both office workers, were always helpful as I rushed in and out of the quarry, trying to do as many loads as possible. They would give me any deliveries that were on my way home to Ilkley at the end of the day.

Another worker there, Arthur, had what I thought was one of the worst jobs in the world. He was a lime drawer, the man who rakes out the burnt lime from the bottom of the kiln. Limestone and coke were fed in at the top and the heat changed the stone into lime as it passed slowly down a huge tube. Arthur worked at the bottom raking out the hot lime for loading onto trucks for the railway and to be bagged for other purposes in industry.

As you can imagine it was very hot. It made him sweat and burnt lime likes moisture. It can burn again causing red irritating skin and worst of all it gets into the corners of the eye or nose, or other areas where there is moisture. This made for a very uncomfortable working day for Arthur, even though he would wear goggles and mask.

I was told the pay was good. It certainly needed to be as it was an unpleasant job but Arthur was a hard man. He was strong and blunt, but he had another job as well. He was the shop steward, the union man who spoke up for the quarrymen. He would often tangle with management to defend the rights of the employees. But things change and people change, too. The quarry manager left and the deputy was promoted to his position. But who could be the new deputy? You've guessed it. Arthur was promoted and didn't hesitate to ditch the union and take the job. Overnight, he changed sides. No more sweating in the kiln covered in lime dust, he now came to work in a suit. He smiled, had time to chat and study his racing paper - I think he had another job as a part-time bookie. He was a changed man.

Every day was an early start. I set myself a target to have two-thirds of my work done by 1 pm. If I managed this it was great to know I was in profit before the day was out. I never stopped for a break unless I was delayed or waiting for a load. I took sandwiches and a flask of coffee, invariably eating the sandwiches as I drove along. My left hand was also the hand I changed gear with. The gear lever shook as I moved it and quite often the meat would fall out of my sandwich ending up on the floor. So I asked Wendy to fill them with something that would stick to the bread - the result was Heinz sandwich spread for months. Morning coffee was taken when I had to stop at a level crossing or queue in traffic.

In addition to hauling lime I also collected basic slag from the steelworks at Scunthorpe. This is a waste product from steel-making containing minerals and phosphate, and was ground down to a fine powder and spread on the grassland as fertilizer.

I'd be so early at the hopper at Scunthorpe I would load the slag myself, as the night shift was still sleeping and the day shift had not yet begun. Fortunately, there was a man in the weighbridge. Usually, I would be overloaded as we were paid by the ton, but he was lenient and never sent me back to lighten the load. I sheeted up, a necessity as the slag was so fine it would blow away if it was not covered. It was important to drive steadily around corners as the slag moved about like porridge until it settled.

On one occasion, I had arranged to meet the tractor driver with the spreader at Bolton Abbey. I dropped into Burley-in-Wharfedale and collected my little boy Jonathan, who liked a ride in the lorry with me. The farm address was Haw Pike, Bolton Abbey, and was located on top of a hill about a mile up a farm track from the main road. But it was a location that was new to me.

I turned into the track and looked up the road, which was steep - and I was overloaded. The track ran straight up to where the railway crossed the road, then turned sharp left, where it wasn't as steep, and then right again onto the last stretch up to the farmhouse across the middle of a big field. I was getting worried. Jonathan was 'brum-brumming' his own engine noise. I drove up the track towards the farm with my foot hard down to the boards and only one gear left. I was beginning to think I shouldn't have been so greedy, overloading just to earn more money. Had I known about the farm I would have arranged to meet the tractor and spreader by the main road, tip part of my load onto the spreader then follow him up the hill.

I was in trouble. The brakes were not made for the load and were never any good going back as they were designed to stop you going forwards. I was sweating. Jonathan was jolly having a ride with dad, but dad was nowhere near as happy. I looked around to make contingency plans. If I stalled the only thing to stop the wagon rolling backwards down the track was to put it on full lock and try to turn the wagon onto its side. We were in the middle of the field with nothing to run into or stop us. I was now in bottom gear and slowing even more as the hill became steeper. I could see the top of the farmhouse over the brow but felt I wouldn't make it. Diesel engines will work at very low revs before they stall, but I was already at the lowest!

Then I had an idea. I remembered that the excess fuel button used for starting in cold weather was on my side of the engine. I reached for the clips that held on the cover, turned the screws and tore back the panel. The injector pump was near the bottom and I could just reach it. As I groped around for the button we were almost at a standstill. As my thumb pushed it in there was an immediate response from the engine. I half expected it to explode as black smoke belched out of the exhaust. We didn't exactly surge forward but we did slowly pick up speed and were able to continue up the track. I kept my thumb close to the button for the rest of the way in case it needed another shot!

Jonathan was still smiling and enjoying his ride, oblivious to the crisis. I pulled into the farmyard, parked on the level, got out and looked back down the track. I breathed a sigh of relief and took a few more deep breaths as I looked at the magnificent view of the moors and Beamsley Beacon. Going down would be no problem but I'd learned a lesson. That weekend I bought a set of Ordnance Survey maps covering the areas in which we worked.

A Chill Wind

It was almost fated that the next time Jonathan came with me there was another serious problem. This time it was during that exceptionally cold winter of 1962-63 and the lad almost froze to death. I had loaded early at Scunthorpe, or should I say overloaded. I picked him up and the two of us went to meet the tractor and spreader driver at a farm near Appletreewick. When we arrived there was no sign of him. The farmer showed us where the slag was to be spread on some rough land at the edge of the moor. It was along a lane about two miles from the farm. We found the place, parked by the gate and waited for the spreader. It was a bitterly cold day with a light dusting of snow on the ground and a biting wind blowing down from Beamsley Moor. We waited in the cab with the engine running to get a little warmth, though there wasn't much comfort as diesel engines run cool when not working hard, and the cold wind cancelled out what came from the engine.

I tried to amuse Jonathan and keep his mind off the cold. An hour went by and there was no spreader. We just had to sit tight and wait. We climbed out and played in the snow. Jonathan was coping very well for a three-year old. After two and a half hours Barry arrived with the tractor and spreader. His last job the day before had been near Pateley Bridge and this morning he had to travel from there.

He loaded the slag and set off over the moor to spread it. I was pleased that we'd made a start, but it would be two or three hours before we were finished as slag is spread so thinly. In fact, it would take thirty minutes per load and five more loads to empty my wagon. The afternoon dragged by with us in and out of the wagon. We had a walk on the moor just to keep Jonathan moving. The wind made it feel like Siberia, but he didn't complain and I was amazed at his resilience. I still have a photograph of him standing on that hillside in the snow.

Another time we were spreading slag on a farm near Settle. The spreader had gone across the field with his first load as I sat in my lorry waiting for his return. I could see him in the distance across the fields followed by a cloud of dust, then I saw a man running towards me. He was a tubby man, indeed quite fat, and wasn't built for speed. He was handicapped further by great wellies up to his knees. Between gasps for breath he shouted, "Stop spreading, stop spreading. You mun stop till t'wind drops. It's blowing on't neighbour's land!" He stood there red-faced, still gasping for breath. I thought he was having a heart attack at the thought of giving his neighbour something for nothing. We had to stop and sit around, "till t'wind dropped!"

Many of the farms we delivered to in hilly areas were often up an old track that had never had a fourteen ton vehicle on it. Often, I would hold my breath when crossing an old bridge on a lane built hundreds of years ago for horse and cart traffic. Some of the worst experiences were driving over the canals around the Hebden Bridge area. These were very steep and you couldn't make a dash across. They seldom had a weight limit sign so you had to risk it while not looking down into the deep, dark canal water.

One day, I was sent with a load of road-stone to a farm near Silsden. It was late afternoon and this was the last trip of the day on my way home. Within sight of the farm I came to a canal bridge, where there was a sign clearly displaying '9 Tons Max'. Maybe the farmer forgot to tell the quarry or perhaps the quarry hadn't remembered to tell me. Here I was, total weight fourteen tons. I was stuck. I took a good look at the bridge. Most bridges will stand an overload; in fact, they are built that way to hold a further 20 or 30 per cent. But withstanding an additional 50 per cent weight was stretching things a bit.

This bridge was a flat steel and wood construction. I looked underneath and saw steelwork and big sound timbers. I tried not to look but couldn't avoid noticing how dark and deep the water seemed. It had been a long day and would become dark in thirty minutes. What should I do?

Fortunately the road either side was level and straight so I could get a run at it. Decision made, there was no turning back now. I reversed my wagon about thirty yards so I'd have momentum and set off towards the bridge, foot hard to the floor. I changed into second gear as I passed the 9 Tons Max sign giving me a final reminder. When my front wheels hit the bridge the front dipped down and the other side of the bridge lifted almost a foot in the air. As I moved forward I felt my rear wheels drop the same amount as they followed onto the platform, then my front wheels hit the road at the other side with a jolt that almost took the steering wheel out of my hands. I wasn't clear yet as there were still nine tons sitting on my rear wheels in the middle of the bridge – but at least I was going forwards rather than downwards. The rear wheels bumped onto terra firma, as the bridge sprung back into place with a deafening clunk!

I stopped and breathed a sigh of relief then walked back to inspect the bridge, wondering who else might have heard the noise. I looked around but there was no sign of anyone. I was pleased to see that the bridge was still in one piece and looked no worse for the experience. The navvies certainly did a good job when they built these canals. The farmer however was a little surprised when he signed the delivery note and saw the weight. "I asked for a small load, six ton maximum," he said with a smile. "But you've done me a favour and it appears now the bridge has a new weight limit!" "Well it won't take it again from me," I said. "If I come again I'm going to be carrying no more than six tons!"

Shovelling Snow
Deliveries of lime were sometimes made all the way from Buxton in Derbyshire to farms in the Oldham and Huddersfield areas. I didn't like this trip but it was good money. The lime came from ICI at Tunstead. This was burned lime and didn't you know it if the dust found any moisture on your body. My wrists and neck often burned in summer. If it rained you were in trouble as the dust stuck to you and made

your skin sore. You couldn't avoid it as you loaded and unloaded. It was awful stuff. We were given some balm-like grease called Crodall which helped a bit, but you couldn't put it in the corners of your eyes where there was always some moisture.

My plan was to come out of Tunstead loaded and sheeted up by 8 am when the day shift workers were just starting. This meant an early start at 5 or 6 am, often in the dark. I worked long hours and would leave home in the dark, returning after nightfall, often seeing Jonathan only when he was asleep.

One cold winter's morning in early 1963 I set off early from Ilkley for Tunstead going via Bradford, Halifax and then Holmfirth. As I climbed up the long hill out of Holmfirth, a few snowflakes were blowing in the wind and started to settle on the road. Not a heavy fall but as I got higher there was just enough to stop me; with a light and empty vehicle I had no grip. I made several attempts but found myself skidding sideways into the verge where I ended up with a black and white marker post jammed under the wheel. I dug it out and threw it into the darkness, then thought, "How am I going to get moving?"

There were no other vehicles using the road and I was stuck all alone. I picked up my shovel and found that the snow was so fine I could waft it away. So I walked up the hill swinging the shovel from side to side as fast as I could. It worked and I cleared a strip up the middle then went back to my wagon to do a second strip for my other wheels. I scraped grit from the side of the road, threw it under the wheels then set off before coming to a halt near the top. I had to repeat the procedure, but next time I managed to get over the top and slither down the other side. Fortunately, the snow ran out before the hairpin bend. Then it was across the Sheffield-Manchester road and on to ICI Tunstead. Loading facilities were good and I was soon loaded and on my way to Oldham to meet Gordon driving the tractor spreader across from Waterfoot. He was quite a character and we enjoyed working together.

A few weeks later I was on the same run, but this time in daylight. The snow was gone and as I climbed the hill out of Holmfirth I spotted the place where the black and white marker post, now missing, had stood. I stopped but when I looked in the direction I had thrown it, it was way below. Apparently, when I'd been stuck in the snow I was only a few feet from the edge of a 200 foot drop! Had I known I wouldn't have sat in a grounded wagon, let alone spin my way back on to the road. I'd been close to disaster and not known about it. I may have said this before but sometimes it's better not to know.

Dos't Tha Want a Drink o Tea?
All over the country road works and construction sites were closed during that hard winter of 1962-63 and work for our lorries dried up. I had to scratch around to find projects and took on one of the worst jobs I've ever done, delivering bags of coal for the Guiseley and Yeadon Coal Company.

As a driver you had to shovel the coal out from railway trucks or from the stockyard, and it was often covered in snow. You had to fill sacks that were frozen solid making them difficult to open, even more so when filling them with best household coal as it came in big lumps. The sacks were then loaded onto the wagon and delivered to customers in the area. You had to carry the hundredweight sacks on your back with the sharp lumps digging into you, often up long drives or pathways and usually around the back of the house. Your hands would go numb with no gloves to wear, and you'd be hardly able to grip the corners of the sack. As is often the case, the worst jobs are also the worst paid.

After a week of this I was pleased when I took a phone call asking if I could transport lime to Scotland. ICI supplied lime from their Horton-in-Ribblesdale quarry by rail to a steelworks near Glasgow, but heavy snow had blocked the Settle to Carlisle railway line and it remained closed for weeks. It was imperative that the steelworks continued to get their lime as they couldn't close down their furnaces like turning off a tap! The lime would have to go by road, which was fortunately still open though a bit touch-and-go at Shap, just north of Carlisle.

In all the misery of that winter, this was work made specially for strong arms and determined attitudes like mine and Howard's with our wagons. Better still, we were happy because it meant we could escape the coal deliveries.

It was a long drag in those dreadful conditions with only a narrow track over Shap Fell. Snow was piled higher than our wagons on either side of the road, making it a long slow grind loaded to capacity for the maximum tonnage payment. When you hit bottom gear you stayed in it for a very long time. We made many trips, travelling at all hours of day and night until the railway line was cleared. The money was first-rate!

Many farmers lead a hard life often living in primitive conditions in remote areas. One such place near Hebden Bridge was well off the beaten track, up a long narrow lane close to the edge of the moor. This particular old farmer lived on his own in conditions similar to how Hannah Hauxwell had lived in Teesdale. (Hannah lived for years in Low Birk Hatt Farm, a dilapidated 80-acre farm that she ran by herself following the deaths of her parents and uncle. She had no electricity or running water. Life was a constant battle against poverty and hardship where she worked outside tending her few cattle in ragged clothes in temperatures well below freezing.)

When we arrived, the farmer took Gordon the spreader driver and showed him the land to be treated. It was rough land next to the moor and took us most of the afternoon as I couldn't get close with my wagon and the spreader had to make a long haul with each load. When we finished and were ready to leave I took the farmer the delivery note for a signature.

He greeted us with the words, "You lads 'ave done a grand job. Dos't tha want a drink o' tea afore tha goes?" Lime dust gets in your throat so a drink is seldom refused. We followed him into the house, down two steps into a low dingy kitchen. It was a hovel with bare stone flags and an antique Aga cooker, as filthy and cold as the flags it stood on. Under the single small window stood a sink that had once been white, with a big brass dripping tap. There was no sign of hot water. The stair door leading to the first floor was open and I could see bare wooden steps and old stained brown wallpaper hanging loose. I wondered what it was like up there.

The kettle was singing on a gas ring that had a pipe leading down to a gas bottle tucked under the sink. In the centre of the kitchen was a long table half covered with a tatty old piece of oilcloth. Where it hung down you could just see a faded flower pattern from the 1950s. Laid on the other part of the table was a yellowing newspaper. I squinted to see the date but it had been covered by tea stains, big brown rings the size of the bottom of a pint pot. There were two long benches, one on either side of the table. We sat down and looked at each other thinking the same thoughts but saying nothing. The kettle boiled and he made the tea standing with his back towards us, then turned around and placed a pint pot mug of steaming tea in front of each of us, then picked up his own. "Dos't than want anything's eats?" he said.

We looked at the dirty mugs, then at him and his filthy hands before chorusing, "No thanks, the tea will do!" I had trouble getting the dirty mug to my mouth. I looked round the rim for the cleanest part before taking a sip and Gordon was doing the same. The farmer noticed our dithering. "Dos't than want a bit more sugar?" he asked. It could have eased down the awful tea but we said, "No thanks. It's just right." It was just a little lie!

Most farmers are pleased to see a new face and like to talk, but he was a man of few words. I tried to weigh him up. His age could be anywhere between sixty and eighty. There was a big old-fashioned mahogany sideboard but no photographs and no signs of a woman, just an old cracked glass bowl in the centre. I wondered why he lived such a life: circumstances or by choice? He wasn't saying and I'll never know, but I couldn't help feeling sympathy as I observed the hard life he led with neither comfort nor pleasure.

As I was sipping I heard a loud squirting noise from under the table. He reached under with his stick and gave an almighty whack. "Get outside you ****," he cried. A cat squealed as it scurried from under the table and shot outside, whilst a vile sulphur smell rose from below. When I looked I saw a large brown steaming pool. He cursed the cat then carried on with his tea as if nothing had happened.

I dared not look at Gordon. We wanted to get out of the place but didn't want to be rude and made an effort to sip a little more tea. My mug was light brown on the outside (like the sink it had once been white) but inside it was stained dark brown. As I reached a little over halfway I came to the tea leaves. The bottom of the mug was full of them, large leaves that looked to me as if this was not the first brew they had made nor the first hot water they'd been in! At least I would finish sooner, as there was less to drink. I was relieved to put down the mug and stand up to leave with Gordon a few paces ahead of me. We thanked him and made our getaway into the fresh air. I noticed the mangy cat skulking under a pile of wood waiting to get back in. The first pub we came to was at Packet Well. We dived in for a quick pint to take the nasty taste out of our mouths, relax and have a laugh about the cat incident before setting off home.

But No Criminal Record
I was now trading as Ken Walker Transport, but while I was considering in which

direction to expand, I found myself in trouble. A little incident occurred that almost brought me a criminal record.

We still lived in Burley-in-Wharfedale but the wagons were garaged at a yard we rented in Ilkley. I didn't have a car and caught the early morning bus with the bus crews going to work. As we jumped off in Brook Street one of the West Yorkshire drivers picked up a piece of paper, looked at it and handed it to me. "Someone's lost their tax disc. It needs handing in." He walked on leaving me with the disc. I put it down in the garage on the window ledge and went to work. Over the next few days I looked at it once or twice and thought I must hand it in to the police. But I was late finishing work and anxious to get home, and didn't get round to it. Month-end came and one of my wagons needed its road tax renewed. I had an idea.

Anxious as I was to save money, I stuck the tax disc on the cab window where it wasn't easy to see the registration number. We carried on as normal but after two months my luck ran out. I didn't tell anyone what I'd done, not even my brother who happened to be driving the wagon at the time.

He parked in Skipton to buy fish and chips, and as he returned to the wagon a policewoman was getting out clutching the tax disc. We found out later that it was her self-appointed job to scrutinise vehicles for expired road tax. She had spotted the disc, climbed into the wagon and snatched it. "I'll keep this," she told Howard, who stood there with his mouth open. She proceeded to write out a ticket. I was in trouble and would have to appear in court in Skipton.

This was serious. I needed a good solicitor. "See Jack Mewies. He's who you need," someone told me. "All the villains go to him and he gets them off." Ha ha! Nevertheless, I rang Jack and explained my predicament. "Why did you do it?" he asked.

There was no point in denying anything. "Because I was short of money," I answered.

"Well be at my office an hour before the hearing and bring £25 cash." I went to his office on the appointed day with the money ready in my pocket. He was busy on the phone and stayed talking for a while longer bringing us very close to the time of the court appointment. I became anxious and noticed a young man sitting at a desk at the back of the office, head down working away, but obviously listening to what was going on and learning his trade. At my many subsequent visits he was always there, but it wasn't until years later that Chris Varley became my solicitor. In the meantime, he could not have had a better tutor.

At last, Jack slammed down the phone and shouted, "Come with me," leading the way to his car. I climbed in, worried as we had still not discussed the offence.

"You don't seem to be interested in my case," I said. He turned to me, "Well if you're not happy get someone else."

"You leave me no choice at this late hour," I said. "Well, leave it to me then and just listen," he replied.

I still felt very nervous, which was in contrast to him. This is what he did every day and Jack was relaxed and confident. I was called to stand in front of the court. The offence was read out: "Stealing by finding and evading road tax."

It sounded bad. I felt bad. Jack stood up and addressed the court. "This young man has a clean record and has just started in business after putting his savings into buying some lorries. He works long hours to pay the hire purchase and to support his family. When he found the tax disc he was waiting for a large overdue cheque and only decided to use it until the payment came through. He would then have funds to tax the lorry. Unfortunately for him the offence was detected before the payment arrived. The vehicle has since been taxed."

I gazed at the coat of arms above the magistrate and found it difficult to keep my face straight. Though it was accurate in outline, he had strung it together as he went along, putting it over so well they swallowed it hook, line and sinker! The first offence was dismissed and I was handed down a nominal fine on the second. Overall, I'd saved about £30 on the road tax. By the time I'd paid the solicitor I was only a few pounds out of pocket and had no criminal record. Jack was a clever man and we became friends. He had been a prisoner of war in the Far East and returned home as one of a handful of survivors. Somehow, he had managed to study law and when he came home set up a successful practice in Skipton. He was another to whom I am grateful for help in building my business.

Wendy's Ambitions

My ambition was to buy more wagons and perhaps a nice car. Wendy's ambition was different: she wanted to have a nice place in which to live. Our cottage in Burley-in-Wharfedale was rented, but with a growing income - and an expanding family - she wanted us to buy a home of our own. On 19 October 1962, a second son and a brother to Jonathan had been born, who we called Andrew. He was easier than his brother and slept better. We needed space and Wendy set about making plans for an investment in property.

She'd seen a house advertised by the estate agents Tipping and Lea that she liked. This was in Strathmore Road, Ben Rhydding, Ilkley, very near to where she'd grown up. The cost was £2,200, which required a deposit of £200. My fuel bill for the four lorries I owned by this time was about £200 per month. It was a simple matter of falling behind in settling my fuel account for one month and using the money as the deposit. The deal was done and we moved in late 1962. I was now a property owner and I still have the invoice!

Mind you, when we'd settled into our new home I started looking at new cars again and soon found a lovely red MGB, just a year old. I took Wendy to see it and we both liked it so much we agreed to the purchase. I collected the MGB from Shipley one Saturday lunch-time, driving it back to Ilkley with the sun shining through the blue tinted panels in the special Bermuda hardtop. I relaxed into the seat and thought, "Now I've really arrived!"

On the way up Hollings Hill a car flashed his lights at me and I flashed back, though I didn't recognise the driver. As I drove into Ilkley I saw an MGB coming towards me and he also flashed his lights. Again, I flashed back and it was only then I realised it was customary for MGB owners to greet one another whenever they passed. I felt part of a special club.

Wendy liked it so much I didn't get much chance to drive it for the next few years. Skipping ahead to 1967 I had by now accepted the inevitable and the MGB was firmly my wife's car. Instead of worrying, I bought a Mini Cooper, paying out £750 for what was my first ever brand new car. Less than a year later the Mini Cooper S came out and I had to have one. It cost in 1968 a few pounds short of £1,000. At the time I thought to myself, "I must be mad to pay that much for a Mini," but it didn't stop me and, of course, I loved it. The Minis would come to play an important role at the end of the decade when I started motor racing but I am getting ahead of myself.

Back a few years: by now I'd been accepted into the Threlfell family. We were living around the corner and the jaunt to Gretna Green was long forgiven. Wendy's father Bill took an interest in my business, occasionally offering a little advice. "Now Ken, I think it would be wise to build up a reserve of capital, then if you face problems you can still manage to keep going."

This was sound advice but that reserve could also be useful as a deposit on another wagon. This meant I could take the opportunity while the work was there to be done. My brother Howard agreed with me, we ran the business very closely together. The two of us remained hard workers and the quarries knew we could be relied on. Work was available and I wanted to expand. If I used our reserves to buy a new wagon on HP, over time it would be paid off. When this happened it could be traded in to make a deposit on one or two more vehicles. The more work that came our way, the more I kept expanding the fleet. Because we worked alongside drivers from other haulage companies, we knew who was best and cherry-picked them to strengthen our team. It meant paying higher wages but the work continued to come in and our reputation grew.

Howard and I set high standards with these drivers. We knew it wouldn't be possible to get a paid man to work as hard as we did, but we sought out the best who would get close to it. Working at the quarries we studied the others. One man had stood out - Walter Biggins. I had kept an eye on him. He was very conscientious getting to the quarry early, and he looked after his wagon. When waiting in the queue for a load of tarmac he would spend time cleaning it. In a dusty quarry that isn't easy, but his vehicle shone inside and out. He even had an air freshener dangling from the mirror. I chatted to Walter and told him that I'd ordered a new tipper, it would be arriving soon and I needed a new driver. The seeds were sown and I said no more. Two days later we were again queuing for a load. Walter was dusting off his wagon and he walked over to where I was parked. "When does the new wagon arrive?" he said. I told him month-end, only two weeks away. "Do you pay the union haulage rate?"

"No Walter, I pay more than the minimum."

"Who'll drive the new wagon? Don't you want to drive it yourself and hand this one on to the new driver," he asked, pointing to my wagon.

"It depends who I get, Walter. If I get a driver who looks after his vehicle he can have the brand new one."

"What about your brother?"

"He won't mind. Like me he'll drive anything."

Walter had worked a long time for his present company. I was new on the scene but I could see him thinking about the wagon. "Could I take the wagon home with me? I have a good safe parking place."

"Yes," I said. "But you'll have to decide quickly as I haven't advertised yet." I told him the terms. "I know you've worked for Windles for years, but make up your mind and don't mess me about." We shook hands and Walter Biggins joined Ken Walker Transport. So started a long and very satisfactory relationship, which was largely untroubled but for one slight hiccup a little while later.

The Hiccup with Walter

With work expanding we had taken over a yard and small garage which doubled as an office by the railway arches on Regent Road, Ilkley. Occupying part of the yard was a diesel tank where all the drivers filled up. As I was out driving most of the time, we had a message board where drivers pinned their time sheets inside the garage. I'd collect them when I came in from work on Thursdays and work out the wages at home. I'd make a point of being in the yard early on Friday afternoons, which was pay day, to hand out the men's weekly cash.

Walter continued to drive at the same quarry where he had worked prior to joining us. He liked an early start and would often get the load of other drivers who didn't turn up. Initially, it worked well for both of us. He got the time in and I was paid for the extra load. But after a while Walter became greedy. His time sheet was showing too many early starts and some suspiciously late finishes. I should have jumped on him, but as I considered him otherwise reliable I didn't say anything. The resentment built up though, as I paid him an hourly rate higher than he could get elsewhere. He was always the first to get a new vehicle with his old one passed on down to a new driver. I would have to keep an eye on him and his time sheets.

A few months later things became worse and I knew I'd have to pull on the reigns. I went home one night taking the time sheets to work out the wages. I took his sheet, crossed out the hours he'd added, then worked out his PAYE and tax deductions, sealing his pay packet with what I thought was his entitlement. The afternoon came and I handed him his wages. Walter took his and slipped it into his inside pocket unopened; perhaps that was his wife's privilege.

On Monday I was late back to the yard. When I looked on the message board there was a white sealed envelope addressed to 'Mr Walker'. I opened it and unfolded a single page neatly written by, at a guess, Walter's wife. It read, 'Dear Mr. Walker, I would like to tender one week's notice and leave on Friday. Signed, Walter Biggins.' I was shocked. Instead of nipping it in the bud, I had let the whole matter go on too long. Perhaps it would have turned out the same way but now there was bad feeling on both sides. I could lose my best driver and he would lose a good job. Both of us would miss out.

Over the next few days I avoided him and he did the same to me, but this standoff had to end. One day, I looked at the fuel sheet and saw that he hadn't filled up. So

I waited and sure enough he came in, pulled up by the fuel pump and filled his wagon avoiding my look. He then came in to enter the details on the fuel sheet. He looked across at me, "Did you get my letter," he stammered. "What do you think?"

"It's not what I think Walter. You're the one who has given in your notice. Are you going?"

"I don't want to," he said. I took the letter out of my back pocket and held it in my hand.

"Walter, you won't find a better job and maybe the same is true for me, I might not find a better driver. I'll pay you for all the hours you work and I won't ask you to work for nothing. At the same time, you mustn't ask me to pay for work you haven't done. If you agree, let's tear up the letter that your wife wrote so neatly for you and shake on it." He took the letter and tore it up. The air was cleared and he continued driving for me for many years.

Who Will Drive the JCB?

By 1963 we had six tippers. Most were Fords as they were the cheapest commercial vehicles. They were also light when empty, giving you a high payload up to the legal maximum weight. Though they were sold as seven tonners we could legally carry up to ten tons.

My ambition was to have better vehicles that weren't worn out by the time they were paid for. I'd recently obtained work hauling coal to the power stations, bringing coke from Rotherham and Leeds into Menston Coal Yard, so we needed wagons with bigger bodies. I bought a Commer, a larger vehicle with an alloy body and a two-stroke engine. The exhaust note from this engine was different to the normal diesel. In fact, when Jonathan was just three he could recognise the sound when one went past our house. We later moved on to Leyland and then to Albion six-wheelers, which were better quality wagons that would last longer and clock up more miles before needing to be replaced.

I've always been observant, I think. As I looked around Ilkley I saw a lot of house building going on with sites to clear, roads to cut, or drains that needed digging. I also noticed that all the diggers appeared to come from Leeds or Keighley. I must do something about it. I thought, surely a local man would have preference? To test out the theory, in 1963 I bought a second hand JCB 3c from Wests at Morley, who also promised me some work until I became established locally. When I got it home I sat inside and practiced working the levers that moved the hydraulic digger arm. Neither me nor anyone else in my firm could drive it, so I decided to learn. But before I had the chance West House Builders rang.

"Can we hire a JCB to work at Morley tomorrow?"

"Of course," was my immediate response. I replaced the phone then panicked: who would drive it?

Early next morning I set off. There were no problems on the road though it did wander a bit due to the worn steering. But with the vehicle standing still, operating the levers to dig a trench was not going to be easy.

My first job was to load a wagon with bricks, which meant scooping them up with the front bucket and tipping them into the back of a lorry without dropping any. Needless to say, this was much harder than driving the machine. I was struggling and kept hitting the side of the lorry. The driver was understandably annoyed and started jumping up and down. The day dragged by. I kept making excuses that I hadn't driven this kind of machine before and was relieved when evening arrived and we could go home. Any relief evaporated, though, when I arrived home. Wendy was grinning at me. She had taken a phone message from Wests during the day.

She read it out, "Will you please send another driver tomorrow, preferably one who knows what he's doing as this one is useless. Otherwise, the machine is off hire."

So I was useless! We had a good laugh but they didn't know it was my first time on the machine, and I didn't want to lose the hire. Summoning up my nerve, I went back and told them the regular driver was ill but should be back the next day. Only I knew that he would not! Could they manage with me temporarily? "I'll do my best," I said.

I was playing for time but I had to learn fast. They gave me the same damn job scooping up bricks with the front bucket. Hit them at the wrong angle and the bucket would shoot up over the pile of bricks and you wouldn't get any; if you went in too low you dug up the soil. I was sweating again. I don't like being watched at the best of times even when I know what I'm doing, but as I struggled in front of the site manager's office I was aware that three pairs of eyes were following my every move. Whose idea was it to get a JCB anyway? I tried to make friends with them, but it didn't work. They wanted me off the job. Still I did manage to last the week out and was very relieved when it was time to make tracks home. What's more I had a hire sheet signed for forty hours at £1/5 shillings an hour.

Strange as it seems, they never phoned again!

My next job was just what I needed, work for the County Council. Once you were listed as an approved contractor, you would only go 'off hire' if you worked too fast. Now I could learn properly how to use this JCB. The work was easy and I had time to think which lever to push or pull. We were digging a small drainage trench and I was given a man with a shovel to go into the trench and tidy up. His name was Brian, but his nickname was, "How am I doing?" Maybe his father was like mine and never gave him any praise, as he obviously yearned for some. He worked hard, did his job well and certainly deserved credit. I gave him some and he followed me everywhere and would do anything for me. In fact, I would say he dug more of the trench than I did with the JCB!

I found more work for the digger and at last was able to employ a full time operator. I had learned how to operate the machine but never handled it with any great skill. It was obviously better to pay for an expert and that's exactly what I did. His name was Eddie Thorne, a friend of Howard. Eddie always came to work dressed up - perhaps he told his mother he had an office job. One day I took him with me to look at a job digging trenches on a building site. I walked up to the site office and knocked on the door. It opened and a man came out, walked straight past me and started talking to Eddie, who obviously looked more like the boss!

Taking Stock!

The sixties were unfolding as the most influential decade of the twentieth century. Things were changing and people were questioning old rules. It was a fun time with a growing family and an expanding business. Ken Walker Transport was now an established organisation with a number of wagons of different types, plenty of work and a good reputation with contractors and employees. From 1964 we added more wagons to the six we owned, adding tractor lime spreaders and three excavators to the JCB.

Ilkley builder Vincent Dobson was one of our customers. He phoned one day to hire a JCB, and I called him back to say when it would be available. When the phone was answered I said in a joking manner, "Is VD there?" What followed was a short silence, then an indignant voice which said, "Vincent Dobson here." I said, "Vincent, when your mother christened you, didn't she realise what else VD stands for and that you could be ribbed over it?" The reply was rather curt, "Obviously that thought was far from her mind." I had to back-pedal, I didn't want to lose a hire!

Ilkley is in a valley, which meant that most of the building sites were on a slope or hillside. So developers needed excavators to dig out the roads and level the housing plots. Again, most of the companies able to do this came from Leeds or Keighley and we thought there would be an opportunity for us, giving better service and prices. The most popular mechanical excavator was a Drott, a small digger/loader on tracks. Buying one would be my next move.

Barry Taylor was a rough diamond as people said, but I liked him. He drove a Drott for a company in Bradford. "Get one," he told me. "I'll test drive it for you." A new one was out of the question, so second-hand it had to be. My long-term faith in auction sales came to the fore: you get what you pay for at a market price I'd said when I bought my old Ford Prefect. But this didn't always work out, as I was again to learn.

The auctioneer firm of Walker, Walton and Hanson was to hold a sale of second-hand construction equipment at Acaster Malbis, near York. We went to the sale and looked over the Drotts. Barry tried them as he was the expert.

I bid and bought one for £600. At the time I wasn't fully aware of the system. Good machines taken in part exchange by the main distributors were sold second-hand, but anything older or needing repair was put in the sale. Well, we bought a dodgy one. It started all right. Barry drove it around and the gears were ok. But what we didn't notice until it was paid for and back at Ilkley was that the track frame had broken. Now it was my problem!

It was a mammoth task to fix as you needed special tools and equipment, but somehow we patched it up and had it working in a few weeks. Until the work built up I wasn't able to afford to get an operator, which meant learning to be the driver myself. This meant another steep learning curve. I called on all the builders in the area looking for an easy job to start with, and finally one came along,

A local builder called Alan Butler had a job for me. I was very pleased and arranged to meet him at the site. He was building a house on a little plot of land on the hillside below the Cow and Calf Rocks overlooking Ilkley. The site was covered with small fir trees about fifteen to twenty feet tall.

I didn't have a low-load trailer to move my Drott, so I had to trundle it along the road at a quiet time of the day, as usual in the early morning. Unfortunately, the tracks left marks on the road and the police followed these and threatened me with prosecution.

Will They Grow Back?

I was at Alan's site early to meet him and get the location plan. But there was no Alan, no message and no mobile phones either at that time. I waited, anxious to get working and to start earning. I looked over the site which was a beautiful place to build a house, but the trees would have to go or there would be no view at all. I waited and waited. I walked around the site. I hadn't seen a plan but envisaged where the house would go and where the drive and entrance from the road would be. It was obvious the high hawthorn hedge at the entrance would have to come down.

I started bulldozing a gap in the hedge for the driveway, pushing the branches into piles to burn. Then I worked on the driveway and pushed some fir trees over. I was enjoying myself and got carried away, and when Alan still hadn't shown up I carried on knocking more trees down. It was good practice driving the machine and an easy job. By mid-afternoon there were not many trees left standing, only a few round the outside of the plot. The centre was clear, ready to be set out for the house.

At last Alan arrived with a large rolled up plan in his hand. When he saw what I'd done he almost fell over! At first he could hardly speak, but when he did he soon caught up. The only words I remember are not printable so I'll edit the conversation. He unrolled the plan. "The house was intended to sit in the middle of the plot surrounded by fir trees. Will any grow if you put them back in?" he asked.
"I'll try," I said, and I did ... but they didn't.

The house was built with a view somewhat different to that which had been planned. Months later when I was driving past I felt like calling in and telling the owner he could thank me for his beautiful views over the moors to Langbar and Beamsley Beacon, instead of looking out just at fir trees. I thought about it, but never called in.

After that first job things could only get better. I struggled with a few more small tasks then I had a bit of luck! The snow that could cause havoc on the roads in winter was like gold dust to me. I had made it known at the local Council Highways Department that we had excavators available for emergencies like snow clearing. We were awarded the job of clearing a section of the Skipton to Harrogate A59 road near Bolton Abbey. My brother and I were the operators and worked long hours, and I was able to present the Highways Department with a hefty bill.

When there was snow on the ground it was also time to have fun with the boys. I'd rush home from work where my sons, Jonathan and Andrew, would be waiting, get them into the car with me and we would go for a drive in the snow around the country lanes, skidding round corners, sometimes travelling sideways. They loved it and so did I, but as I write this many years later I'm not so sure it was such a good idea!

On 10 February 1968, Timothy was born. We now had a house full with three young boys falling over each other and making plenty of noise. With the increase in our business fortunes came more money and we made plans to move again, this time to a spacious, detached house on Valley Drive, which ran between Ben Rhydding and Ilkley. I had turned thirty and Wendy was in her mid-twenties. We were becoming a prosperous young family and had the world at our feet.

I landed a bigger job and employed a Drott operator full time. He name was Richard Bell, a man who always talked with his hands, *Con los Manos* as the Spaniards say. He was good at his job and didn't like to be told how to do it. For my part I didn't know how to work the machine properly so I couldn't tell him. All I could do was just outline what needed to be done and let him get on with it. He had great skill with an excavator. I couldn't judge the angle of the front bucket as you can't see the bottom edge where it scrapes the ground, but he could do this to within an inch. Listening to the exhaust note and watching him juggling the hydraulic controls it was clear he was an *artiste* at his trade.

I'd read in the paper that the International Wool Secretariat had announced the building of a new research centre at Ilkley on a site not far from where I lived. I drove past the field every day on the lookout for any sign of activity and eventually saw men erecting a sign. Mowlems was the main contractor and I introduced myself to the site manager and offered our plant hire and tipping lorry services.

The Mowlems' manager, a Mr Harrison, was a nice man and we struck up a friendship that led to me getting a lot of work and hire for the excavator. Previously, the site had been a playing field so the soil had to be stripped off and removed. He hired our machine to excavate and our tipper lorries to move it. The next part of the contract required a temporary road to be laid on the site so that heavy cranes and other machinery could be brought in. Mowlems contracted with us to deliver hundreds of tons of hardcore for this, which we sourced from a demolition job we were handling elsewhere. We also hired a machine to level the material. When the temporary road had to be removed after the cranes had finished, they paid us to load and cart away the hardcore to the tip. That was the idea, but I found a market for it and sold it again.

This job proved very profitable. It's wonderful to sell something twice without cheating anyone. I made sure Mr Harrison enjoyed a bottle of whisky that Christmas.

New Drivers

It was now 1968 and I had just bought another wagon and needed a new driver. In the past, my policy of cherry-picking the best from other companies had been very successful and I had a good team working for me. This time though, before I made a move I was approached by a driver looking for work. I was immediately wary. First of all, good drivers seldom have to look for work and as I studied him I was not impressed.

He was short with thick black hair and a bit untidy-looking. What added to my unease was that he had a heavy gold chain around his neck, several large rings on his fingers, tattoos on his neck and hands, and looked a bit like ... well, a Gypsy. I didn't know what to say. For certain, I didn't want to judge him by his appearance, but first impressions are hard to ignore. I'd worked with foreigners and felt empathy with them and now I wanted to do the same with this driver. I dug a little deeper and asked him a few questions. First I asked something that wouldn't be allowed now and maybe shouldn't have been then either.

"Do you have good health? I can't afford to have my wagons standing idle while you're off work."

"Never ail a thing," was his reply in broad Yorkshire.

He had only recently moved into the area, which was a good reason for not having work. When I asked where he lived, he gave me an address at Cowling, a village near Keighley and said that he'd just bought a house there. I warned him that it was a hard job working for me, early morning starts and long hours.

"Well that'll be no bother to me," he said. "I'll work day and night if ah'm getting paid, and ah'm not bothered about holidays except two days a year: the Boroughbridge Horse Fair and the Appleby Trot. I mun have those off."

Well that confirmed my feeling, he certainly was a Gypsy. But there was something about him I liked. He was switched on and his eyes were bright. The hands that wore the rings were work-worn and he seemed willing. I was impressed and decided to take a chance on someone who was new to us. I had a wagon standing idle, which was not earning money - and neither was he.

"I can start straight away," he said. "Ok, you've got the job on a trial period of one week," I told him. "If at the end of that we find we can work together, it's permanent." When he shook my hand his firm grip squeezed his rings into my fingers. It turned out to be one of the best moves I ever made. Bob Johnson was his name and the longer I knew him the more I liked him. He was a first class worker, 100 per cent dependable and always true to his word. He would set off as early in the morning and worked as late at night as we required. I couldn't fault him and made sure he had those two days off for the Gypsy special meeting days. Of course, we made sure he had other time off too, when it was raining or if we weren't busy.

Bursting at the Seams
Up to now it had been fine at our yard by the railway arches on Regent Road, but as we expanded further we began bursting at the seams. When the vehicles all turned up for a service on Saturday mornings they had to park in the street outside the garage and you would occasionally see a driver greasing his lorry in the road.

The time had come to find new premises, which we found at East Parade, Ilkley. This had a nice new building, giving us the benefit of a separate workshop and offices, and a spacious yard. The owner wouldn't sell so I took on a lease and in 1968 we moved in. Greater opportunity for growth meant I could stop driving and spend more time in the office, organising the existing work and looking for new business. I was also able to engage office staff and a full time mechanic to take over the repairs and maintenance that Howard and I had done since we started.

A stroke of good fortune was finding a bank manager, Roy Johnson, who was another man who helped me on my way, at least for a while in those early years. His bank was in Leeds but he came to Ilkley every fortnight in his old Ford Consul, a vehicle he ran for years.

"Why not buy a newer car Roy?" I asked him on one occasion. "Well you see Ken, I get expenses for my car. This one is very cheap to run, so I show a small profit on the deal," he said with a smile.

We discussed business in my office on his fortnightly visits then went out for a pub lunch, taking turns to pay. This went on for a number of years. I started with a modest overdraft so when I suggested an increase he would say, "Just keep going. I can see your business is expanding. If we ask Head Office they may turn you down. Don't worry I can fix it." That is what he did and my overdraft increased in the following years. But it backfired – and that's a later story.

As the Ken Walker Transport business grew it became difficult to control the cash flow. The nature of our operations was that we were always owed a lot of money. I employed good office staff, three girls in total. One of them had the almost full-time job of phoning around to debtors, though often the only way to get a cheque was by making a visit, which meant another job for me. Eventually I decided it was time to employ someone to take over credit control and an advertisement was placed in the local paper. Several replies came in and I conducted interviews, shortening the list to three. To be sure I picked the right man for this position I asked David Crowther from my accountants to help with the final decision.

David was a switched-on young man who checked our books, invoices and ledgers, and prepared them for the annual audit. He would scrutinise every invoice to make sure they were legitimate business expenses and not a private purchase charged to the business. He once rejected an invoice for tyres when he noticed they weren't the right size for my lorries, though right for my racing car! I was impressed and asked him to join my company but his prospects were good where he worked. He had the opportunity of a partnership in the future so he declined my offer.

Together, we interviewed the last three applicants for the credit controller position and agreed on one who seemed to be just right. He was pleasant, quietly spoken and, in fact, didn't have a lot to say. But I wasn't looking for a salesman and in any case he had a degree in economics. David and I decided he was the best man for the job and I appointed him. With my lack of education I felt a bit intimidated by him, but told myself that employing a man who was better than me in that department would ensure the further success of my business and leave me time to get on with what I did best.

The first day I explained what was required. "We have a cash flow problem and I want you to control it. There are thousands of pounds owing to us and you must chase it by all possible means. If necessary you should go and visit them to get the cheque. Secondly, we owe money to suppliers but in this case you must delay, though not too long to get us a bad name. This way you can earn your wages on saved bank overdraft charges."

He set to work and I saw little of him, leaving him to get on with the job. Occasionally, I would call in his office to ask how he was getting on. He would say that everything was fine, which took a load off my mind and allowed me to concentrate on looking for new business. After he had been with us for nearly three months he took a day off work. I looked in his office and noticed that the huge scribble pad in the centre of his desk didn't seem to sit evenly on the surface. I lifted it up to find out why and imagine my surprise when I saw at least six county court summonses for non-payment of debts!

The next day I asked him to explain. "I'm sorry. I did what you said but some accounts just slipped through the system."

"Well I'm sorry too," I said. "You'll have to slip through my system … you're fired!" He may have had a degree but as the great Russian author Solzhenitsyn once said, "Education doesn't make you smarter." I had to unravel it all when he'd gone. By visiting those we owed money to and asking for time to pay I ensured this didn't turn into a disaster. There was plenty of goodwill and people understood our position. I made sure everyone had their money as quickly as I could manage.

After the year-end audit, I'd always sit down with the auditor David Crowther to analyse the accounts. As we looked at the expenses column he said, "You know Ken, your biggest single item of expense is wages;. If you can make even a small saving there it will add up to a large amount over the year."

"Can't do it," I replied. "If you pay peanuts you get monkeys. All my men are good at what they do. They are well above average and they must be paid over the odds. I'll never try to save money that way. They contribute to the success of our company and must have their share." On reflection looking back forty years, I still think I was absolutely right as many men worked for me for years and were as sad as me when the bubble finally burst. But I'm getting ahead of myself again.

Tragedy at Work

What follows is a part of the story that I find difficult to write about. It was one of the worst things that happened in the 1960s and took the form of a dreadful accident involving two of my men, taking one life and wrecking another.

Tony Turpin was one of my best drivers and a lovely man. When he came to work each morning he'd park his Ford Cortina 1600E with great care, check the windows were closed, lock the doors, then walk round trying each one. His car was handled with great care and looked like new and he treated the wagon he drove for me in the same way.

On this particular Saturday morning, he set off very early to collect a load of special bricks from a yard near Doncaster but while going down the motorway a wheel-bearing collapsed and a wheel came off his wagon. Tony managed to pull off the road onto the hard shoulder. He phoned in and we immediately sent down spare parts and a wheel with a young apprentice mechanic. Working on the hard shoulder they jacked up the wagon, and were leaning under the vehicle fitting the wheel when a twenty-ton articulated vehicle ploughed into them at over 40 mph, pushing the vehicle along the road with the two of them trapped under the wagon.

The young eighteen year-old apprentice was killed instantly and Tony was so badly injured he was in hospital for weeks and was never the same again. Forever after, he walked with a bad limp and even his speech was affected. I always felt terrible when I saw him limping round Ilkley and often thought that while he had enjoyed working for me, if he'd worked elsewhere maybe this awful accident would never have happened to him.

Apparently, the driver of the vehicle that hit them had fallen asleep at the wheel. He later admitted to a late Friday night drinking session, followed by little sleep then an early Saturday morning start. He received a derisory small penalty for the life he had taken and the grief he'd caused! The insurance company eventually paid Tony a fairly large sum in compensation. Shortly after receiving it, he came round to see me and kindly offered to invest some in my company, the company that he might have felt had ruined him. I couldn't take his money.

Years later if I saw him in Ilkley, I would stop for a chat. He was always pleased to see me and smiled as I shook his deformed hand. Sadly, the compensation made little difference to his life. His family broke up and Tony died early.

A Radio For Key Vehicles
Every day when things happened I realised the importance of communications; important but often difficult in those days long before mobile phones. Drivers out on the road would have to find a public telephone box to ring in for instructions or to report a problem. Invariably, many of these boxes were out of order, wasting time, effort and money. Taxi companies were virtually the only commercial operators to have two-way radios but I used to think how much better our working lives would be if we had them too. So I looked into the possibility of getting radios, a control room and a radio mast all of our own.

Right at the top of Ilkley Moor were two police radio masts but I quickly learned there was no hope of planting mine beside them, so I looked around for somewhere else. Further along the ridge towards Addingham looked a good possibility. It was high and had ground suitable for a mast, and was close to an electricity supply. I carried out a survey by driving around the area in my car, then trekked over the moor on foot and eventually found an ideal spot close to Doublerstone Farm.

Now all I had to do was 'sweeten' the farmer who owned the land. Farmers are a strange breed. I've known many in my time and have generally found them good to deal with. However, they live a very different life to most folk, often in remote corners meeting very few people from one week to the next. And when they do see someone new they liked to talk. Well, I can be a good listener if it will be of ultimate benefit. I went to see Mr Fothergill, the owner of Doublerstone, and listened to him. It wasn't hard going as he was an interesting old character and, like us all, had a tale to tell. After about an hour I had the chance to say my bit and it was his turn to listen. I needed his permission to put up a forty-to fifty-foot mast on a part of his land overlooking Addingham and Ilkley, which would be located about a hundred and fifty yards from his house in a spot convenient for the electricity supply to a base station.

Wisely as it turned out, I didn't ask for everything at once. I only mentioned the mast on this first visit, it was clearly a better idea to reveal the whole plan bit by bit over several visits. This first meeting served to sow the seeds. It worked better than I might have expected as, lo and behold! when I mentioned a figure for rent he agreed. We shook hands and I left feeling very excited.

Of course, this was just the start. I would still need a licence, which I knew wouldn't be easy, and a GPO landline would have to be run down the moor to a GPO connection, and then to our office. However the wheels had been set in motion and eventually it all fell into place.

Our excavators and JCB drivers did the work, setting up a base station made from large concrete manhole rings dug into the ground to make a chamber. This could not be visible above ground and had to be accessed only by a steel cover, kept locked and secure. We dug a trench for the GPO cable across the moor and down almost to Addingham, to link in with the main line. We bought a second-hand mast from a company near Hull and when the system was up and running, we had a radio in the office, my car and all the key vehicles. We were moving with the times, becoming a user of the most up-to-date technology and gaining hugely in efficiency.

Immediately, we saw a vast improvement for the business as the drivers and men on sites were in constant touch with HQ, as I was with them. It also meant problems could be dealt with immediately. The skip wagons in particular could deal with orders as they came in, which was a big improvement in service to our customers. It was a wonderful time to be in business.

As things were going so well now, I felt it was important for me to take the occasional break. Sometimes when it was hot in summer and I finished early, I would go down to the Ilkley swimming pool, park my car close to the hedge that ran round the pool area, leave the radio on and the window down and go inside for a swim. I'd find myself a nice spot to sit by the hedge, close to the car and take a little sun while monitoring the calls on the radio. I could hear every call and knew exactly what was going on at work.

David's Low Loader

Ken Walker Transport now had a good number of tipper lorries and excavators and in addition to hauling road stone for the quarries we would clear sites for building work, taking spoil to the tip. There was a problem, though, when we needed to move a machine as you can't go far on the road with an excavator on tracks, as my earlier conversations with the police had shown. In fact, you shouldn't go on the road at all. We had to pay another company to come and move our excavators, which was both expensive and an inconvenience. So I bought a second-hand low loader.

Originally, this had been made by a clever man called David Gilson. He cobbled together a loader using wheels and axles from an ex-Bradford Corporation trolley bus he had found in a scrapyard. The front tractor unit pulling the loader was a rather ancient Leyland. David hadn't quite reached fixing the rear trailer brakes when we bought it. Come to think of it, neither did we! Anyway, it was used only a couple of times a week, and as the sole drivers were either Howard or me, it was decided we could manage. This made us independent in terms of moving the excavators.

One day I took a machine to a location near Manor Park, dropping off the excavator at the site. I was then confronted with having to turn round. The Leyland and loader together made a long vehicle of over thirty feet. In addition, it didn't have power-steering, and manoeuvring in tight spaces always proved difficult. As if this wasn't hard enough, the whole vehicle sat low to the ground and would easily hit the deck on uneven surfaces.

Manor Park is a lovely estate with expensive houses. By taking a great deal of care, I thought I'd be able to turn around the triangular piece of grass at the entrance. I drove in from the main road, taking extra care to keep off the grass, and started a three-point turn, that eventually became a twelve-point turn.

I was shunting and struggling when a door opened and a woman called out in a cultured voice, "You are not supposed to come in here with that thing."

I just smiled back at her, sighed and continued. I think the smile made her angrier and she called out again, "Did you hear what I said young man? This estate is out of bounds to the likes of you."

I was struggling with the truck and felt like saying something strong and fully to the point, but I managed to contain myself and just smiled again. By staying calm and keeping focused I eventually turned the vehicle around without putting a wheel on the precious grass. On the way out I passed her door where she was still standing, glaring at me. "I'll report you," she shouted and I noticed her look at the cab door with my name and telephone number on it.

When I arrived back at the yard, I drew up outside the garage and noticed my office staff looking out of the window having a good laugh. "What's so funny?'" I asked, as I walked in.

"Well you've been reported and you're in big trouble," explained one of the girls, greatly amused. "We've just had a phone call from a rather irate lady at Manor Park who says one of our drivers with a large lorry has just turned round by her house, cutting over the grass and leaving ruts in it. When I spoke to him he came out with a stream of abuse, she said. The driver had a beard and an Alsatian dog sitting in the passenger seat. I think he should be reprimanded and told not to come down here again."

We all had a good chuckle, though it wasn't really a laughing matter. She was a fancy-talking liar and had it been one of my drivers she could have caused trouble for him. She was obviously well educated and lived in a fine house, but her education apparently didn't stretch to telling the truth.

Another time I had to move an excavator from Horsforth to Otley. When I loaded the machine onto the low loader the excavator driver had put a forty-five gallon oil drum full of fuel in the front bucket, as was normal practice. I set off up the long hill towards the village of Rawdon. The old Leyland was slow on hills – frankly, it wasn't much quicker on the flat! As I approached Rawdon, a car came past waving frantically and pointing to the back of my vehicle. As soon as I reached a wider part of the road, I pulled over and stopped, then went round to see if there was a problem.

There certainly was! Looking down the road the way I'd come, I saw it was awash with diesel oil, a strip a metre wide running back as far as the eye could see. The oil drum had chaffed on the bucket teeth as we travelled over the bumps, wearing a hole in it. I walked back down the road to where the oil was already melting the tar. The road surface was shiny and tacky. I turned the drum round but it was too late, as it was almost empty. If the police or any council workers appeared I'd be in big trouble, even bigger trouble if the police noticed that I was running on 'trade plates'!

There was nothing I could do, so my best plan was to keep moving, and ensure there would be no further trail. Also, I was better off putting some distance between me and the slick as quickly as possible. Never had that old Leyland been pushed as hard on those back roads towards Otley. Driving along I found it hard to take my eyes off the rear view mirror.

Eventually I arrived in Otley, unloaded the excavator at the site, and then stayed out of sight. I used the time to clean the trailer before sneaking back to Ilkley, still nervously eyeing the road behind me. Days passed before I was able to breathe easier when I took it back on the road.

The swinging sixties were coming to an end, but the world felt a good place to be in. My business was booming, with all our different activities in transport and contracting complementing each other. We made £27,000 profit in 1968, which was a lot of money in those days. There was lots of building work in and around Ilkley, and we could beat outsiders on price, quality, service and speed. Our excavators and lorries worked almost non-stop and I was paying good wages; most of the time we had a waiting list of drivers and machine operators wanting to join us. We had more than thirty vehicles and excavators, dumpers, cement mixers and rollers that were hired out to local builders. Including office and garage staff our workforce numbered over forty.

Ken Walker Transport hadn't been in East Parade long when our solicitor, Jack Mewies, suggested I make the business into a limited company. "You are expanding all the time and it would be a wise move to protect your home and private assets," he said. I took his advice and formed 'Ken Walker Transport and Plant Hire Limited'; 'Ken Walker Contracts Limited' was created the following year. In that way we planned to keep the contracts business as a separate entity. I felt proud when I drove along the road and saw one of my green and white lorries coming the other way.

It was time, I thought, to go motor racing; afterall, even Fangio had been once a bus driver!

My first tipper with Jonathan stood on the bumper 1961

Our first two wagons that we used on the M6 motorway

Spreading slag on Barden Fell 1962

Jonathan aged 4 in the snow on Barden Fell 1962

Alan Atkinson and Melinda
not long before his tragic accident

Alan Atkinson spreading lime at Marsden,
later killed in a tractor accident

Lime spreading 1964

With new wagon 1964

Tipper with Special Body for lime work

Fleet line up Regent Road Ilkley 1964

Howard with wagon 1963

Richard Bell with my first Drott loader 1965

Snow clearing 1966 - A59 Blubberhouses

CHAPTER 8
1969 TO 1972
MOTOR RACING

My road car was a Mini Cooper S, a superb little motor and I liked driving it as fast as I dare on the Ilkley roads. I enjoyed all fast cars, or should I say I liked driving any car fast. It was a thrill! However what I really wanted was competition against others on a circuit. Nothing much had changed since I was a sixteen-year old sliding my motorbike around the corners on the Melmerby grass track arena. After that expensive pile-up on the hill climb years before, I had changed my priorities to building up a business and gaining financial security for our young family; racing had sat firmly on the back-burner. But here I was in 1969, a prosperous businessman with all my operations earning good money. It was time for something new.

A few years earlier I'd joined the local Ilkley Motor Club and competed in one or two road rallies and treasure hunts with David Hatfield as my co-driver. It was not enough for me now: I wanted to race. I looked around for advice on getting started, having a chat with Peter Procter, a local man who had been involved in a terrible accident at Brands Hatch when racing a saloon car. He was badly burned and this led to him quitting racing. Frankly, though, he was not particularly helpful and didn't give me any pointers.

One of my friends was John Bosomworth, a rather spoiled only son of a wealthy father who owned Wonderloaf Bakery in Bradford. His father, Jack, was an old-fashioned Yorkshire businessman who believed you started at the bottom and worked your way up. He applied this to John, although his mother Agnes undid most of any good by giving John everything he wanted.

When John was old enough to drive, his father put him to work on a bread van, calling at all the local shops in Ilkley. John would sell until opening time at the Rose and Crown, then his van could be seen in the pub car park … sometimes with my Mini next to it. John and I would be at the bar enjoying a pint of lager courtesy of Wonderloaf!

This didn't deter his career progression and John's father bought him a garage in Skipton, further away from the Rose and Crown but still close enough for us to get together on a regular basis in the evenings. One night we were enjoying a drink when John told me he'd bought a McLaren racing car, which he was planning to use in the next Harewood Hill Climb. I couldn't wait to see the car and about a week later it arrived. It was a beautiful F1 racer, fitted with a Rover V8 engine and was ready for competition. Along with the car came a mechanic, John Ward, to advise on tuning and maintenance and it was through a friendship with him that the doors to motor racing opened for me.

That night I went home and told my wife about the McLaren car. "I've always fancied a racing car."

"Well why don't you get one? We'll all come with you," Wendy replied.

"Because I have responsibilities to you, our three young boys, and the business."

"Don't get old and end up sitting in a rocking chair always wishing you had done it," she said.

So that was my green light. Over the years I have quoted her many times, and of all the women I've known she is the only one who would have given me that answer and the support that followed. Many families would prefer to go to the coast, lakes or theme parks for the weekend. We went motor racing and loved it! Some of the happiest days of my life were spent at race circuits – and, fortunately, I'm still not in that rocking chair yet.

Waiting for the Flag to Drop

John Bosomworth liked to drive his E-type Jag or Jensen Interceptor fast on the road - and frequently off it, accidentally. But he wasn't a keen racer. He wanted a racing car to pose with at the Harewood Hill Climb, along with others like himself who had more money than talent. From the time I entered motorcar competing, I drove in only one hill climb as racing against the clock left me cold. I wanted company, a start line with twenty to thirty cars revving up waiting for the flag to drop.

I began to see more of John Ward, and listened to him. Originally from South Africa, John had come over to the UK for motor racing. He was very experienced and had driven different racing cars including Minis, but suffered a bad accident that damaged his leg and foot, leaving him with a permanent limp. I liked John from day one. He was quietly spoken and smiled a lot. He had a vast knowledge of motor racing. I listened to what he had to say about the sport, and he became my mentor. At thirty-four I was old to start motor racing, but with John's help and knowledge I found a few short cuts which helped me catch up with the others ... and I certainly did that!

John suggested I buy a cheap 850cc Mini, race-prepared, and this way I could drive in races and learn the circuits without going fast enough to kill myself. We looked through the ads in various motor magazines and found what we wanted in *Autosport*. John actually knew the car, as the owner was moving up a class to 1000cc. We bought the mini for £600, complete with trailer and spare wheels. A tow bar was fitted to the family estate car and now we were in business!

I was excited. Even though the car wasn't road legal I couldn't resist a short run round the block. It felt dreadful, noisy, rattling and as solid as a skateboard. My practice run completed without incident, I next sought a competitor's licence from the RAC. I joined two clubs: the British Racing and Sports Car Club and British Automobile Racing.

My first event was at Croft Autodrome near Darlington. We were there at the crack of dawn with the whole entourage comprising wife, three boys, John Ward, David Hatfield and my brother Howard.

John and I walked round the circuit, inspecting the surface bumps, and hollows, especially those at the corners where the tarmac met the grass and you might be able to cut over. Then it was time for the practice session which would decide the grid positions. I went out with twenty other cars and had the shock of my life! On the roads around Ilkley I was quick in my Cooper S, no one passed me there. But here among real racers I was left standing. I had to think hard and get my act together. Many cars passed me and disappeared into the distance but I managed to keep calm, learned the circuit, and started to understand the car. It was very different to a road car and wanted to go straight at corners, but as I began to speed up the car felt better - it was made that way. There was also the good feeling of being able to use the entire road, knowing there wouldn't be anyone coming the other way - except for the odd occasion when another car spun around to face you.

In my motorcycle days I'd read a magazine article by Geoff Duke. For those who have never heard of him he was a brilliant Norton rider who won many TT Races in the 1950s. In the article he took you on a lap of the Isle of Man circuit complete with diagrams showing the fastest line through the corners and wrote, "Always look down the road as far as the eye can see." This map was in my head and I used his line for the corners. As I lapped around Croft I soon became quicker and managed to keep up with the slower cars. I would have to wait a bit longer for my turn to do the overtaking, but it would come.

I started behind the field on the grid and enjoyed a good race with the back markers. More encouragingly, I wasn't last and I kept out of trouble. My philosophy from the very beginning was to be there at the end when the chequered flag was waved. To lead for five laps, spin off and then watch the remainder of the race from the trackside was not my idea of a good day out. I wanted to cross the finish line, with both driver and car in one piece to race another day. Try as I might, I must confess this was not always the way things unfolded, as in the heat of the moment my race plan could change - and occasionally did.

We raced at a different venue every weekend. On most Saturdays we would set off for circuits in the South of England with a car that was reliable and competitive. I was learning and finishing in better positions. Best of all, it was a family affair with everyone enjoying it. Each week when the entry list arrived in the post, my eldest son Jonathan, now eleven, would go through it and assess the opposition. When we arrived at the circuit he would walk round the pits checking on the cars and drivers. After the practice laps, he would go to race control and get the times and grid positions, then tell me who I could beat and who might beat me. He knew the opposition better than I did.

After the summer holidays, I went with Wendy to a parents' evening at his school. When I picked up Jonathan's English book I saw an essay he had written. The class had been asked to write about the best day of their holiday and Jonathan had described a day spent racing at Croft in great detail, from the time we got up at 6.30 am to our arrival home at 8.30 pm. He included practice grid positions, names of the opposition and even their finishing places. It was good enough to appear as a report for *Autosport* magazine.

During that first year we raced at Croft, Rufforth, Mallory Park, Silverstone, Cadwell Park, Oulton Park, Thruxton, Llandow, Castle Coombe, Snetterton, and Brands Hatch – names that will reverberate with any motorsport fans.

First off the Grid

At the crack of dawn I walked round every circuit with John Ward before practice. I can still see him now, tall and lanky, limping along by my side. I listened to him and made very fast progress towards becoming a proper racing driver. It would have taken years on my own to learn what he taught me in those months. In the process, we became firm friends.

John taught me to watch the starter, the man with the Union Flag who began each race – there were no lights then. Before my race, there were usually other races and I would scrutinise the starter, watching his technique and the way he dropped the flag. No two are ever alike. One starter might slowly lift the flag, hesitate for a moment, and then bring it quickly down. Another would take it slowly up and then fast down. Yet another would have it up and down in a flash. John told me to watch each one to see if I could anticipate the drop by a fraction of a second and get away first. You had to be careful not to go too early or you would be penalised. The aim was to gain places that otherwise could take several laps. I put the theory into practice and my starts were superb. I started off the grid like a bullet and in the whole of my racing career never once suffered an early-start penalty.

The starter for the British Racing and Sports Car Club was a man called Dennis, whose technique was difficult to follow as it changed as the day wore on. Most of the marshals were volunteers who enjoyed motor racing, getting involved in running weekend events and the socialising that went with them. Denis would bring out his steps for the first race, set them down on the grass by the start line, then climb the three steps to the top. He'd wave his flag and the cars would be off - and so was he, but in a different direction towards the refreshment tent for a pint. He'd return in time to start the next race, and this would be repeated all afternoon. By the time the last race came around, he would have become rather unsteady on his feet, even before he tried to climb the steps. When he reached the top he had trouble raising his arm with the flag. Often the cars were away before he could ready himself to do it properly.

I heard many years later that Denis had been robbed and beaten in Leeds where he lived. Sadly he didn't recover. He was a nice man and worked hard for the Club.

Going to Brands Hatch was a much looked-forward to and eventful occasion. Brands was a very important circuit at the time, hosting national and international races. I had to get to know it. We made our customary early morning inspection on foot, John giving me a few pointers. "Take special care at Paddock Bend," he told me. "The road dips, turns sharp to the right and seems to disappear. Drivers cannot see the exit, and as you go into the bend the car becomes light on the steering, making it hard to keep pointing in the right direction."

I took John's advice and got through Paddock without problem but then made a mistake when approaching Clearways. I skidded off the road, onto the grass, spun round and crashed into an advertising hoarding for the *Evening News*. Fortunately the wood wasn't strong and had been built to expect drivers like me, so the sign immediately collapsed on to my car. For a moment it was dark inside, but there was no serious damage and I wouldn't have to pay for the collapsed sign.

As we left the circuit for home, I looked around and spotted the wide gap in the advertising signs where the *Evening News* had stood earlier in the day!

We set off, heading north up the motorway. I was driving, towing the trailer with the Mini. We had a long way to go so I got a move on. The Mini was nose-first on the trailer which put most of the weight on the drawbar to the car, making it stable for fast towing. The vehicle and trailer handled well at 90 mph, which was tempting to drive at though quite a bit over the speed limit. As dusk fell, I was in the fast lane when I noticed a police car following with flashing lights. The traffic was heavy but I slowed and eased into the middle. He went past motioning me to pull over, so I moved into the slow lane. As the traffic was so dense he had to go much further up the road to move across, by which time I had stopped on the hard shoulder and changed places with Wendy. She drove slowly up the hard shoulder to where the police car was waiting. And I fell asleep!

The policemen were surprised to see a woman at the wheel. "You shouldn't be towing in the fast line - 70 mph is the speed limit and 50 mph for you with a trailer. I'll have to book you."

After he'd written out the ticket I woke up suddenly and asked, "Why've we stopped? What's happening? Why are the police here?"

I proceeded to give Wendy a ticking off in front of the lawmen and said, "If there's a fine it will come out of your housekeeping money." The officers laughed as they left, though not as much as we did when they were out of sight. I kept within the speed limit the rest of the way home. We managed to get away with the change as my hair was as long as Wendy's at the time. She was fined £27 with two endorsements and, naturally, I gave her the money.

Winning in the Rain

The next race was at Rufforth and we drove in atrocious conditions. The rain had come down all day and Rufforth is one of the worst courses in the wet. It was originally a World War Two airfield, just a great open space with no buildings or shelter. The motor club used it three times a year, marking out the circuit with straw bales and oil drums. I once did half a lap with an oil drum stuck under the car.

On this occasion, I didn't have any wet-weather tyres. After discussions with John Ward, I put on the tyres from my road Mini Cooper. These Dunlop SP sports were quite narrow, making them better for cutting through the pools of water on the track. On my road car they would 'scrub off' after 3,500 miles the way I drove, but for these conditions they were just right. The track surface was uneven with water sitting in huge puddles up to three inches deep. While I don't suppose this bothered Lancaster bombers in World War Two, for light motor racing cars in the wet it was hopeless. Cars flew off the track one after another, aquaplaning over the pools, with the drivers finding it impossible to maintain visibility and keep pointing the right way in the downpour.

On this day, saloon cars both large and small would run together in one race. My little 850cc Mini was well down the starting grid, but as the race got underway many cars fell foul of the weather, crashing or pulling out. After a while I found myself near the front. My pit signals read 'fourth', then next time round 'third' and then 'second'. My skinny tyres were cutting through the water and though I was driving much slower than if the track had been dry, I was making good time. Nevertheless, it was still a surprise when I caught up with the leader who was just returning to the circuit after a spin on the grass. I tucked in behind him and saw he was having great difficulty controlling his high-powered car.

Beneath my feet were holes in the floor and water was shooting up like a fountain inside the car, hitting the roof then dripping back down. I was tempted to try and pass him but, as I could see how hard he was struggling, I thought it best just to wait for him to spin off again. It didn't take long and I saw him disappear in a cloud of spray.

Now, I was in the lead. As I passed the pits my crew were jumping up and down with delight holding out the pit board with a huge number 'ONE'. The rain had been my saviour. Next time around I saw the driver who had been leading – actually Brian Robinson - standing by his car cleaning his glasses. He told me later that they had steamed up and he couldn't see a thing.

When you cross the line ahead of the field that first time, the feeling is very special. This was a most memorable win, although I didn't so much win as inherit the race due to other people's misfortunes on the rain-drenched track. Still, I had concentrated hard to cope with the conditions and had earned that special feeling when Dennis waved the chequered flag.

Another time at Rufforth, the racing was made more exciting for spectators and drivers by the appearance of a top rally driver, Hannu Mikkola from Finland, driving for the works Ford Rally Team. He was lightning fast and had come to Rufforth to polish his skills on tarmac. His technique was interestingly different, as I was to find out. We were in the same saloon race and I was going down the long straight as fast as my little 850cc Mini would go. At the end was a sharp right-hand corner, and I was almost at my braking point when a Ford Escort shot past me, going so fast I felt sure he wouldn't make the turn. Suddenly my path was blocked by his car sideways on, then it shot off to the right and around the corner. I followed, amazed at his driving and car-control. I don't think he touched the brakes, but just threw the car sideways to scrub off some speed, and was already pointing the right way to exit the corner. He disappeared, leaving me struggling with the corner as if I was stationary! It was spectacular to watch Hannu and it was obvious he was world class.

By the end of that first year, I'd driven in fifteen races at nine different circuits. I had won three, and gained a few second and third places. It was a satisfactory result for a debut season and most importantly, I had learned a lot.

At the annual dinner and prize presentation I collected my trophies: three small cups and a stop watch.

In the top-fifty league table of club racers, I was forty seventh. Next year, I planned to do better! What about next year? John Ward had left, going back home to South Africa. I gave it a great deal of thought. I was thirty-four years of age. I had no ambition to go into single-seater racing as I preferred saloon cars. I felt confident in my ability to go fast in a Mini, but what next? I decided to go up a class to 1000cc saloons, a more competitive section, racing against Ford Anglias and Hillman Imps.

Taking the Mini Up a Class
The 1969 British Saloon Car Championship was won by a Mini powered by an engine prepared by Jim Whitehouse at Tamworth-in-Arden, south of Birmingham. I went to see him. He was a very clever engineer and showed me around the little Arden Engineering workshop where he built his special Mini engines. I was impressed, listened to his advice and ordered one.

I was prepared to use the same car as the year before but decided I would sell the engine and replace it with the Arden unit. The engine from Jim cost £1,000, which was a lot of money in 1969, when you could have bought a complete new saloon car for less. Club racing was for amateurs and for having fun, but it was at its most enjoyable when winning, so I decided to buy the best I could afford and do it properly.

My brother Howard preferred motorbikes. In fact, he rode in the sidecar of a grass track outfit with a local rider namely Roy Cunliffe. But Howard was keen to help in preparing my racers and so we set to work.

For the uninitiated, I should mention there are two ways to make a car go faster: more power and less weight. One must go up and the other down.
I'd ordered the best engine, now I must fix the car. I took out the old 850cc engine and sold it. Before installing the new Arden it was time to lighten the weight of the car. I had already stripped bare the interior and had fitted a fibreglass bonnet and boot. I cut out the door panels and replaced them with aluminium. Next I took a step many people didn't agree with, as it took away the strength of the saloon. I cut off the roof and replaced it with fibreglass. When I weighed the roof panel I was amazed at how much lighter this made the car. It did mean, though, that there was an occasional problem when someone came to talk to me, leaning an elbow or arm on the top and causing the roof to cave in!

During the winter months in early 1970 I spent many hours improving my car. The Mini subframe was heavy so I replaced it with a beam axle, using the cutting torch to take out the rear floor section complete with subframe. I stood inside the car with my feet on the ground through the hole I'd made, and wondered, "What next?" The rear bodywork was flopping about. "What have I done, or overdone? Will it all go back together," I asked myself.
I looked at the lovely new beam axle kit by the side of the car. How would it fit? Well, with the help of my garage mechanic who fortunately was a good welder, it was soon in place and set up. These changes made the car substantially lighter.

Jim rang from Arden Engineering to say that the engine was ready. I went down and parted with £1,000. I had bought a Jack Knight slip differential and fitted it into the gearbox along with a new final drive ratio, and screwed it all together. The first time it fired into life I felt a thrill! The exhaust note was so crisp it brought that old sense of music back to my ears.

When it was finished we took the Mini to the local paint shop and had it painted white and green, the same colours as my wagon fleet.

With what was largely a new Mini I prepared for entry to the Northern Saloon Car Championships. All races were at circuits within a hundred miles of Ilkley, which was convenient. On free weekends, we decided to go further south to take part in other events.

Round one was at Croft. I went out to practice and almost immediately was black flagged for inspection as an observer had reported a loose exhaust. I drove to the scrutineering bay where my bother Howard joined me. "We'd like to check the exhaust," said the examiner. "We think it's loose."

"Not so," said Howard. "It's mounted on springs to allow for the engine torque. Would you like to have a look?" He picked up the rear end of the car and held it waist-high for the inspection. The scrutineer was amazed! He knelt down and peered underneath, checking that it was secure and gave the ok. But it took a long time for the look of surprise on his face to fade. The car was so light it was actually flimsy, as by now I'd taken out most of the strength with the cutting torch and replaced metal with fibreglass wherever I could.

You might ask what the car's top speed was. Top speed wasn't as important as acceleration, braking and the handling characteristics of the car. But I recall one time at Silverstone when we were out in the practice session with all of the other saloons. The bigger engined cars went by us smaller ones without trouble, but if I tucked in behind one of the faster racers I could get a 'tow' in its slipstream. I timed one tow just right, and was sucked along behind. But then my engine started to misfire and I looked at the rev-counter which read 10.000 RPM, well over the maximum recommended. I eased up as I didn't want to blow the engine and went into the pits. When the times were posted up, I was pleased to see I had an excellent grid position thanks to the tow. Later at home, I did some calculations: 10.000 RPM which, with the gear ratios I had, converted to over 120 mph. Not bad for a 1000cc Mini!

Before I came on the scene at Croft, the saloon race up to 1000cc had been controlled by two drivers, Andy Barton and Cedric Bell, both of whom also drove Minis. They were quick, experienced and knew the circuit at Croft and shared wins between them. They were not happy when I came along and started beating them. One day they walked down the paddock together. "We'd like a chat with you Ken," they said. "OK," I replied. "I'm listening."

"Before you came on the scene, we'd entertain the crowd by changing places until the last lap, then race each other to the flag. What do you think about joining in?" "That sounds fine to me," I replied.

For the race we all three lined up on the front row of the grid. When Dennis dropped the flag I took off and led flag to flag while they raced each other a short distance behind. I didn't trust them, after all they were long term friends of each other. Together, they could easily have prevented me getting to the front on the last lap. They were not very happy with the outcome.

A Whiff of Perfume

The next time I was at Croft was the 1970 Battle of Britain meeting. After winning my race I was presented with a large silver trophy. As it was Battle of Britain Day, many ex-servicemen and their wives were there for the presentation. A rather elderly lady stepped forward with the trophy. She was well dressed and well spoken, with a whiff of expensive perfume. We shook hands and she leaned her rather wrinkly powdered face forward for a kiss. I made for a patch of rouge on her cheek but she was having none of it - smack on the lips! I couldn't argue with that, though her husband stood at her side and my wife was not far away. The crowd warmed to it encouraged by the announcer on the public address system. When I broke away they all cheered, so I went back for an encore to more cheers. She was a good sport and enjoyed the fun.

After our usual get-together at the club house we set off home, calling at the Beeswing Pub in East Cowton where my old school friend Wilf Jackson lived. I took the cup to show him. We looked at the names of previous winners engraved on the trophy. Some had gone on to bigger things and became famous - and there was one who had become infamous: Roy 'the Weasel' James, who drove the get-away vehicle for the Great Train Robbers, getting a thirty-two year prison sentence for his role. He was a silversmith by trade and while in prison made a silver trophy for the British Racing and Sports Car Club.

One circuit at which I liked racing was Mallory Park near Leicester. It was quite easy to learn and I was soon going quickly, eventually taking the lap record for my class. But on one occasion when practising, my gearlever broke near the bottom where it goes into the gearbox. Drivers face many problems, some big, some small, when motor racing and this was a big one. We didn't have a spare part. We'd travelled a long way down from Ilkley and it was very disappointing not to be able to race. Then, one of the drivers told us that a competitor had a workshop in the back of his car transporter and, what is more, he thought he had a welder. I went over but as I approached the transporter I saw his name in large letters along the side, 'Roger Williamson Racing 1000cc Ford Anglia'. He was in my class and in my race. What prospect was there of him helping? I hesitated, then walked up to him holding the two pieces of the gearstick in front of me. He got the message straight away, "Do you want that mending?" he asked.

He lit the welding torch, slipped on his goggles and set to work. In no time at all it was done and he splashed water on the weld, before handing it back.

I thanked him and asked, "How much?" "Nothing to a fellow competitor; you are racing aren't you?"

"Yes Roger, in the same race as you." He looked a bit surprised, then a broad smile broke across his face – a bit like the singer John Denver. "You didn't tell me that. But I'm not going to cut it in half. In any case I don't have a hacksaw with me," he said, still smiling. I shook his hand and thanked him again.

Roger may not have realised he was helping the opposition, but it turned out that I was no threat to him. He led the race flag to flag, and I was third with Terry McNally getting in-between.

It was obvious that Roger Williamson had talent. He went on to greater things and eventually drove in Formula 1. Sadly, before he could show his full potential he was tragically killed in a horrendous accident during the Dutch Grand Prix, his car catching fire with him trapped inside. His teammate and friend, David Purley, tried in vain to save him while the race marshals stood around. David eventually got hold of a fire extinguisher that went off like a damp squib, lasting only a few seconds while poor Roger burned in his car. It brings a tear to my eye as I write: I can still see his smiling face as he passed me the repaired gearstick.

Formula Three

In 1970 I had a taste of Formula 3. A friend from Bradford called Barry Maskell drove in this class, which was where many future champions started their careers. Formula 3 involved very close racing with young, highly competitive drivers keen to make a name for themselves. If they did well the next move was on to Formula 2, and for the very talented, very lucky or very rich, they could hope to step up to the ultimate: Formula 1.

Barry offered me the chance to drive his spare car when he didn't need it. As it happened, he rented a garage from me and was always behind with the rent, so I suppose he thought this would square the debt. I jumped at the chance to gain more racing experience in a different car. His proviso was 'bend it-mend it', meaning I had to put right any damage. For me this was a great opportunity when it didn't clash with my saloon car racing programme.

Formula 3 was to be quite an eye opener. I was confident enough driving a front-wheel drive saloon, but this was totally different. Just to sit in a F3 car was worlds apart. You slid into the driving position until you were almost flat on your back with hardly an inch to spare on either side. It felt claustrophobic. Bending your head forward to look out you would see great wheels on either side of the car. After being used to sitting in my saloon with the wheels protected by bodywork I felt lost. At least if you rubbed door handles with another car in a saloon it was not a crisis, and I often finished a race with tyre marks on my Mini. But Formula 3 was something else: here you only had to rub tyres, locking them together for one car to launch over the other. I didn't feel at all confident. What was I doing lying here? But I heard myself say, "Yes Barry, I'd love to drive the spare car at Cadwell Park next weekend!"

We arrived at Cadwell Park early in the morning. I'd raced my Mini there before so there was no need to walk the circuit. Barry was late as usual, so while waiting I took the car for scrutineering, then went out for a practice session. As I left the scrutineering bay I'd forgotten how wide the back wheels were and caught the fall pipe. It crashed to the ground bringing a section of spouting with it, just as Barry appeared. I glanced in the mirror to see the look of horror on his face! He must have been thinking, "If he can't get out of the scrutineering bay what will happen to my car on the circuit?"

I took things very steady, slowly getting the feel of a very different racer. It felt strange lying down so close to the ground, but Cadwell Park is such a pleasant and interesting circuit it was fun just to drive round without trying to break any records. As I became used to the sensation, the excitement of driving in a proper racing car began to build in me.

All went well in the race. I didn't win but then I wasn't last either. I kept out of trouble and stayed well to the left when I saw Barry behind me. He was very quick on his day, though often weak in his preparation. It was good experience to drive a F3 car even though I had to be extra careful. F3 was dangerous and there were many serious accidents. By and large, drivers in these races had a different philosophy to mine: they had to win at any cost or die in the attempt. Fortunately, none died when I was around. They would race down the straight in a line of up to twenty cars, slipstreaming each other like a long snake only inches apart, then try to out-brake each other and be first into the corner. The results were occasionally disastrous, with bits of cars flying in all directions. I kept well out of their way.

My next race in Barry's spare car was at Oulton Park. I made a much better start than Barry. In fact, I kept in front of him for the first lap but he couldn't let a Mini driver in a borrowed racer stay in front. Soon, he came flying past. I kept out of trouble again, finishing well down the field but enjoyed the race. A few weeks later I raced at Thruxton on the same day that Graham Hill won the Formula 2 race. That was my third and as it turned out last F3 event, and it had been an exciting and enjoyable experience.

Shady Characters

In those days motor racing attracted some of the more shady characters from the motor trade and secondhand dealerships. It was easy then to buy ex-fleet cars cheap in an auction with 100,000 miles on the milometer, then turn the clock back to 25,000 miles. One of these 'clockers' walked around the motor auctions complete with a small toolkit, similar to a watchmaker's in his pocket. He would buy a fleet car with very high mileage, take it to a quiet part of the compound, wind the clock back, then go back and enter it for the next sale. Like this, he would buy and sell a car on the same day, often making a huge profit.

Fortunately in the interests of justice, I know that particular man ended up in the 'nick', though many others doing the same trick did not. The innocent purchaser looking at cars on a garage forecourt could end up buying what he thought was a lovely low mileage vehicle. He would have paid his hard-earned money, often making payments for the next two or three years, whilst the 'clocker' relaxed in Spain or, more likely, bought an even better racing car.

If you looked around the paddock at motor racing events, the best and most expensive cars often belonged to a villain. Unfortunately for honest men, they were usually the quickest and the race winners.

I was talking one day to a farmer friend and said, "You know David, I think some of these car dealers are descendants of the horse dealers of the past."

"No Ken, you're wrong," he said. "They're descendants of the horse thieves of the past!"

One particular family I often saw at the auctions were Gypsies who had recently settled and sold their caravans. They were sharp and made a lot of money, much of it due to 'clocking' cars. What I could never get used to was how many of the car dealers could look you in the eye and tell you such lies when describing the car they were trying to sell. "Mint condition" was the term so often used - but more often misused. You could stand by the car listening to the sales spiel, while actually seeing the areas that been filled in and repainted. Telltale paint marks around the windows and screen rubbers where they hadn't masked properly were common, as was over-spray between the doors. I once saw a man stuffing newspaper in rust holes then putting filler over before repainting. They were interesting characters. Some I became acquainted with, but I never bought anything from them. I felt more comfortable drinking than dealing with them.

When he couldn't raise funds, one racing driver was so desperate to have the best car he sold one of his family's haulage vehicles without them knowing. It was a sport for fanatics!

One of the most successful drivers I knew was Tony D..., who seemed to win every race he ever entered. What's more, he had the best car that crooked money could buy. He had a used-car pitch under some railway arches at Castleford. If you looked at the site you would think, "How does this little place make so much money?" Well, it didn't. Tony was a smart guy and much of what he made came from other sources.

There was a sports car race series called Can/Am held each year in Canada and America. Tony used to go over, taking his car in a huge transporter which was actually a specially converted bus. He took part in the races then drove down to Jacksonville and loaded up with King Edward cigars at a very low price, hid them in his transporter and returned to Castleford. I don't know how it was managed but each year he got away with it, making good business selling them at the motor auctions where he was well known with dealers.

After I quit racing I didn't see him for while, but a few years later, I decided to go to the car auction at Bradford to buy a car. The car park was full and it was difficult to park, but as I walked through the entrance I noticed a brand new red Ferrari left on the footpath by the gate. As I walked round looking at the cars I saw a face that I recognised. He smiled, I walked over and we shook hands. "Good to see you Tony," I said.

"And you Ken," he replied. Tony always had a tan from his travels to sunnier places but on this occasion he looked very pale.
"You haven't been ill have you Tony?" I enquired.

"No Ken, I'm quite well but where I have been there is not much f*****g sunshine."

He went on to tell me that he'd just come out of Strangeways Prison after eighteen months inside for smuggling. His cigar trade had been going on for a number of years but eventually the police caught up with him. One day at an auction a man walked up to him and asked when would there be more cigars? "I'll bring some next week," he said, and thought no more about it. When he appeared in court he saw that same man again, but this time as a witness for the prosecution! They had been watching him for weeks before they trapped him.

"Was it rough inside," I asked. "Not at all Ken," he said. "I would do it again for what I made. The first six months at Armley was tough, but when I was transferred to Strangeways I was put in charge of the library, which was a piece of cake!" Needless to say the Ferrari was his so they hadn't completely cleared him out. Perhaps crime does pay!

See What You Can Do Against the Locals
Going racing at weekends was a real family outing and we used to miss it if there wasn't an event. On one particular weekend when there was no round in the championship I decided to seek an entry to another race somewhere in the country. There was nothing doing at most venues, but eventually an opening came at the South Wales Motor Club at Bridgend.

"You can come with pleasure; we've heard of you. Come and see what you can do against the locals." So off we went to Llandow.

It was a long journey and we set off early on the Saturday morning. By the time we arrived at Llandow, though, it was late and we had trouble finding somewhere to stay. At last, we found a bed and breakfast. It was awful but as it was so late we took it. Dirty, untidy rooms didn't make for a good night's rest, but they did make us a good breakfast in the morning, which restored us somewhat before we left for the circuit.

The practice session went well. The track was an oval and quite easy to learn, but I was only fifth quickest, putting me on the outside of the five-wide front row with the local ace, Ken Bowen, in pole position.

Before being called up to the grid, my normal procedure was to start the car and warm it up to running temperature, then Howard would put in the race plugs and I would proceed to the race area. On this occasion, we had to wait much longer than normal as there had been an accident in the previous race and the debris was taking time to clear. When we were called to the start line my engine had cooled and was misfiring badly on the race plugs. I struggled round to the start, revving hard but when the flag fell I was left behind as the other cars disappeared into the distance. I spluttered off, the last of the twenty-six starters. After three laps I'd lost half a lap. I was going up one side of the oval circuit while the other racers were coming down the other. I was embarrassed and felt like quitting, but I hadn't come all this way to be last. I pushed on as both me and the engine began to warm up. I could see my boys standing by the trackside looking glum; this was not what they were used to seeing. It was a twenty lap race and though we'd done eight or nine laps by now, I felt I had to go for it. My car was running sweet and I was wound up, slowly pulling in the cars ahead of me. The last driver (me) was soon second last, and on I went through the field. The crowd seemed to be with me, although I was not Welsh, and they seemed to sense that here was someone able to topple the local boy. Perhaps he had ruled too long. I ruthlessly carved my way through the field and eventually on lap nineteen I caught and passed the leader, almost putting him onto the grass in the process. I had just one lap to enjoy being in front but it was a lap to savour before taking the chequered flag.

It was one of my best ever races. Afterwards I was overwhelmed by the local people. Most had never seen me before but I obviously made an impression in my white Mini. Rarely was there much in the way of autograph hunting at club-level races but that day I signed 'Ken Walker' on scores of programmes. One woman was so excited that I had blown off the local "big head" as she called him, she stayed with us until we left the circuit for the long journey home. Having turned a near disaster into one of my finest victories, the drive home was blissful!

The question asked all those years before during National Service about what sport I might be good at was at long last being answered.

Northern Champion

That year, 1970, I took part in all the championship rounds and as the year went by I found myself leading the points table, closely followed by Geoff Wood in another Mini. It was a great season for me, the team and the car, and I continued to pull in the wins, totting up twenty-three first places. I held onto the lead and won the Northern Saloon Car Championship.

When the national league table of club racers was published I was third in the top fifty, which was certainly a big improvement on my previous placing of forty-seventh!

The annual Northern Motor Club prize-giving was held at the Craiglands Hotel in Ilkley, very close to where I lived. It was a special evening and I felt quite famous as I walked up to receive my awards, all twelve of them including, best of all, the Northern Saloon Car Championship trophy.

Now I needed to make plans for the 1971 season. I'd agreed to buy an ex-works Chevron B16 from John Bridges. It was originally spoken for by Peter Lawson but when a friend of his was killed in a racing accident he changed his mind. John asked if I'd like to be his co-driver in the next round of the European Sports Car Championship at Imola in Italy, and I was delighted to accept. This was to be my first race in a proper sports car, having only driven once before on a private practice day at Oulton Park, and it would be my first race abroad.

We flew to Italy from Leeds Bradford Airport. My travelling companion, Brian Redman, was also going to Imola, though in his case to drive a JW Gulf Porsche. We soon made friends. He came from Bolton and had started his racing career in a Mini so we had that in common, but now he was a top works driver.

It was a wet day and I always felt nervous about flying. I looked out the window, and noticed that the old turbo prop aircraft was vibrating, especially when the pilot revved up for take off. I won't say the rivets were dancing in their holes but where the wings were attached to the body there were grey streaky marks caused by friction. I looked away as there was nothing I could do. If the rivets on my racing car had looked like that I have would stopped and not driven again until I'd replaced them all.

Despite my anxiety, the flight was smooth until we were close to Florence when quite suddenly we started to descend. My ears hurt with the pressure; it was just like needles were being pushed into them. My thoughts went immediately to the wing rivets. I looked out and fortunately they were still in place - and so were the wings! I looked around and saw that many passengers were clearly uneasy.

Next to me was a little Italian man who was bouncing up and down and getting very agitated. He was poking his fingers in his ears and shaking his head. "The pilot, he must be crazy;. When we land I will speak to him," he cried.

We continued our descent and were soon on the ground. My ears were still hurting and the Italian was still complaining. He jumped up first, and I noticed when I passed the cabin door that he was talking to the pilot, still agitated and waving his arms about. Later in Customs I spoke to him, "What was the problem?"

He replied, "The pilot, he say many aircraft waiting to land and he had to hurry. He is sorry but I still think he is a little bit crazy."

John Bridges, the Chevron B16 owner, met us at the airport having come over on an earlier flight. He drove us to Rimini through the mountains then along the coast. Here we met the rest of the team and made straight for the beach. It was a lovely warm evening, even at ten o'clock, so we stripped off our clothes and swam naked in the warm water of the Adriatic. It was a wonderful experience.

We drove from Rimini to Imola to the superb hotel, full of the motor racing fraternity. It felt good to be one of them, but I didn't let the occasion keep me up late. I needed a good night's sleep. Next morning we drove to the Enzo e Dino Ferrari Circuit. There were crowds of people everywhere, even before the morning practice session was due. Security was so tight we had problems getting onto the circuit even with our team passes. Finally we succeeded and found our mechanics already there preparing the car for scrutineering.

Red Hot in Imola

All drivers must have a medical before they're allowed onto the circuit for practice sessions. The Italian doctor checked me over, first blood pressure, then heart rate, and then he checked them again. "Your blood pressure, it's quite low," he said.

"That's good," was my reply. I supposed it would seem low to him when he was used to checking those excitable Italians.

I didn't walk around the circuit as there was plenty of practice time. I took the Chevron out and soon discovered it was the quickest thing I'd ever driven. The circuit was not easy to learn: it was long, and undulating with many twisty sections and a long, fast, sweeping bend called the *'Tamburello'*. Another new experience for me was the dizziness brought on by G-force going round this bend at more than 120 mph – goodness knows what experience F1 drivers go through! It took a lot of courage as you couldn't see the exit. There was a tall hedge on the inside and the road slowly unfolded as you sped over the bumpy surface with your foot hard to the floor at the same time hanging on to the wheel. It was changed years later after the deaths of Roland Ratzenberger and Ayrton Senna in that area.

After a few laps I got used to the G-force, my dizziness passed and my lap times came down as I learned the circuit. The more laps I completed the more comfortable I felt in the car. Practice over, it was time to return to the hotel to unwind.

Next morning was race day and the throng of spectators was even bigger. Sports car racing was very popular in those days and drew huge crowds, nearly as big as Formula 1. It was again difficult to get into the circuit even as a driver. The tension was rising. It was a hot day – a very hot day!

The race distance was 500 kms, which is a long way to go in scalding temperatures. John Bridges started the race while I watched from the pit wall, nervously waiting my turn. Both Ferrari and Porsche had works teams and the competition was intense as they fought for the lead, changing positions every couple of laps. Opposite the pits was an enormous grandstand packed with patriotic Italian Ferrari fans. When the Ferrari appeared first they all stood and a huge cheer went up, rocking the stand like a goal being scored at Wembley. On the next lap, if the Porsche was leading the Ferrari fans sat in silence while it was the Porsche fans' turn to cheer. I found it very entertaining.

John came in after twenty-four laps and I took over, gently easing into a steady rhythm, thinking to myself, "there's a long way to go." As well as looking where I was going, I had to keep an eye on the rear view mirror as the big five-litre lead cars came up fast and I certainly didn't want to tangle with them. A few laps later I noticed black smoke pouring into the sky on the other side of the circuit. When I came around, I discovered a car had gone off the track, crashed and burst into flames. The fire was under control by the time I got there - the marshals waved me past and the race continued.

The smell of petrol was stronger than normal, but the car appeared to be running perfectly. The heat of the day, though, was causing the track to break up and the tar to melt. On many corners we had to cut across the grass. It was becoming very hot in the driver's seat. John had fixed a little Tupperware dish in the door recess which he filled with bits of chopped up fruit. I rationed myself to one piece every two laps.

The smell of petrol was by now sticking to my nostrils. I felt a cold patch on my bum and realised there was a petrol leak. The tank was on the right-hand side next to the seat, which was made of fibreglass and shaped to fit my bottom. The petrol was leaking into my seat and then soaking into my fireproof overalls. Now what was I to do? Fire was a thing I didn't like the thought of and I became scared! When I started motor racing I was aware that accidents can and do happen. The worst were when a driver is trapped in a burning car, dying a horrible death. On a scorching hot day with one car already gone up in smoke, and where one tiny spark could mean me going the same way, was unsettling. I didn't want to quit. Because I had been a Mini driver some in the support team clearly didn't rate me highly in this big, international league. There was nothing else for it: I would have to show them, or die in the attempt.

The petrol was now burning my backside and there was the constant risk of a spark engulfing the whole car. I resolved to press on and not think about it. "The faster I go the sooner I'll finish," I thought. As long as there was enough fuel to complete the race, of course. It would be dreadful to suffer for forty laps only to run out of petrol just before the end. I could see myself wringing out my racing suit into the petrol tank just to get to the chequered flag.

The heat was taking its toll on the track and cars. A number of drivers had retired due to their cars overheating and had parked on the inside of the track. My bum was also overheating, but each time I passed the pits there was one less lap to go. The crew were starting to get excited as we were now second in our two-litre class. John was waving to me, all smiles. It was among the most uncomfortable moments of my life but the further I raced, the shorter the distance to the finish and the less inclined I was to quit.

At last, I was on the final few laps. Fuel had continued leaking into the seat but I had become numbed to the pain, and had put the fear of fire out of my mind. Finally, I saw the finish. When the Italian official waved the chequered flag I didn't know what feeling was stronger, thrill or relief! I cannot explain how I felt. The longest distance I had driven in my Mini was twenty laps, or half an hour. Here, I had been in a strange and more powerful car, on an unfamiliar track, for thirty-six laps in scorching heat and dangerous conditions. After the race I went from zero to hero with the support crew. The team loved me and lifted my petrol soaked body from the car.

I was rushed to the medical centre where they painted a solution on the red bits to cool them. But nothing could cool the glow inside me. We had finished second. I had tasted the big league and played my part. The medical check-over showed that I'd lost almost 7 lbs, sweated off during the day. But it could so easily have been burned off!

Later, John insisted on me going with him to collect the prize money, millions of lira. He handed me a wad of notes. "No John," I said. "The deal was that I'd be your second driver for expenses only. I'm happy with that."

"Without your effort we wouldn't have any prize money," he said, pushing the wad back to me. I thanked him. It was such a wonderful experience I'd have paid him for the drive. Now, I was a paid racing driver, a true professional. I converted the thousands of lira to over £150. John had paid for my airfare, hotel and almost everything else leaving me a nice return on the experience.

Back at the hotel that evening we celebrated and drank a little wine. I took mine standing up, much to everyone's amusement. When I eventually reached my bed that night I slept on my stomach! What a great day, though when I closed my eyes I could still smell petrol!

European Sports Car Racing
The race had given me confidence to feel I could step up to the sports car class. At the moment I was a big fish in a small pond driving Minis, but didn't want to stay

that way. I relished a new and bigger challenge. At thirty six I was too old to think of single-seater racing but, instead, long distance sports car racing looked just right.

John Bridges was a director of Chevron cars at Bolton, Lancashire. I had agreed with him to buy the B16 car driven at Imola at the end of the season. When the time came I rushed over to Bolton and brought it home to Ilkley, excited at the thought of driving a new and very different car, and competing in Europe. John was a very fair man to deal with and threw in many spare parts. He also gave me valuable information about the car's set up, including a list of gear ratios he had used for most of the circuits in the UK and Europe.

The car had been raced under the name of Red Rose Motors and, as you might expect, was painted red. That was the first thing to change and we had it painted white with a green stripe to match the Ken Walker Transport wagon colours. I engaged a race mechanic and prepared for the 1971 season and the prospect of competing in the European Sports Car Championship.

I needed a proper car-transporter as you can't tow a car across Europe on a trailer. Also, I needed equipment and spares. I bought a Bedford coach that had been specially converted to carry a race car in the back, as well as providing accommodation for the crew. Things were slowly coming together.

What I also needed was to get more practice in the car so I entered a race at Oulton Park. It was a wet morning, but the rain had stopped by the time of our practice session. I went out and spotted a dry line around parts of the circuit. I was feeling quite confident after my drive at Imola and speeded up to get a good time for my grid position. Going into the bend before the start and finish straight I overtook a slower car which put me off the dry line. As I accelerated round the bend I lost it completely and spun off, hitting the bank first with the front then with the rear. Bits of expensive fibreglass flew in all directions. I came to a halt stuck hard into the banking. The session was stopped while the car was recovered. At first sight this seemed a catastrophe, especially with an important event coming up. Fortunately the damage was mainly superficial, though nevertheless expensive. We took it home for repairs feeling rather deflated, but after new parts had been fitted the car was ready in time for the next race, which for me was the big one!

This was the BOAC 1,000 kms international race, to be held at Brands Hatch. We set off in high spirits. I had just managed to get a little sponsorship from the Wendy Wools company, and their representative arrived with the decals for the car.

Race day was another on which it rained and rained and rained. In practice I'd been slow as I didn't like the wet and the £1,000-worth of damage it had caused last time out. John Bridges was my co-driver, but I drove for over four of the six hours.

It was a nightmare. Some drivers actually liked the wet and could handle it. But I couldn't and thought it was like driving at speed on ice with the car 'twitching' from side to side whenever you pressed the accelerator. When John was out driving I watched from the pit wall as Pedro Rodriguez came down the pit lane in a cloud of spray, the car twitching this way and that way, with him catching, correcting and keeping in a straight line. He was absolutely brilliant in the wet. Later in the year when Wendy and I were flying to a race in Europe I looked across the aisle to see him sitting there with his partner. "Give me something to write on, Wendy?" I asked. She tore a page out of her diary and I reached over and asked for his autograph. This was shortly before he was tragically killed in a racing accident.

That we finished the race at all was some achievement considering the conditions. My ambition to be there at the chequered flag was tested to the limit, and it was good to finish in one piece after driving for so long in those atrocious conditions.

Now it was back to Ilkley to attend to my business for a while, giving time for my mechanic to work on the car, strip it down, check it over and prepare for the next event in three weeks: the Paris Grand Prix at Montlhéry, a circuit just outside Paris. I had seen old films of cars racing round banked circuits like Brooklands but had never driven on one. Montlhéry was steeply banked so this was going to be a new and exciting experience. About half of the circuit was on the road, a very bumpy surface of stone sets, while the other half was on the banked section using half of the original oval.

Drivers would leave the road and enter the oval halfway along the side, driving up the banking and around the bend, before turning down and launching back onto the road with the extra momentum created by the gradient. It was very difficult to get the balance right. If you drove too far up the wall, you slowed the car and lost time. On the other hand, if you didn't go high enough you lost the advantage of the launch off. It took a lot of practice to get it right.

It was a good race and by the end I was starting to find the perfect line. I was there for the chequered flag and had a new and thrilling experience to add to the others. The next race abroad was again in France, this time at the famous circuit known as Charade at Clermont-Ferrand, a beautiful area of the Auvergne. The long 8 kms circuit ran into the mountains on a road cutting through volcanic ash, before diving down almost to sea level. With all the bends and undulations it was an interesting but difficult to learn circuit. It was where the film *Grand Prix* was made in 1966.

Like the course, the race was long and hard. I completed the distance, though with a struggle as my car wasn't running right. Still, it was thrilling to be in such a famous place with top racing drivers, many of whom also drove in F1. It felt good to drink in the bar with such company and to recognise various locations from the film.

One of the supporting races was for little Citroen 2CVs. This was entertaining as there were about thirty of them buzzing round in close formation, leaning over in unison at the corners at such an angle it looked as if they would all turn over, though none did. I don't think they exceeded 60 mph, but as they were all equally matched it made for very good close racing.

The next round followed three weeks later in Portugal. It was decided that my mechanic, his assistant and girlfriend could take their time driving overland from France with the transporter, enjoying a holiday on the way. In the meantime I needed to get home and tend to my business. So, Wendy and I drove from Clermont-Ferrand to Bordeaux, parked the car, removed some electrical parts to immobilise it, and caught a flight to the UK for the short spell back at work.

A Journey Through Spain

When we returned to Bordeaux two weeks later, I was nervously thinking about the car as we came in to land. After all, it was a brand new Ford RS 1600. The engine was the latest design used in successful Ford rally cars, and I had visions of it sitting on the car park minus the engine. I needn't have worried, as we found it exactly as we'd left it, with a little extra dust. I refitted the distributor cap and other electric parts and it fired up straight away. Next stop was Villa Real, Portugal.

We drove south from France into Spain, then headed across the wide open Spanish landscape towards Portugal. As we travelled through the dry central country there were few villages or houses. We had driven for miles without any sign of habitation when over to our left we spotted a group of very small huts with a low mud wall around them. I was curious and went to look, and couldn't believe my eyes! The wall was made from mud and straw blocks, as were the low huts. A woman in a black dress stood in the doorway of one which itself was not much higher than her. Two women were washing clothes in the centre, children were playing in the dust and a few goats wandered about. It felt as if we'd stepped back in time. As we gazed around, the villagers gathered to look at us. They were as curious as were we. It was time to leave.

The recommended route was to travel across Spain to the south-west and enter Portugal in the south, before travelling up country to Villa Real in the north. I looked at the map and thought, "That's a long way round when there are roads shown on the map giving a more direct route. Maybe they're being over cautious. I have a car that will cope with any old road and a trip through the mountains could be fun!"

Never squeamish, Wendy was game for an adventure, so we headed for the hills. There was very little traffic and as we climbed into the mountains the only traffic was on foot or hoof, an occasional peasant and his donkey. The road worsened, becoming just a dusty track. On the steep parts the surface had been sprayed with tar to hold it together. There, it was smooth and soft with the heat of the sun, and every twenty yards or so were silver streaky marks where a snake had been run over, baked by the sun and pounded into the road by passing vehicles.

We pulled off the road for a break, spreading a blanket on the dry scrubby grass and took off our clothes to catch a little sun! It was peaceful and isolated with not a sign of life. As we looked down the track into the valley I spotted a man walking towards us with his donkey piled high with hay. I heard the tinkle of a cow bell, higher pitched than the dull-sounding ones you hear in Switzerland. The man plodded slowly along and after thirty minutes reached us. As he passed he gave a nod, his weathered face breaking into a smile.

We decided to move on. I picked up the blanket and as I gave it a shake, hundreds of huge ants fell to the ground. Wendy screamed with horror as she ran to the road. Had she seen them before, there would not have been a stop and certainly no clothes would have been taken off!

We continued west towards Portugal, winding our way down into the valley bottom where the road followed a dried-up river bed. We eventually turned right across the bed and along the other side. That was when I noticed a little wooden shack on my right at the side of the track. I was driving slowly and as I drew level an old rusty chain rose quickly from the dust. My eyes followed it to the shack where a man in an untidy uniform was sitting on a chair on the veranda, holding the outstretched chain in one hand and slowly raising the other in a stop signal.

I didn't speak Spanish and he knew about as much English, but he made it clear that we could go no further. I tried to persuade him saying we were low on petrol and couldn't go back. Then I noticed his rifle propped against the shack door and any thoughts of making a dash for it evaporated. There was no apparent reason why we couldn't go on. Perhaps it wasn't an official crossing point from Spain into Portugal, or it could have been that the road ahead was impassable. For several miles it had been deteriorating and was now no more than a farm track. We gave him a few English cigarettes as a goodwill gesture, which seemed to please him. I thought this would work and indicated the road ahead and motioned for us to continue. The smile disappeared quickly and he pointed firmly to the road back to Spain.

We retraced our track through the mountains, going back to the recommended but roundabout route. However, it hadn't been a complete waste of time as it was a lovely part of the world and well away from any tourist trails. We travelled south and into Portugal, turning north to Villa Real.

Our accommodation was a short drive from the town. When we arrived I couldn't believe my eyes. Up a wide drive cut through a forest of trees it looked like a palace. In fact it had been one: the Vidago Palace to be precise. It had been taken over by the government and turned into a first class hotel. When we walked through the front door it opened into an area as big as a ballroom. All the racing personnel were staying there. What was more, it wasn't expensive and would not make much of a dent in my £345 'start money'.

In the centre of town was the local British Leyland distributor's garage. This was to be our base to prepare the race cars. The Leyland Minis, Maxis, and Allegros had been moved out and parked around the back, leaving the place to ourselves. As I helped unload the car and equipment I noticed two young boys watching. Eventually one came up. He could speak a little English.

"My name is Jamie, can I help?" he asked. "I will do the shopping and any running about for you, and I'll clean the car." He was pleasant and willing, and I was happy to give him the job. I noticed other boys had joined all the teams. Jamie was a great help and never left us all the time we were there. One day when he was off on an errand another boy came and hung around, but when Jamie returned he soon chased him away. I understood him to say, "This is my team!"

Racing at Villa Real

The race covered 250 kms over public roads between the towns of Villa Real and Mateus, the latter famous for its rosé wine. Many parts of the course were very narrow, often little more than a track. It started along the main street of Villa Real, running out of town onto a country road, over a railway crossing and on towards Mateus. The barrier pole of the rail crossing was leaning out at half-mast, neither up nor down. Each time I passed I couldn't resist a quick eyes left, eyes right along the train track to see if anything was coming. Thank goodness, nothing did! The race returned on a different road, entering Villa Real over an iron bridge back into the main street and the finish line.

Practice was early the next day, following which there was time to look around the town. The Portuguese were very friendly and made us welcome with good food and plenty of it. Photographers were everywhere, with pictures of race cars and drivers posted in all the shop windows. On race day the town was packed to capacity and you could hardly move. It was obvious that this was one of the highlights of the year and visitors came from far and wide to watch.

The race was another new experience for me, being very different to most European races where there were proper racing circuits. There the roads were much wider than on this track. Here were crowds of spectators, many standing so close to the roadside you could have reached out and touched them. I don't know how often races were held in Villa Real, perhaps just once a year, but it reminded me of what I knew of pre-war motor races like the Targa Florio and the Mille Miglia, though not as long or hazardous.

After the race, all of the cars lined up at the side of the main street and we were besieged by autograph hunters. If they didn't have a programme to sign any piece of paper would do, some even plucking leaves from the trees. It was fabulous and for a short time I felt quite the celebrity.

The journey back home was also enjoyable, though this time we travelled with other drivers and their friends in a convoy of four cars - and kept to the recommended route! We drove together the whole way, stopping for food, usually bread and sardines, or boiled eggs, cheese and tomatoes, all bought en route and eaten at the roadside in the sun. What could be better!

The next round of the European Championship was to be held in Germany at Wunstorf near Hanover. I was very disappointed to miss it - business considerations took a hand - as this was the very same town at which I had been stationed during my spell of National Service. It would have been like going home, and I would have enjoyed racing around the RAF camp where I had once marched, ridden a motorcycle and, of course, cleared the snow.

Though I missed the Wunstorf race, I took part in the next round. This was held at Silverstone in this country, and was one of the first ever to be shown live on BBC television. It was nice to think I was in the public eye, even though the race itself was uneventful.

By now the European season was drawing to a close and I was starting to think of the following year, 1972. Sports car racing had been a wonderful experience but I felt uneasy about continuing. To remain competitive was very expensive.

When I was at Silverstone I learned that Dunlop had developed a new tyre which would have gained me half-a-second a lap. Then I heard that Cosworth had new pistons, which meant an expensive engine rebuild to have them fitted. The pistons would give me another half-a-second and if you didn't buy when everyone else had, you were bound to slip further down the grid.

Unlike the fathers of some of the other drivers, my dad wasn't in a position to shell out wads of cash to fund my sport. When I sat on the grid and looked around at the other cars, most belonged to very wealthy people. For instance, one driver was the son of the owner of a large yellow excavator company; another had a father who owned an electronics company; a third was the son of an actor; another came from a family of property magnates. While not poor, I couldn't afford to compete financially. I was starting to feel under pressure yet the original idea of going motor racing was to have fun. I'd had some wonderful experiences but I was a bit disillusioned with the expense of the sports car competition, so I decided to sell the Chevron B16 and return to local club racing.

After the last European race of the season my wife Wendy told me something she had kept to herself for some time. A friend was going to see a fortune teller and she had gone with her. The fortune teller chatted to Wendy for a while then asked if she was married. She replied, "Yes."

"And does your husband drive fast cars?" "Yes, again," Wendy replied.

"Well I can see a lot of cars driving fast on a long straight road and suddenly one is flying off the road and crashing in flames. I can't say more as it's too horrible." She then changed the subject and talked of other things.

A few weeks later there was indeed a dreadful accident in the famous Le Mans 24-hour race, which happened at the end of the Mulsanne straight. There was a crash and one of the cars flew off the track and crashed into a tree, bursting into flames. The driver, Jo Bonnier, was killed instantly. While not quite my double as he was a bit taller, we had the same build and same colour hair, and he too wore a beard! Wendy was very upset.

While I wasn't about to change anything in my life because of what a fortune teller had said, neither would I make light of it. She had certainly seen something!

Motor Racing Comes to a Halt
When I advertised my car in *Autosport* magazine I had numerous enquiries including some from America, and it was soon sold. So what was I to do in 1972? I had already decided to return to club racing at local circuits. I had raced a saloon and a sports car, so I thought maybe it was time for a proper racing car, an open wheeler.

I'd enjoyed driving Barry's Formula 3 car and I thought I could manage a bit more power. So I decided to buy a Formula 2 Brabham. Earlier I had made friends with a driver called Peter Kaye, who had raced his own sports car but had become short of funds. He was now without a racing car, but he was a very good mechanic and prepared cars for other drivers. Any that he had worked on looked immaculate and were very reliable. It was often difficult to get a good mechanic, as I had found to my cost during my sports car season. So Peter and I struck a deal: he would prepare the Brabham for me and in return I would loan him the car to compete in hill climbs. It was a very good arrangement and worked well. For a whole year my Brabham never let me down and always looked first-class. However, I had one small complaint: he liked to use my wet weather tyres in the dry, as they were sticky and ideal for the short squirt up the hill climbs. The tyres gave him the extra grip he needed, but would wear out after three meetings!

During the sports car racing season we made many new friends and the social side was most enjoyable There is nothing better than a group of like-minded people getting together to eat drink and talk about their common interest. Regularly on Tuesday nights, anything up to twenty of us would gather in the Troutbeck Hotel in Ilkley. The hotel belonged to the Fielding family and they always made us welcome, allowing us to stay until the early hours. Landlord Harry would sit on a little stool at the end of the bar in-between orders. As the night wore on and the 'in-betweens' got longer, Harry would nod off then wake with a start when a glass was placed on the bar beside him. He would blink, a dreamy smile would cross his face as he filled the glass, then he would return to his stool.

The Fieldings were a lovely family and we spent many happy hours there. I liked playing darts, though it was something else to add to the list of things I was not good at. I could only be competitive with a very good partner. One Christmas, the other players presented me with a little dartboard trophy engraved on the bottom, 'Sportsman of The Year 1974'. I wonder if they were trying to tell me something! I still have it with my other trophies.

When the 1972 season started the first race was at Croft. This marked my return to fun racing. My car was blue for a change, and was polished and gleaming with the alloy wheels shining like chrome; Peter Kaye could be proud of the preparation. During the year, I raced only at Cadwell Park, Rufforth and finally at Aintree.

Aintree had been a famous Grand Prix motor racing circuit at one time but was now used only for club races. The circuit ran inside the Grand National horse racing course. When we arrived at the track I took an entry form and looked through the other entries to assess the opposition. We noticed that the lap record was held by a local man with a Brabham BT30, the same car as mine, meaning he was the man to beat. We arrived early as this was my first time at Aintree. Though John Ward had long before returned to South Africa, I remembered his training and thought of him as I inspected the circuit.

The time came for the practice session. I always took it easy for the first few laps, especially at a new venue, slowly learning the circuit and building up speed as I felt more comfortable. Suddenly a car flashed past me. It was the driver of the other Brabham. At the next corner he span off, skidding spectacularly across the grass before disappearing. I couldn't see where he'd gone and carried on with my practice. Next time around there were race marshals waving red flags. I slowed down and noticed an ambulance parked near to where the car went off. The session was immediately stopped and I returned to the pits.

I later learned that the local man who had been keen to show me the way around had spun off and gone backwards into Beechers Brook, coming to a sudden stop under the steeplechase fence. Fortunately there was no water in the brook, but he suffered whiplash as he hit the bank backwards and needed hospital treatment.

So that was the main opposition removed and I went on to win the race. I didn't take the lap record, though, which was still standing when we left - as was the fence at Beechers Brook! My competitor fully recovered and was discharged fit from hospital.

My wife, the boys and my brother all enjoyed that last season of club racing, though it was nothing to the first two years in the Mini when I went out every week and won. It's good to compete but far better to come first! We had all lost some of the enthusiasm, I think.

I had started rather late and now, at thirty-seven, I felt I was over the hill for motor racing. It was time to call it quits and I sold the Brabham, closing a special chapter in my life.

Some thirty-eight years later I went back to Croft for the first time since I had raced there. I met a man who had part of the Brabham bodywork with my name clearly written on it. He kindly gave it to me - but that's another story!

Cadwell Park 1970

A happy family day out Croft 1970

Me at the wheel of Barrie Maskell's F3 car, Thruxton 1970

Oulton Park 1971

Portugal 1971

Rufforth 1971

Howard as passenger - Grass track Silsden 1973

CHAPTER 9
1972 TO 1977
LIFE GOES ON

My friend John Bosomworth rang one day, He sold second-hand cars from his garage in Skipton. "How do you fancy a half share in a Healy 3000?"

"What would I want with a half share in a Healy 3000?" I replied.

"Well I think it could be of interest to you. If you trust me, send a cheque for £385 and I'll cut you in." Though I'd known John for a long time I didn't totally trust him. After all, he was now a car dealer and even if he'd been trustworthy before, by now he would have been corrupted by others. Nevertheless, something about this intrigued me. An Austin-Healy 3000 was a famous British sports car that won its class in many European races. I decided to take the risk.

I sent John a cheque and a few days later called at his garage to inspect my investment. He was talking on the phone when I arrived, so I wandered around and spotted the Healy 3000. When I noticed the number plate I couldn't believe my eyes, 5KW! John was right, that would be of interest to me.

We agreed that I'd have the registration plate and John would have the profit on the car when it was sold. I was pleased with the deal and a few weeks later the number plate was duly transferred to my Porsche, the first of many cars that would carry my initials. A few months later most of my investment was returned to me when he sold the Healy.

I was thrilled to have a personalised number plate at such a low price. As my business prospered John sold me several cars, no doubt making a good profit on each. He knew I'd be back for more. His number plate at the time was SWT 1 – he referred to this as 'sweet one'.

Not many months had gone by before he rang again. "I have just the car for you Ken, come up and have a look."

I drove to Skipton, looked at the car and had to agree with him. It was a beautiful Ferrari Dino. Being bronze, though, it was the wrong colour as in the view of many people all Ferraris should be red. But I could live with that as it was such a wonderful car. We struck a deal and I traded in my Porsche. It was exciting to drive the Ferrari back to Ilkley, handling just like a racing car: the faster you went the better it felt. Later as I looked closer, I noticed the numbers on the mileage recorder weren't in a straight line, a give-away sign that it had been clocked. Sure enough, the next day they all moved around out of sync. I knew the name of the dealer who had sold the Ferrari to John and had it confirmed when I quizzed one of his mechanics. The man was notorious for winding the clocks back and I'd have never knowingly bought from him. I decided not to make a stink of it and get John into trouble, so I let it pass. Fortunately the car was sound mechanically, it looked good and was a pleasure to drive.

Mr Bamford on the Line
One day I was showing the Ferrari to Edith Threlfell, my mother-in-law. "Would you like a ride in it?" I said proudly. "Yes, Kenneth I would," she replied and climbed in, which was not easy as it was so low. I drove out of Ilkley towards Addingham on the new road, where I soon wound it up to 100 mph. "Are you all right Edith?" I asked. "Yes, Kenneth I am. It's very smooth and comfortable. I like it," she replied.

"We're doing 100 mph," I told her.

"Oh slow down, slow down," she cried out. She was obviously quite happy until she realised how fast we were going. It would have been the fastest she'd travelled in a car in her life or for that matter was ever likely to, as Bill, my father-in-law, drove a sedate Morris Oxford.

Business continued to flourish and we were living comfortably. One of the reasons I was able to make quite a lot of money was the tax system. To encourage businesses to buy new equipment the government gave generous tax concessions on purchases, so I kept buying more wagons and plant. Even my cars could be written down against profit and thus minimise the tax liability. My accountant warned me it could, "Come home to roost" if I stopped buying, but all the time I was expanding I was safe.

I decided to buy two new JCB excavators and phoned the distributors, Tates of Leeds. The rep was soon round to see me but we couldn't strike a deal. I wanted a discount with no trade-in, a clean deal for them, but he wouldn't budge. Tates were of the opinion that their diggers were so good they didn't need to discount them. They were right in as much as the JCBs were the best on the market, but I thought they were being greedy by not offering even a token reduction, so I decided to buy from Whitlock, a cheaper make. A few days later I was in my office when Christine, my secretary, buzzed me on the intercom, "There's a Mr Bamford on the line for you." I was talking on the other line and snapped back, "I don't know a Mr Bamford. Ask him what it's about."

The reply came back, "About buying a JCB." Just then the penny dropped! "Put him through," I said. The name of the owning family of the world-famous JCB earth moving machines was Bamford.

"It's Joe Bamford here. I understand you're in the market for new machines." I explained my problem with Tates, then asked him why he had bothered to ring such a small operator. "Mr Walker, 80 per cent of my customers are like you, small operators, and I don't like to lose one. I'll have their rep come to see you. In the meantime, will you come down to our factory at Uttoxeter? Bring someone with you. We'll make you welcome and show you around."

I thanked him for the offer and promised to talk to the Tates' rep, Norman Summersall, who dropped in the same afternoon with his tail between his legs.

But it was sadly too late, I had placed the order elsewhere and wouldn't back out of the deal.

Joe Bamford was a very successful man and not all of it was due to his undoubted engineering expertise. He paid close attention to customer relations. The year I had competed in the European Sports Car Championship, his son Anthony had driven in the same series. We had the same make of car, Chevron B16s, but had different colours: his were JCB yellow of course, with his sponsor's JCB letters painted in black.

The Family Grows Up

The family had settled into our large house on Valley Drive in Ilkley, and both Wendy and I drove nice sporty cars. Wendy had recently changed her little Lotus Europa for a Mach 1 Mustang, a big American car that she loved. She also had money for nice clothes. We had our first holidays abroad and could afford to eat in the best restaurants. I always felt proud when the five of us sat together around a table: a very attractive wife and three lovely boys who knew how to behave and handle a knife and fork. In fact, we had everything we wanted, health, wealth, and happiness. Despite this I would occasionally feel a small twinge of guilt: did we have too much when many in the world had so little? Were we getting more than our fair share out of life? Could it last? I told myself that we were working for the money not stealing it, so it was ok. The feeling would pass and I'd go back to living life to the full, striving to expand the business while enjoying hectic social times.

I have mentioned money many times but my main driving force was to be successful. Naturally money would come with it but, in the society we live in, success is too often measured solely on how much cash a person makes.

Now we had money, there was something else very important to do. Jonathan and Andrew were growing up; Jonathan was 13 in 1972 and Andrew was fast approaching his teenage years. I wanted them to have something that was never given to me: a good education. I discussed this with Wendy. True, they were both doing fine at the local school but I wanted them to have better chances. We looked at private schools and eventually narrowed down the choice to one we liked. Unfortunately they would have to board, which meant them coming home only at weekends. Neither boy liked this idea one little bit and made a fuss. We pressed them and told them they would benefit from the experience, and that they'd be home for a couple of nights a week in any case. But it made little difference, they were solidly against the idea.

I was exasperated, thinking of my time peeling potatoes when all I'd wanted was to be at school to learn. It caused friction in the family. Wendy had seen her brother pressured at school almost to breaking point by her ambitious father and eventually said to me, "We can't make them miserable, forcing them to a school that they don't want to go to."

Maybe this was one of the times in my life I should have stood my ground but, as I've said before, I was a compromiser by nature and gave in. They stayed at the local school. How strange it was that what I most wanted at their age they wanted the least. Whether they are better or worse for it I don't know. Today, Jonathan makes a good living as a builder working with his hands. Andrew became interested in education and went to university where he gained a degree. He is now a music producer. The youngest, Timothy, is also in the building trade specialising in drainage and excavation work. They appear to be happy with what they're doing.

However, there was a cloud passing across our family life, a problem that was to become serious. At the same time as increasing prosperity had improved our way of life, Wendy and I started to grow apart. Without wishing to go into details, our marriage was coming to an end.

A Day Trip to Darlington

Some friends of ours, Alan and Maggie Bolton, had a shop selling ladies fashion clothes and as it happened Wendy was one of their best customers. Wendy fancied a shop of her own so after a lot of discussion and time spent looking for the right location, we eventually opened a shop on the corner of Brook Street and Church Street, Ilkley, selling lingerie, underwear and bras. For her it was a hobby, but she failed to follow my grandfather's adage, "If you have a hobby make it pay". This was one hobby that certainly *did not* pay, though for a while she enjoyed running it, chatting with her customers. In the fitting room was a huge mirror on the wall covering the old fireplace. Some time later when we closed the shop and moved this mirror we found almost a hundred coat hangers hidden behind. It seems likely that many customers had simply walked out wearing what they had gone in to try on!

Ilkley was a popular area for house builders with people moving from Bradford and Leeds to this most Yorkshire of towns. Houses were going up on every bit of land where planning consent could be obtained. Work was never far from my mind so in the evenings or at weekends I would drive around looking for signs of new construction sites opening up. I also checked the local newspaper's listings of building applications and wrote to developers offering my services.

I had seen an advertisement in the *Commercial Motor* magazine for Walker's Trailers at Darlington (no relation). We had an idea for a new type of tipping trailer suitable for hauling road stone and tarmac. I was interested in Walker's range of trailers and wanted to look at them. I picked up the phone and rang asking for details.

"What's the nearest airport to you?" the salesman asked. I told him Leeds Bradford at Yeadon. "Well, can you be there tomorrow at 10 am and bring your transport manager or mechanic."

"Slow down a bit, I only need some literature to look at," I told him. He was not to be put off.

"Just say you will be there and we'll send our plane to pick you up. There's no obligation. Just come and have a look round the factory at our products." His persistence was impressive, so I agreed. The next day Howard and I were at Yeadon. We were met at the airport, escorted to a small four-seater aircraft and flown to Teesside Airport from where we were chauffeured to the works near Darlington.

Here we were met by a line-up of Walker's management and shown around the factory.

They had an impressive production line and a compound full of different types of trailers. Next stop was at an expensive restaurant in the town where we were wined and dined before being returned to the factory for the sales talk. After all the attention they wanted an order and put on the pressure. The order form had been already prepared and all it needed was the number of trailers required and my signature where the 'X' had been pencilled in. But I was not for signing and this caused problems. We were crowded by the head salesman, the managing director and Mr Walker himself, but this Mr Walker was not to be moved.

"You only have to sign to place your order in the queue as we have a heavy production programme. Otherwise, when you finally decide you'll have to wait."

My brother was feeling a bit uneasy. He looked at me and out of the corner of his mouth said, "Are you going to sign?"

I shook my head and told them quite firmly that I'd made it clear from the start I only wanted more information. It was their idea to go to all the trouble of bringing us here. I said I was impressed with the trailers and their organisation, and when I was ready to buy they would get an order. They looked disappointed but realised I was not going to be pressured and gave up.

The chauffeur took us to the airport where he met a girl, who flew us back to Yeadon. Apparently, she needed to get in some flying hours with a qualified pilot for her licence. As we came in to land I felt uneasy. She lined up the plane with the runway, then as we approached she slowed down too much. The engine coughed and we lost height just as we were passing over the landing lights located on top of tall poles. We were very close but just skimmed over. The pilot took control and turned the power back on, as we landed with a hop, skip and a jump. We shook hands and thanked him for his trouble although he was a bit surly. Perhaps he had commission on sales, but he wasn't getting any today. Howard said he was surprised I had held out without signing. We made for the Rose and Crown to see our workmates after what had been a most interesting and enjoyable day. Later on I was as good as my word and we did buy two trailers from Walker's.

After visiting a site near Skipton I was on my way back to Ilkley when I heard on the radio a call for a mechanic to go out to a machine that had broken down near Keighley. I decided to call in and take a look. The excavator had been working on a building site levelling and grading the ground around the completed houses. The machine had picked up a scaffolding clip in one of the tracks, which had jammed the track and damaged the running gear. This was quite a big problem. I was annoyed as scaffolding clips should be collected when the scaffolding is removed and not left as an unnecessary hazard. I spoke to the site foreman but nothing could be done. His workmen had just been careless and now it was my problem.

Then and there an idea came to me that I thought would stop it happening again. I told my machine operators a bonus of £1 would be paid for every scaffolding clip they brought to the garage. This way they would look out for them when grading which would avoid it happening again. Well, as a plan it backfired! After a week they had brought in more than 150 clips, in the process earning good beer money. Unfortunately many had been stolen and when one builder rang me to say he'd lost twenty-five and if they weren't returned he would throw our machine 'off hire', I had to cancel the arrangement!

There was a factory in Addingham that produced plastic baths and toilet fittings. Business was good and they were expanding with plans to build a new factory. I paid them a visit and made friends with another man whose assistance would prove of great benefit to my business. His name was Luigi Rognoni, an Italian. As the man in charge of the firm's building work he hired my excavators.

Luigi loved hunting and I found farms where we could go to shoot rabbits and pigeons. The company he worked for had a bad reputation for not paying their bills, but Luigi always got me a cheque when I pressed him. The work went on for a long time and he also placed a contract with us for removing plastic waste, burying it in a railway cutting.

Death of my Father

Then I received some bad news from Keighley. My younger sister Connie rang one afternoon to say that our dad had been taken ill and was now in Airedale Hospital. I made arrangements to meet her and my mother as soon as I could get away from work. I took Howard with me and we arrived in the waiting room at the hospital. My father was in Intensive Care and was unconscious. In my usual optimistic way I tried to lift their spirits.

"Dad is as strong as an ox. He'll be all right, don't worry," I told them.

Sadly I was wrong, he never recovered. He was only sixty years old and had enjoyed good health all his life. This illness - he had suffered a cerebral haemorrhage - came out of the blue and we were all devastated.

How my parents came to be in Keighley needs some explanation. At the time Wendy and I married in 1958 they were still running the fish and chip shop in Burley-in-Wharfedale, but dad didn't settle there for long. Early in the 1960s they moved to another fish and chip shop near Redcar where my two aunts had gone to live but a couple of years later they moved back to the area, buying a fish and chip shop at Haworth. Again, dad soon lost interest and they moved to Keighley, where dad took a job as a minibus driver for the local college. Connie, who was always closest to him, was now married and was living nearby in Bingley when he died.

On the day dad was taken ill, he went home from the college for his lunch as usual, telling my mother he would return early to wash his car and adjust the brakes. They found him later that afternoon when someone noticed his legs poking out from under the car and called an ambulance.

The next day was one of the worst in my life as I had to go to the hospital for his clothes and personal belongings. I collected them and came out into a bright, sunny day. As I walked slowly across the car park towards my car I was a little dazed, clutching a carrier bag with his wellington boots poking out of the top. Inside one of the boots was his well-worn wallet, bulging as he always had a few hundred pounds in it. There was a handful of loose change from his pocket, a bunch of keys, two spanners from his overall pockets and a grubby hankie. These were the last possessions he had on him. I took them to my mother who was heartbroken. They hadn't always seen eye to eye as I had witnessed in my youth, and she spent much of the time in his shadow 'keeping the peace'. But though they never sat holding hands they had grown closer as my father mellowed with age. She was now lost without him. It was a comfort that Connie lived close by and gave our mother great support not only then but for the rest of her days.

My mother was to live a long time on her own; in fact for another thirty years. In later life I remember her once saying to me, "You know Kenneth, I've never got over losing your father. I have to get on with life on my own but there is never a night when I don't think of him as I climb the stairs and get into bed on my own."

Like my mother, I had faced most of the harder side of my dad's nature. But I missed him too, and still do. I have often wondered why he had such a short fuse to his temper. I'd heard from my granny years before that he'd been shy as a boy. Maybe it came from that.

I learned some positive things from him, like how engines work. On the negative side, I'd always resented his stock answer to being questioned. "Because I say so," he would say. These were words I would never use with my own sons. I didn't beat them either, except on a single occasion when one stole from another.
However life goes on. It doesn't stop like a bus for someone to get off.

Chippy Walker
The Ken Walker Transport and Plant Hire yard at East Parade was about half a mile from our new house in Valley Drive, so occasionally I'd walk home for lunch. On the way I passed a shop that had been shut for a long time. Through the dusty, cobwebbed windows I could see an old fish frying range and as I stared I was taken back all those years to my chip-chopping days. Though the shop wasn't being used, someone lived in the adjoining house. I knocked on the door, and an old man appeared.

"I'm Ken Walker and my garage is in the next street. Can I have a chat?" He was a nice old man and we had a long conversation, before striking a deal. The outcome was that I'd bought the shop!

The property comprised a small shop with a flat above. I immediately set about refurbishment. The shop was completely re-equipped and fitted with new pans and the latest counter range models. Years before in Masham, I had been known as 'Fishy Walker', and I wasn't going to be called that again. But I did like 'Chippy Walker' and this was the name of the business we formed. I had the name painted above the door.

My older sister Freda had been manager of a fish and chip shop in Redcar until shortly before this development. She was now free and we came to an agreement for her to manage the shop and live in the flat above. Initially, it was hugely successful as it was the only fish and chip shop in the area, but Freda became sloppy, forgetting to order supplies. She would make excuses and blame the wholesaler or a late delivery. The problem was she always knew best and couldn't stand me pointing out her mistakes, so we soon fell out. She had a good education, much better than mine, but this didn't give her management skills. She left and I sold the shop, which was a great pity as it was a thriving business with no cash flow problems!

I was constantly looking for areas to grow into and one that suggested itself was demolition work. Tippers and excavators were needed for this and it would help me expand the fleet.

Announced in the early 1960s, the Beeching reforms of the railways (which meant the axing of hundreds of stations and lines) were having a profound effect by the 1970s. Dr Beeching had believed that the railways should be a business and not a public service. Therefore railway lines that didn't pay had to be closed. The Skipton to Ilkley line was one of those, with services ending in 1965. A few years later British Rail was ready to decommission the infrastructure.

I tendered for the work and soon we were moving railway embankments, demolishing bridges and taking up the tracks. One of the disused railway cuttings between Ilkley and Addingham ran across the fields at a farm called Reynard Ing. I came to an agreement with the farmer, Tom Mason, and used it as a tip for excavated material. It was eventually levelled and grassed over; fields divided by the railway line almost a century now became whole again. Tom was a nice old man. He lived with his wife in the farmhouse that had changed little over many years. The ancient fireplace had a bread oven at the side and I think Mrs Mason still used it. Tom showed me round the house one day and upstairs to the bedroom in which he had been born more than seventy years before.

The Walls Come A' Tumbling Down

After my success with Ilkley I managed to get on the council list of approved contractors for the Skipton area and secured a job demolishing ten houses and an old hall at Milligan Fields, Cross Hills.

Insurance for this type of work was difficult to obtain and expensive. I put this job down as low risk as it didn't border any main roads, so I didn't arrange any specific insurance. This saved about £1,000 and I assumed all would go well - an assumption that proved ill-founded.

One of my best and most reliable men, Derek Symonds, was appointed to run the job. The houses were the first to come down, then we moved to the hall. At the end of the site next to the road was a small church, a single-storey stone building that was not to be demolished as it was a spiritual meeting place. Between this and the hall was a house that was to be removed in order to leave a space. This would reduce the risk of damage to the church.

Once the house was carefully cleared away we started on the hall. Derek had a long wire rope fastened around the wall of the hall some thirty feet up, with the other end secured to an excavator. As he pulled the rope, a huge crack opened in the gable end and the whole wall came down with seventy to eighty tons of masonry crashing to the ground in an enormous bang! The unwanted consequence was the collapse of the little church.

When I drove to the site Derek was standing speechless. He had a stammer when he was excited but he couldn't even get that working. He stood with his head down only giving me the occasional glance, mouth wide open but not capable of saying a word. I had a reputation as a hard taskmaster and was sometimes intolerant when mistakes were made. But Derek was careful and I knew it must have been an accident. I calmed him down and investigated the damage. The church was flattened. We always had a few spectators but this time we had many more. I spoke to an eyewitness who described what had happened. He told me that as the walls of the hall came thundering down it caused such a draught as it landed that the roof of the church lifted up and one of the walls caved in. The roof came back down, finishing on top of the pile of rubble. Derek hadn't miscalculated and the wall hadn't actually hit the church at all. It was the impact of tons of stone landing so close to the church wall.

We were in trouble. A man appeared and demanded to speak to the owner of the demolition company. I put my hand up.

He said, "My name is Mr Martin and I am a member of the Church committee. I would like the name and address of your insurance company." Well that was going to be difficult. I could have said, "You're talking to him; I am that same man," but I didn't.

However, I apologised to him and asked for his name and address so that our 'insurers' could contact him. He gave me his details and we looked over the damage. Three walls were still standing, though the pews, pulpit and lectern were buried under the rubble. Derek was distraught and didn't know what to do. I gave him a few words of comfort, although I needed some myself. The committee man was raking about in the dust and rubble with a long face. It was clear that I would have trouble trying to make peace with him. I told him, "Not to worry, it will be put right. We're a reputable company and have adequate insurance cover. I suggest you remove anything of value and my men will help you."

I left him poking about in the rubble and drove back to Ilkley thinking, "How do I sort this one out?" Back at the depot I heard that Mr Martin had already been on the telephone asking for the name of our insurance company. My staff were well trained and told him that he would need to first speak to Mr Walker, the owner. My pint at the Rose and Crown that evening didn't taste anywhere near as good as usual as I pondered the problem.

Next day, I told Mr Martin that my insurers had authorised me to talk to him and arrange to make good the damage. "Good," he said. "One of our members is a builder and can give you a quote. That way we'll know the work has been done properly and to our satisfaction. In the meantime I will prepare an inventory of the damaged contents."

He wasted no time presenting me with the list: oak pulpit, oak lectern, silver cutlery, Axminster carpet, velvet curtains, etc, etc. Clearly, the church committee saw this as an insurance opportunity and they were going to make a meal of it. I looked through the debris. There were old knives and forks with yellow handles; the lectern was oak but worm eaten; the pulpit was pine, but very old and split; the Axminster carpet was threadbare and badly frayed, the crockery had cracked long before the roof fell in. They were not being reasonable. I was quite prepared to make good the damage done, but certainly was not prepared to finance their betterment. What kind of churchgoers were they?

The press heard about it, the story appearing all over the area. One headline read, 'Oops! Sorry about the Church'. Reporters were soon on the phone to my office asking for an explanation.

My standard reply was, "Demolition is a hazardous job. However careful you are occasionally things go wrong. My foreman is very experienced and took all necessary precautions. He was not to know that the gable end had been cemented over at some time in the past to hide a huge crack. This caused the whole wall to come down in one go rather than just a section at a time. I have discussed it with the church representatives and our insurers, and it will be put right."

The church was eventually made good and we went to a great deal of trouble to replace the fixtures and fittings. As I expected, members of the church committee weren't satisfied nor would they ever be, that was the kind of people they were. The name of our insurance company remained a well kept secret.

The Old Mill
Our next demolition job was an old corn mill at Steeton between Keighley and Skipton. Unlike Cross Hills, this job went according to plan. The Old Mill, dating back to the seventeenth century, was a five-storey stone building, originally water driven but in recent years converted to diesel and electric power. It had stood empty for a number of years and now looked derelict. Even the rats had left, though there was plenty of evidence that they'd enjoyed living there. While it didn't look like a big earner, it turned out to be very good for the company and helped offset losses from Cross Hills.

The building stood at the side of a main road, though just far enough back for safety. It was an ideal 'sales' location. In the event, we were able to sell almost every bit of the Old Mill, much of it to passers-by, with the exception of firewood. This was given to anyone who could collect it and much of it was taken away by one old timer who came every day with his barrow. Yorkshire stone, roof slates, bricks and even the rubble was sold for hardcore.

The Old Mill was full of oak and pine timber. When we removed the roof slates we discovered that the purlins were made from four-inch thick oak boughs that had been only roughly flattened on one side where the slates sat. Some of this oak still had the bark on. I sold every one for £1 a foot. Colin Johnson bought some, along with other pieces of oak for an Ilkley nightclub, the Minstrels Gallery, he was setting up. At forty foot long the pine floor joists were the biggest I've ever seen and were still sound. They were not difficult to sell, only difficult to move.

I noticed that some of the larger pieces of oak were an irregular shape and didn't look as if they'd been made for the task they were doing. When I made enquiries I learned they possibly came from a previous demolition job! When the old sailing ships were made redundant some of the virtually indestructible oak they were made from was brought inland and used to repair buildings. The use of ships' timber in the Old Mill explained the misshapes. I was told on good authority that many of the old buildings on the Duke of Devonshire's Estate at nearby Bolton Abbey also had been repaired using old ships' timber. These days whenever I go into an old building with oak timbers I look for the ones that don't look purpose-made. It's good to think they may have been round the world several times.

At the back of the Mill were buildings that had been cart sheds. They were quite narrow and low with stone arched entrances. A man came onto the site one day and asked if he could buy one of the arches and would we take it down stone by stone and number them? He wanted it to make an inglenook fireplace in a barn conversion he was working on. We agreed a deal and he returned the following week with a trailer to collect the stones. I was pleased as I now knew how to sell the other two arches, getting an even better price after advertising them as being suitable for inglenook fireplaces.

Later, when I pulled down railway structures I became interested in how they were built and read about the men who had put them up and how they had worked. It had been a remarkable achievement with most of the labour being done with picks and shovels, plus the occasional 'steam navvy'. The engineers of that era, men like Stephenson and Brunel, were certainly clever and the navvies were tough, tough men - they had to be to achieve what they did. My small excavator scooped up more than a ton at a time, and I pictured the railway navvy pushing his barrow up a plank out of the cutting. If he was lucky there would be a man at the top pulling with a rope. About ten barrow loads would have been equal to one excavator bucket full. The stonework on the buttresses and arches was a work of art. The joints were so thin the blocks sat literally stone on stone. Sometimes when I visited a site I'd spend a pleasant hour checking the masons' marks on the stones trying to find any that matched.

One day we found an old tobacco tin which fell out of a wall as the stones were removed. It was still in good condition and when I opened it I found a mixture of tobacco, clover and hay seeds. Amazingly it still had a strong smell. The seeds had been added to make the tobacco go a bit further. We assumed that someone had played a trick on its owner and walled his tin into the stonework when he wasn't looking. It had stayed hidden for sixty or more years.

Before we started pulling down the houses or buildings on our many demolition jobs I liked to have a good look round. Empty houses can tell you a lot about who lived in them. Though rundown, some former residents had tried to make the best of them through painting, decorating and cleaning. Others were like slums, neglected by owner and occupier. Occasionally we would find a tiny garden that had been cared for by the last occupier while others in the same row might be piled high with rubbish.

I liked demolition as it could be both interesting and profitable. It wasn't just a case of smashing things down. There was a procedure to follow which made the job easier and less dangerous. It also stirred my interest in social history. In my time I have demolished houses, buildings and railways. Sometimes I felt like a vandal, and wondered if what I was doing was right. On a few occasions I was sure it was the wrong thing, just as it had been when Beeching's axe fell on the railways. But cleverer and certainly better paid men than me had made the decisions, and I was only earning a living.

An Honest Man

Whenever we opened a demolition site people would soon appear, clamouring to buy timber, doors flags, slates and other building materials. On each job of this kind there had to be an honest man, or as the workers would say, "A boss's man." One of my most honest workers was Mick Winsor, a wonderful gentle giant of a man; gentle that is until he stepped into the ring as a professional wrestler: then things changed! He liked the heavy work on a demolition site to keep fit.

Once when I visited a site Mick was swinging a 7 lb hammer, breaking cast iron central heating pipes. A triangular piece of iron about the size of a 50p coin flew up and dug in his eyebrow, only missing his eye by a fraction. It stuck there, firmly embedded and a trickle of blood ran down to his chin. Still holding the hammer in one hand he reached up with the other and plucked it out, holding it for us all to see before he threw it into the skip. He wasn't a bit shaken, but smiled and said, "That was close." There was no question of him seeing a doctor or going to the hospital. We just plastered him up and he carried on working. If anyone was used to taking a few knocks it was Mick!

By contrast, a fellow named Brian Glover who was one of the machine operators was not as trustworthy. When working on a large clearance site he dug up an old copper cable that had been disconnected but left in the ground. The cable ran right across the site and was worth a lot of money. He took it to a scrapyard and sold it for several hundreds of pounds, giving some of the money to others on the site for their silence. You can't truly buy silence like that though, and it didn't take long for me to hear about it. I hauled him into my office for an explanation. The problem was that we were working for another contractor, so any scrap recovered was their property not mine, leaving me in a difficult position as I could be accused of theft. He lied and denied everything, leaving me with little choice but to sack him. However, he had a large family and was a good machine operator. We had plenty of work and in many ways we needed each other, so I gave him a stern warning. "Anything happens like that again, Brian, and you and me will part company." He left my office rather sheepishly, believing he had got away with it.

A few months later we were not as busy and I was offered some work on a pipeline in Wales. The machine that Brian operated was the only one suitable for the job.

I spoke to him, "I'd like you to go to Wales for a few weeks but you will get home Fridays for the weekend."

He replied, "I'm not going there."

"Well Brian, I've offered you work, if you don't want it I have nothing else for you to do, so you'll have to leave." He did leave but, listen to this, took me to an employment tribunal. Not only that but he won his case and was awarded several hundred pounds in compensation for unfair dismissal!

Another story occurs to me that indicates how everyone you employ is different. A new driver had started. All my staff were paid weekly, working a week in hand, and this was his first pay day. That Friday afternoon I was in my office when I heard the clunk of slow, heavy footsteps on the stair then a rap on my door. In came a big woman: "I've called for David's wages," she said.

"Well you can't have David's wages," I told her. "I give the wages to the wage earner, if he then chooses to give them to you that's his affair."

She stood her ground. "But I've always collected his wages," she retorted.

I could be equally as stubborn. "Until now maybe you have, but not today. If he comes to me and says I'm to give them to you that will be fine, but as it stands now the answer, sorry, is no, he must collect them himself." She didn't like this and left in a huff. Clearly she took it out on poor David who then gave us the necessary authorisation to hand over his wages to her. The next week she was back, picked up his cash in a haughty way and I was left in no doubt who wore the trousers in that relationship.

After a lull in business which prompted me to be cautious about any more expansion, we won a couple of demolition jobs linked to the high level of railway closures that blighted the early 1970s. The first was the biggest and most challenging demolition project we had ever handled.

Our company was held in favour by Mirfield Council. Twenty-four houses had to come down, plus a length of railway viaduct some forty feet high with five arches that was part of the old Spen Valley line. Dr Beeching's axe had fallen on this and the viaduct was now disused. It was a new and exciting challenge.

The viaduct was built from Staffordshire blue engineering bricks, some of the hardest ever made. When I worked out the estimate I wasn't sure how it would break up. I was in for a shock when we started. Brickwork built using black mortar (not cement) could be expected to separate at the seams when hammered with the bucket teeth of a huge twenty-ton excavator. But this was a solid construction and each time we swung the bucket only a few bricks fell to the ground, making progress painfully slow.

I had to find a better way. Explosives were forbidden because of the proximity to houses and the main Huddersfield Road. I had read in *Construction* trade journal about a new revolutionary concrete breaker, a far cry from 'Paddy' with his jackhammer. I would have to get one.

I found the nearest agent and immediately hired an excavator with the breaker fitted. I was on site to watch it being unloaded and spoke to the operator, showing him the job to be done. He was full of confidence. "No problem!" he said.

He tracked the machine down to the first arch. The 'pecker' was bolted onto the long arm of the excavator, leaving a thick steel rod protruding from the end. The other end of the steel rod was connected to a hydrogen cartridge. When pressed onto a hard surface it set up a vibration that ran through solid rock or concrete causing it to crack and break up. The first time I saw the pecker in action I couldn't believe my eyes, for the brickwork just separated at the seams, bricks falling to the ground, clean and ready to sell.

In my estimate to the council I'd priced for the bricks to go straight to the tip as having no commercial resale value. Once the pecking started, though, the bricks tumbled down and I was able to sell every one. Good clean engineering bricks were always in demand.

Another job at Mirfield was doing well. I'd made friends with a council member who was in control of the demolition contracts. We had originally tendered for work, done a good job and left sites tidy upon completion. He was impressed and wanted us to do all their demolition in the future. We negotiated individually for each job which allowed us some leeway in order to get a good price. The council member took me to look at an old hospital, which happened to be a single storey wartime construction of timber covered in steel sheets.

"There's nothing in this to cover my costs," I said. "It's just a load of hard work." (It is worth pointing out that on many demolition contracts you were expected to reduce the contract price if there was stone or scrap to recover and sell.) I told him we would need £1,000 to clear the site. He said that he would put it to the committee.

A week later he rang and asked, "When can you start?" We agreed a start date and my first job was to arrange insurance — I'd learned my lesson with the church. Fortunately, the insurance cover was inexpensive as the demolition was located well away from other properties and could be considered a low risk.

By this time we had two skip wagons along with about thirty skips. On day one we set out a number of skips, each one to take a different type of material recovered from the old hospital. I went with my foreman to show him the job and explain what was to be done. I hadn't inspected the building and had only glanced inside, but when we looked closer I had a pleasant surprise as it was full of scrap, all good for selling for cash.

The building was like a large Army hut. You entered by an end door and walked through a passageway all the way through the length of the building to the other end. On either side of this passageway were thirty small rooms containing sinks, WCs and heating radiators, all fed by metal pipes made of copper or lead. For us it was like an Aladdin's Cave. When we pulled up the floorboards we found copper piping running the full length of the building, branching off to every room.

We couldn't believe our luck. I knew there would be scrap but hadn't any idea there would be as much as this, or as valuable. The job showed a handsome profit. Mick Winsor got his bonus and some went into my back pocket.

Fire in Burnley

I tendered for and won a large demolition contract over on the other side of the Pennines in Burnley town centre. It was another big job and a very difficult one too. A block of twelve properties, comprising a row of shops and offices facing on to the main street, plus a large area at the rear with houses, warehouses and workshops, all had to be demolished and the debris removed. I realised the job would need a great deal of care and an awful lot of scaffolding.

One of the buildings, formerly the offices of the tram company, had a huge clock fastened to the wall. I was told that for many years the whole of Burnley ran by this clock. We were asked to remove it with special care as it was going to a museum.

Some of these buildings were five storeys high, so the first job was to strip the roofs. I engaged a stripping gang from Bradford to remove the roofs, which included taking down all the slates and timbers. They were rough lads but good at what they did, and that was good enough for me. They raced greyhounds in their spare time and explained some of the tricks of the trade, like borrowing dogs from Ireland to race here under assumed names, or giving them huge doses of drugs that would make the animal run faster than it had ever run before. The downside was severe as the drugs would strain the hearts of the dogs, possibly meaning they would never run again.

The lads were not frightened of hard work and ran across the roofs like cats. The deal was that they stripped the tiles and took the lead as payment. One of the conditions laid down by the council was that nothing should be burnt on site as it was in the centre of the town. This would mean a lot of extra work as everything had to be hauled to the tip. The Bradford lads threw the timbers into a central area with the pile getting bigger by the day.

"When will you be taking the wood to the tip?" I asked them.

"When we have all the roofs completely cleared. Don't worry," I was told. "We'll soon move that lot. By next week it will all be gone." His words proved to be prophetic but not in the way he intended!

On the Sunday morning following this conversation, while it was still dark, the police were knocking loudly on my front door.

"You're in trouble," they told me. "There's been a fire on your site in Burnley and you must get there immediately." No time for breakfast as I shot off on the back roads to Lancashire. It was just getting light as I sped through Colne towards Nelson and Burnley. In the distance I could see a large grey cloud slowly rising like steam from a cooling tower and as I drew nearer to Burnley I saw this was in fact huge palls of smoke. There was no wind and as I reached the town centre the smoke hung close to the ground, filling the streets like fog. I couldn't believe my eyes!

There was a lot of activity with police cars and fire engines everywhere. In total, I counted seven fire appliances. The fire was now out but you could still smell it. I felt like a criminal as the police immediately surrounded me and started firing questions, and the press were not far behind. I told the police that everything was safe on Saturday when we left the site and explained that we never had fires as it wasn't allowed. Someone must have done it deliberately. They gave me a grilling but there was nothing I could tell them, though I had a good idea what might have happened. I suspected that the stripping gang had sent someone in the middle of the night to torch the pile of timber to save them from having to cart it to the tip. The blame would be pinned onto vandals. That way they saved time and money … and so would I for that matter!

When I questioned the gang next day they denied everything, pointing towards vandalism, just as I thought they would. But I knew who the real vandals were and I was talking to them. There was nothing I could do if the police were unable to prove anything, and I couldn't complain too much either as they had saved us both a lot of expense - and the stripping gang knew it. The council were upset but nothing could be done and no one was ever prosecuted. In the end, like the smoke, it all blew over and we carried on, keeping a wary eye out for the next problem.

My brother Howard was driving the huge excavator and was involved in pulling down the walls of the bank in Burnley. This appeared to have been constructed from lovely Ashlar cut stone, but as we peeled off the facing stone we were alarmed to discover that it had been completely rebuilt at some time. Within the outer walls was a new reinforced concrete and steel structure which would be extremely difficult to break up. This was threatening to be a bigger problem than the fire. Initially we hacked at the base to weaken it, then tried pulling with wire ropes. The walls would give a little, then whip back towards the main street. If the walls fell the wrong way there would be a catastrophe as they could land on the busy main road, which was always full of people and cars.

I was worried and discussed the problem with Howard. He told me confidently, "I'll tell you what we'll do, our lad" (that's what he called me). "Tomorrow you stay away, go to another job and leave this to me. Don't worry, I'll fix it." I took his advice and stayed away. Howard was absolutely fearless but he had good sense and I knew he wouldn't take silly risks.

Most days after work we would meet in the Rose and Crown around 6 pm. On that next day I was the first to arrive and ordered two pints. I'd taken a sip of mine, glanced at his glass and wondered what sort of day in Burnley he'd had. I didn't have to wait long before I heard the familiar sound of Howard's heavy studded boots on the steps leading down from the car park. The door burst open and in he came, beaming from ear to ear.

"You can come to Burnley tomorrow," he said. "It's all down." He had removed a big problem for me and I felt great relief. He didn't explain how he'd done it and he didn't need to. I was just pleased it was finished. We drank our beer, "Cheers Howard!"

The Sludge Lagoon

It was time to confront the next problem. In this business there were always problems but that was what made it so challenging and interesting. After all, if it was easy everybody would do it! There wasn't long to wait and the next problem was a real 'stinker'. Literally!

Years before when I bought my first lorry and had no work, I had moved a manure heap. There was a stink with that but nothing like this one. And it came from two directions: the tannery and the water authority.

The contract we were awarded was to empty a sludge lagoon at a tannery in Keighley. Let me explain: when cow hides first arrived from the slaughterhouse they were put through a machine that stripped the hair and any skin or flesh still on the inside. This was a big improvement on the procedures at the Wensleydale Meat Company which had disgusted me when I was a delivery man in my first job after National Service. What hadn't changed though, were the smell and the rotting animal matter.

Once separated from the hides, the hair, skin, flesh and other waste was disposed into a rat-infested lagoon to settle. Also into that lagoon went the effluent from the tanning process. Then, once a year the lagoon had to be emptied. On this occasion we won the contract but soon found out it was one of the worst jobs we had ever handled.

The wagons stood by the side of the lagoon where they were loaded by an excavator. The sludge was carted to an old quarry located up on the moors. Some of the wagon tail doors didn't fit tightly, which meant the sludge dripped out onto the road as the wagons passed through Keighley. To make matters worse, if the traffic lights were red the wagons would leave a pool behind them. At all times, drivers with loaded vehicles had to go slowly around corners or the sludge would splash over the side. Wagons, drivers, yard and our garage all began to stink. There seemed no escape from the smell. When the drivers complained, I had to pay them extra money in compensation. One told me his wife wouldn't let him in the house until he'd stripped off his working clothes and left them outside.

When I drove over to check on progress, the smell hit me as I entered Keighley. A few days into the contract I was contacted by the water authority and told to immediately cease tipping sludge into the old quarry. I was instructed to meet their representative along with a Keighley Council representative the following morning. Next day, I arrived to find five cars and seven or eight suited officials waiting for me. I learned that they had been monitoring the watercourse and its catchment area for the Yorkshire Water Board. They told me the sludge had found its way from the quarry through fissures in the limestone and into a beck. Their technicians had analysed the sludge and told me there was poison in the residue from the tanning process. I could no longer use the quarry to tip the sludge and I was once again in trouble. It was frustrating as suddenly I found myself with six wagons and a loader standing idle, and wages still to be paid. Something had to be done and quickly!

Shortly before this, we had been tipping excavated material in a cutting on a farm near Hawksworth. To get there from Keighley was a longer haul than to the quarry, but my options were limited. I had to get the lagoon emptied and the job finished or I wouldn't be paid. I went to see the farmer and his greedy eyes lit up when he saw the pound notes in my hand. We agreed a deal and the wagons rolled once again. There was no watercourse near his land but we worked as fast as we could to empty the lagoon before the Water Board started checking on us again. When we finished we covered over the tip with spoil and that was that. Now, at last I could send in my account.

Our Marriage Ends

Wendy and I agreed to separate. This became a painful experience for both of us and for our three young boys, the youngest Timothy in particular. For a while there were tears and threats, but this settled down and we moved apart: Wendy and the boys into a new home in Weston Road that I had converted from a garage warehouse, and me staying in Valley Drive just a few hundred yards away. We tried getting back together, as much for the sake of the boys as for ourselves, but it still didn't work out.

We decided on divorce in 1973, though right to the end I was reluctant to take the step and disappointed that this had come about. Wendy was determined we should not go on as we were and, again, I compromised. Whatever else, we were determined to handle the divorce as amicably as possible and let our solicitor, Jack Mewies, over in Skipton, take charge of the whole thing. This kept disagreements to a minimum. Wendy took ownership of the house on Weston Road, furniture and a car, and I started monthly payments for her and the boys. After the arrangements were made we drove back in the car together over the hills back to Ilkley.

It was a sad time and mirrored other difficulties that were to arise in the 1970s. For a time there was an estrangement and I didn't see Wendy or the boys very often, even though we were living so near to each other. Wendy was an attractive woman and it didn't take her long to make a new friend who she later married. His name was Ian Gledhill, a quiet man and a good father-figure for the boys.

Life goes on and I eventually found a new companion myself in Julia Nadal, then twenty-one, who I met one evening in 1974 in the Minstrels Gallery nightspot in Ilkley where she worked as a part-time waitress and barmaid. She was very attractive, tall and slim with lovely fair, almost blonde hair. At the time she was a student at Liverpool University and only came home at weekends.

Initially, we didn't see much of each other but the friendship grew and we felt comfortable in each other's company. After the trauma of the breakup of the marriage it was good to have a close friend again. By the following year a close relationship was underway which was to last through many more events for the next seventeen years.

Julia was a local girl whose parents had a farm at High Austby on the side of the valley overlooking Ilkley. Her mother, Peggy, was a keen horsewoman and her father, Jiulio, looked after the farm's cows. They had met after World War Two when Peggy was with the Land Army in Wales, and Jiulio was a recently-released Italian prisoner of war. After their marriage Peggy's father set them up on the farm where Julia and her sister, Gina, grew up.

Julia left college having gained a degree in Art and Design and took a job in Leeds designing children's clothes for a company in Chapeltown.

It Never Rains ...

By this time we were getting a lot of work from Skipton Council. The man we dealt with was reasonable and we established a good working relationship. I would never offer anyone a backhander (a bribe) but I liked to say thank you. One year as Christmas was approaching and I was due to meet the council representative on a site near Keighley, I took a case of wine saying, "I've brought you a Christmas drink just to say thanks for the co-operation you have shown."

He looked shocked and cried, "Oh no. I can't take anything from you. We don't want another Maudling affair. Just put the box in the boot of my car when I'm not looking!" Reginald Maudling was a Conservative MP who in 1972 became tied up in some shady dealings with a certain John Poulson, a Yorkshire architect. Maudling resigned as Home Secretary over the affair which effectively ended his political career.

As we approached the mid 1970s, we were always busy. Our wagon drivers worked long hours, often above the legal limit. Each driver filled in a daily sheet recording hours worked, loads carried and meal breaks. These sheets were handed in daily to me as manager.

I was shocked and just a little worried when we received a letter from the Ministry of Transport to say that they would be paying a visit the following week to check our records. I would be in big trouble if they saw these, so I spoke to all the drivers and they agreed to come in on Sunday morning to re-write the sheets. Seven drivers gathered in the garage and scribbled out new details with modified hours. Fortunately, I had a good supply of new sheets.

When the job was done I took six of the seven to the Rose and Crown for a lunchtime pint. The one who didn't come was the individual whose wife collected his wages every week, and he apologised, saying he had to go straight home. When the man from the Ministry came a few days later I was a little nervous. We had tried to make the sheets look grubby and used but they still looked new to me. Thankfully, there was no need to worry as he was a reasonable man. He found one or two minor discrepancies and off he went, leaving me to throw the sheets in the bin and breathe a sigh of relief.

We now had tipper wagons and excavators as well as dumpers and cement mixers. We used them ourselves or hired them out to builders and other contractors. In fact, by this time we had all the equipment needed to expand into civil engineering road and drainage work. What we lacked was the know-how.

I needed a contracts manager with experience in civil engineering. It had to be someone who knew how to estimate and manage that type of work. I tried to poach from other companies but failed, so I placed an ad in the local newspaper and sat down with the applicants. The man I selected seemed good, very good in fact. In time I came to realise that he was actually too good to be true.

His name was Mike Schofield and he told me he'd worked in the Middle East on drainage works. He explained how he'd saved his company thousands of pounds by bulldozing sand to form the shape of bridge works before pouring in the concrete, which had eliminated the need to use timber and steel for shuttering. It sounded good to me. I hired him at a modest wage, but offered him a share of any profit he helped create. I also gave him a company car. This way, if he didn't make money for me he certainly wouldn't make much for himself. What I hadn't considered was that neither of us was going to get anything but trouble out of this arrangement.

"We'll have a regular meeting every Monday morning," I told Mike. "I want you to come to my office to give a progress report on all the contracts, letting me know exactly where we stand on each job as we go along."

I took him to all of my local builder contacts who might be able to offer work on new roads and sewers, and introduced him to local authority customers to see if they would allow us to tender for civil engineering. Slowly, small jobs began to come through. I formed a new company, Ken Walker Contracts Limited, and decided the contracting work would be managed separately from the plant hire and transport companies. Things looked good but I took a decision that would have important but disappointing consequences later: after advice and pressure from the bank, I made a cross-guarantee between my transport and contracts companies.

We made a little money on the various smaller jobs in the first few months. One at Cleckheaton, for instance, showed a modest profit. But we were looking for bigger deals where the return would be worth the investment in time and effort. After several months we finally won a major project when our tender for £96,000 was accepted by Kirklees Council for road realignment at Batley outside the Foxes' biscuit factory.

While this was going on, a second large deal came our way to put in drains and a concrete base for a new Coca-Cola bottling plant at Pudsey. It looked promising and showed we could win bigger and better contracts.

The Batley deal was duly signed and we started work. When I visited the site I noticed the smell of biscuits cooking at Foxes. This was lovely at first but by the time we'd finished this particular project I had gone right off. Today, whenever I see Foxes' biscuits in Morrisons, I'm reminded of the pain of that time.

At Pudsey there was a need to get the work underway, but as we were a newly established company the customer needed a guarantee bond to cover them in case of default. This was easily arranged through our bank. We were looking forward to getting started and I was confident we were on the right track.

As the weeks went by Mike and I kept religiously to our weekly meeting on Monday mornings. He would show me the contract prices, reporting on the progress of work and money that was owed to us. Eventually, the first payment for the work near the Foxes factory arrived, but it was much less than expected. Then another payment came in and that was also below what we had reckoned. I brought this up with Mike. "Explain this to me Mike," I said. "We're not being paid as much as you say we should be getting."

"Well Ken, you see, where we've joined the new road to the old road there was a large drain that was not in the drawing or in the contract. We've done a lot of extra work re-routing and connecting it but there's still more to do. They won't pay us until the end of the contract. There will be extras coming our way at that time."

It seemed a reasonable enough explanation, but it went on. Each month we were being seriously underpaid, the value of cheques consistently less than the claim Mike was entering to justify his profit-share. It reached the point where I decided I ought to speak to Batley Corporation. Mike could be a bit abrasive with people and perhaps my manner would be better with the clerk of works.

I drove over to Batley and had a big surprise. The Batley Council clerk of works told me flatly that there were no 'extras'. Apparently, we'd made such a bad job of the contract that damage to the drain was our responsibility, and if we didn't make it good at our expense to their entire satisfaction we'd be kicked off site. Another contractor would be brought in to finish the work and we would be sent the bill.

I was staggered! I had left the responsibility to Mike and trusted in his ability. Certainly, I hadn't stood over him questioning his every move but he never gave any hint of problems when we met on Mondays. We soon discovered he'd made a total 'balls-up' of the job. And while he could easily walk away, I couldn't. I was trapped with both a contract and a bank guarantee. As I drove back to Ilkley, my recently acquired Ferrari was of little comfort as I chewed over the problem. I did some quick calculations and determined that on the figures he'd given me, I'd lost over £20,000 on this one job - and the contract was not yet finished!

I called in Mike, but he waffled - I should have spotted this about him before - and offered no real defence. He had mismanaged the job from the start, so I had no choice but to fire him. In turn, this left me to take over the job myself.

It was extremely difficult to discuss this project with the council clerk of works as my knowledge of road works and drainage was limited and a lot less than his. Because of the way it had been run I was at a great disadvantage, a fact the engineer took advantage of. He totally screwed us. We finished the project eventually, but only by pouring good money after bad.

I later learned that while this job was going wrong, Mike was diverting my men and materials to another job nearby he had taken on in his own name. While he was floating his business he was busily sinking mine.

After Mike left, he went full time into business in his own name. It ran for about a year before he hit the buffers and he went into bankruptcy. If there was one crumb of comfort it was that he had done to himself what he virtually single-handedly had nearly done to me.

On reflection, I thought I'd been keeping my finger on the pulse by holding a review meeting every Monday morning. I now wonder if this rigid check frightened him into covering up his mistakes until it was too late to pull the coals out of the fire.

When I did find out, those coals were all blazing away and it was too late to recover the situation. Also, the attitude of the Batley clerk of works as a paid public official left a lot to be desired.

When I first started in business I'd picked some very good drivers and machine operators and continued employing good men as I expanded. That had been the source of a lot of my success. But when the time came to build up our management capability to help run the business I wasn't so lucky. On this occasion I had picked a real loser and he turned me into one.

… But it Pours

"Well it never rains but it pours," as the saying goes. At the same time as things were going pear-shaped at Batley, a similar story was unfolding at our other major undertaking, the Pudsey Coca-Cola contract. When Mike cocked up, he did so in style. The factory base was a huge slab of concrete with a maze of drains, channels, and pipes set into it. The levels of these were critical both for the flow and the amount of concrete used. Over such a large area, half an inch too much concrete used and you could lose a lot of money, but put down too little and the base was insecure. We had to be extremely accurate, but once again we didn't get it anywhere near right.

The main contractor's surveyor condemned a large area of the concrete we'd laid and ordered it to be taken out and redone. Breaking the concrete out was going to be another massive problem. Normally you could use a vibrating breaker or an excavator, but this was not allowed as it could easily damage the drainage underneath. The only way was to 'nibble' it out with hand breakers. This took days and days, and to add insult to injury the main contractor charged me hundreds of pounds as a penalty for delaying the contract.

We then had to re-lay the concrete. Again we were tied into a contract bond and couldn't walk away. I can assure you, it's not a very nice feeling when you have already lost thousands and then have to pour in more just to get the noose from around your neck. In the final result the contract lost me over £18,000, a staggering sum in the mid-1970s. Added to the Batley job, the combined losses meant that we were now seriously in trouble.

Mike had been pouring money down the drain and nearly wiped out Ken Walker Contracts Limited. The bank had insisted the two companies would be treated as one as far as they were concerned, despite the fact they were separate entities, each one guaranteeing the other on any loan. This had been the case for a number of years but was now putting the otherwise healthy Ken Walker Transport Limited in trouble.

In keeping with usual banking procedure you can have the umbrella until it rains. Well, now that it was pouring down, the bank wanted their umbrella back.

My formerly friendly bank manager, Roy Johnson, was not as helpful anymore. He wanted the bank's money back, extended to me in the form of loans and overdrafts and now amounting to £75,000. The problem was made worse because my official overdraft limit was only £10,000. Roy, himself, was in trouble too as he had sanctioned the increases as my business grew. It all looked good until the losses from the contracting side came rolling in and then the bank turned on me.

Head Office had never endorsed the extra money that had been extended to my companies. But now they were in the picture they decided to turn the screw, and pressure was put on Roy to do the dirty work. He reminded me I had plenty of assets and that I must sell some of them as a way of reducing the debt. The problem was that business assets such as wagons, excavators, skip lorries and skips don't make much in a forced sale. It was much better if we could hang onto them and use them to keep the companies afloat and earning revenue, and pay back the bank that way. They weren't interested and the sell-off started.

As the contracting losses came to light, I realised how much of a hole we were in. One of the first assets to be sold was my car, at that time a very special BMW 3CSL. Unlike the wagons and plant hire, it didn't do anything to generate income and, though I loved it, hard decisions had to be made.

The man who bought it was a market trader. When he came to Ilkley to collect it he arrived on a 750cc Suzuki motorbike with a carrier bag full of cash. I was delighted with the cash as by now the bank was making it difficult when the time came to pay the firm's wages. However, I wasn't as pleased when I discovered the money was about £750 short and he asked if I would take the bike in part exchange. Otherwise, he explained, he simply couldn't afford to buy the car. The bank had me cornered: the cash would pay the wages and relieve the pressure for a while. He had me cornered, too, as the car was not going to be easy to sell at the price it was worth. I was obliged to do the deal on his terms. As I still had a motorbike licence it at least meant I could ride the Suzuki to and from work.

Friday came around and the wages were paid as usual. I always felt a great relief when the little brown envelopes were handed out; my men had been paid and I could breathe again. All my employees did their best to help. The problems I had were none of their making. They were entitled to take their money home every Friday. Once they'd been paid it meant that I had a few days respite before it would begin all over again the following week.

I rode home on my newly acquired motorbike. At about 8 pm the door bell rang and I was surprised to see Howard standing there. "Yes, what do you want?" I asked. "Well can't you see it's raining? You can't go to the Rose and Crown on the motorbike so I've called for you."

I was quite overcome, what a nice thought. Over the years Howard and I had grown close. The five year gap in our ages had been a lot when we were younger. Probably like many younger brothers, Howard was around but was never old enough to join in with what interested me. His standing up to our father over the driving instruction was a sign that here was a young man I could relate to, even look up to a bit myself, just as our mother always said he looked up to me.

Howard was there when I was starting in business and his help was important in getting me through those first few years of real struggle. I knew he would always back me up, and he could be relied on whether it was a business issue, a motor racing problem, a concern over the trustworthiness of an employee or, as now, a personal difficulty. He was a partner as much as a brother.

Now, with the downturn in my business and the breakup of my marriage, it was Howard who stood by me. He still had the use of a company pickup and had come to give me a lift to the Rose and Crown for our regular Friday night drink together. It is a memory I will always treasure.

From 1973 until the end of the decade, Britain's economy was in a mess and it looked like the country was in terminal decline. The miners' strikes in 1973 and 1974 and the Conservative government's refusal to meet their demands had thrown us all into a three-day week. Rampant inflation following the oil price hikes that happened at the same time, sparked widespread misery as hundreds of companies went to the wall and massive unemployment returned to haunt people. The country even had to accept a bailout from the International Monetary Fund, just like poorer third world nations.

I was not unique in the problems I faced. Tough conditions also forced many other companies out of business. Whether banks helped or made the situation worse you decided according to your own point of view. As far as I was concerned we didn't get any assistance.

When my boys were young I had taken out insurance policies that would mature for each of them at the age of fifteen. The intention was for the money to be used on further education or, indeed, for whatever they chose. These policies had been deposited at a previous bank for safe keeping. When I moved banks some years before all my documents had been transferred to the new bank in Leeds. Now Roy had found them and came to see me with the three policies in his hand.

"I want you to assign these policies to the bank."

"They're nothing to do with the business," I said. "They are private insurance for my children's future benefit or schooling, and nothing else."

He replied, "Well that's not important now. You owe us money and these can be used to help repay us." I was very annoyed and refused to sign, but as the weeks went by and further losses emerged, he put renewed pressure on me. Reluctantly I signed them over, feeling very aggrieved.

Off to Cowpasture Road

That didn't keep him quiet for long as the bank held a second mortgage on my house in Valley Drive. This meant they could get their hands on the property, clearing most of my overdraft as the mortgage was only small. I was forced to move out and had to find somewhere else to live. After a search, I managed to get a flat in Leconfield House on Cowpasture Road in Ilkley, living with retired old-timers.

Fortunately, the divorce had given Wendy ownership of the home in Weston Road in lieu of her share in the matrimonial house. This was safe and secure for her and the boys, and protected them from my creditors and the bank.

I had always been open with Roy and shared the company books with him. I did this as I was proud of how well we were doing, but now things were going badly he knew too much and could see clearly how he could recover his employer's funds. Armed with this in-depth knowledge he was in a good position to continue pushing me to sell more assets.

The contracting company which had incurred the losses had nothing much to sell. Instead, it owed thousands of pounds for concrete and other materials. Under the cross guarantee arrangement the bank had led me into, I had to pay for these materials from the earnings of Ken Walker Transport, which now led to cash flow problems for what had been a profitable business.

Obviously, our policy of constant expansion came to a halt, bringing with it much larger tax bills as we were no longer able to offset tax against capital spending on new equipment. This felt like we were being kicked when we were down.

As word spread that we were facing difficulties, the phone rang constantly with people asking for money. My office staff were good at stalling, but eventually it was down to me. I had to talk to suppliers or go and see them and try to arrange extra time to pay. Also, there were problems with getting paid. When customers know you're in trouble many hold back from settling. I was constantly under pressure to chase around to get money from those who owed us so I could pay the wages.

At the same time I was trying to finish off the contracts that Mike Schofield had left in such a mess, while also having to fork out money for materials needed to get them finished. What made things even worse was that the contracts company owed the transport/plant hire business about £26,000 for the hire of equipment. Even though this had been made at discounted rates with extended credit, now when we needed payment there was no money and this aggravated the cash flow problems even further. It was a difficult time and I could feel the noose tightening around my neck!

The excavators, tippers and skip wagons were making money but the contracting company's losses were currently standing at £49,000 and were not done yet. All the time Roy pressed me to sell the only things that were making money. I resisted as long as I could but just to keep the pot boiling and pay wages I did sell two JCBs and two of my newest lorries. I felt sick to see them go, especially at the low prices they fetched. Someone would always gain from my predicament.

When the transport/plant manager, Rod McLaughlin, saw that my BMW had been sold he offered to buy his company vehicle, a Triumph TR6 sports car, at a well written-down price. It was a lovely car in good condition despite having made many off-road excursions late at night when Rod struggled back to his home in Boroughbridge after an evening in the Rose and Crown. Rod could be a hard man to deal with, but this had often worked to my favour over the years, and he was good at his job. His purchase of the car helped with another week's wages.

The transport and plant hire company still had value as a going concern, especially as we had our own tipping facilities for the skip service. So I decided to try and sell that business as a profitable going concern. I placed a rather costly advertisement in a trade journal and soon had several enquiries, meeting a number of interested parties as prospects looked good. One company in particular were very interested, a family concern from Bolton in Lancashire trading as Alan Morgan Limited. Though much bigger than my company they had similar activities and were anxious to do a deal.

The Alan Morgan people came to Ilkley, bringing with them the retired founder of their firm. They had a good look around, then took me out for lunch, appearing friendly and genuine. The founder chatted and asked if I would stay on if they bought my company. I had worked for myself for many years but as things stood I said that providing we came to a satisfactory agreement on the sale I would be pleased to remain with the firm.

They came to Ilkley many times over the next few weeks, seemingly very keen. So I encouraged them and let the other enquiries slip away. The banker, Roy Johnson, knew I had someone interested and kept pushing me to close the deal, but I couldn't tie down the Alan Morgan people to talk money. Maybe I was being naive but at the time I didn't realise what their plan was.

Howard

In a few years the hope and optimism of the 1960s and early 1970s had gone. First, my marriage ended, then the business started to collapse, and now came a third hammer blow. This is the saddest part of the whole story. You can recover from financial problems though it may take time. I still could see Wendy and the boys on a regular basis as we lived close together. But loss of life is tragic and permanent. What came next was far worse than my business collapse.

It was a Saturday afternoon, 20 September 1975. I had finished work for the day and escaped to my flat in Cowpasture Road. Since my business had fallen into trouble I didn't enjoy the Rose and Crown as much as I had in the past. As I looked out the window towards Brook Street I saw a policeman running up the road. I recognised him immediately. It was PC Raymond Walker, a man with the same name but no relation. He was a good friend. Ray looked flushed and was gasping for breath. When he saw me at the window he waved for me to come down. I met him on the pavement edge. He could hardly speak, partly from breathlessness but more from the difficulty of finding words for what he had to say.

"Howard has been in an accident," he managed to gasp. He carried on talking but I don't remember the rest. The message was loud and only too clear from his look - his face said it all. He knew Howard as well as he knew me. In an instant I knew my little brother was gone and suddenly the sinking business was unimportant. I'd lost both my brother and my closest friend.

Howard had been a sidecar passenger in a motorbike grass track race in Lancashire. On a bumpy circuit near Preston he'd been thrown out and run over by another competitor. The wheel had run over his face and he died instantly.

As the shock reduced I started to feel an overwhelming sense of guilt. I had driven my racing car all over Europe, often in very dangerous conditions and had survived, while Howard had fun competing in a few local events a year and this happens!

I don't know who propped up whom, but Raymond was as badly shaken as me. He had known us for years, and had the house next to Wendy and me when we lived on Valley Drive. Policemen get awful jobs and I'm sure this was one of Raymond's worst. His ordeal was not yet over for he now had to go and break the news to Howard's wife, Joan, and their two little children Fiona and Graham.

As I went back inside my flat, I stepped over the doormat where only a few weeks before Howard had stood when he called for me on that wet Friday night.

I felt numb. My thoughts flew back to the motorway where we started with the first lorry, then ran slowly through all we had done together over the past fifteen years. As well as a brother he had been my right-hand man. He could drive every vehicle we owned and would never quit no matter how difficult the job. It was him who solved problems that had stumped me. We had come a long way together and now he was gone.

I then had to tell my mother who hadn't yet recovered from losing my father. There were many tears.

The family of Howard's wife were undertakers and all the arrangements were handled by them. I went for my last look at him. After such a sudden and violent death his face didn't have a mark. I looked at his ginger beard, so much like mine. Both my mother and I thought he grew it to be like me, but he would have never agreed to that.

The funeral service was held in Ilkley Parish Church. It is a large building but the crowds of people who turned up for the service packed it out. There were so many flowers that we draped a sheet over the back of his pickup and stacked them on that too. It was driven behind the hearse by one of our drivers all the way to the cemetery, followed by a long convoy of vehicles. I had not only lost a brother but also a man who had been a close companion all the time I had been building up the business from the very beginning. I missed him dearly and still do.

Finality

It was late 1976 and the companies had limped along for more than a year. I knew I was on borrowed time but though desperately short of cash, I made a point of paying the local traders with whom we had had accounts for many years: Ross Brothers for petrol, Mortens the ironmongers, Clough Tomblin accountants, and the milkman!

Around this time the bank went silent, ominously quiet. I'd been expecting the drama of a visit for some time and I didn't think it would be Roy who would come to do the deed. It seemed certain that things had been taken out of his hands and sure enough when the dreaded day came Roy was nowhere to be seen.

I arrived at work early one morning to see a Jaguar parked outside my office. I didn't pay it much attention but unlocked the front door and went upstairs to my office. Almost immediately I heard footsteps coming up the stairs and a tall, official-looking man walked in, attaché case in one hand and a business card in the other. He handed me the card. I didn't need to study it or him to know my time had run out.

Though I had been expecting it for weeks it was still a shock, but at the same time a relief.

"I have been appointed and authorised by National Westminster Bank to close down your business," he informed me, or words to that effect. "Can you show me around?" I did, but when he asked me if I would help him wind up *my* company I declined. Instead I walked around to the transport café for a bacon sandwich, then went back to my flat.

Later in the day I returned and rang Alan Morgan. I had phoned them so many times as the business ran down only to be stalled with every excuse imaginable while they waited for this day. When I told them it had arrived they drove over from Bolton and were in Ilkley within hours! The scavengers were here to benefit from my misfortune.

It had become clear that Alan Morgan, the organisation that was most interested in my company, had chosen for many months not to close the deal. They had the funding sorted out but were hanging on and had stalled me and my solicitor. What hadn't been clear before but now became apparent, was that they had been waiting for the bank to foreclose. Then, they would step in and pick up the pieces for a song. That is now what happened.

Earlier, Alan Morgan had asked me if I would stay on as manager and run it for them. The offer was still open and I agreed, though I have to say I wasn't happy about working for an outfit that had stolen what my hard work had built up over so many years. But it was a job and would give me breathing space, so I swallowed my pride and accepted the situation with as good a grace as I could manage.

They took over and moved in. What had been green and white now quickly became Morgan blue, something that certainly left me feeling blue. The sign above the front of the depot came down, and another went up carrying their name and colours. I looked up at the new name. Something was wrong. It didn't seem to fit; nothing seemed to fit, or maybe it was me who didn't fit any longer. I was dismayed at how soon some of my staff changed allegiance. Maybe it was only to be expected but it hurt nevertheless, as I had always ensured that when the organisation was successful the benefits were shared around those who helped create it.

Alan Morgan offered me a salary. This seemed quite generous but looking back I realised they didn't plan on paying it for long. They also gave me a company car and this is where they were rubbing my nose in it. After all my years of top class motoring I was given a Ford Cortina 1300cc, a bottom of the range rep's car! I'd drive this over to Leeds in the evenings after my day's work and pick up Julia from her job at the children's clothing factory in Chapeltown, bringing her back to my flat in Cowpasture Road.

I can't say that I settled into my new position but I got on with the job. Part of my new responsibilities entailed going round to my customers, both old and new, and filling in a log sheet every day. This meant ticking boxes showing where I'd been and who I had made contact with. This way they were handed on a plate a comprehensive list of all my customers in readiness for when I would no longer be required.

I only had one more card left to play.

When Ken Walker Transport had moved into the premises on East Parade I'd taken out a lease in my own name. This was before the business had been made into a limited company. Later, I never got around to changing the lease. So it had stayed that way for years. Naturally, the new owners wanted the lease. I went to see my solicitor and good friend Jack Mewies. "Don't assign them anything until you get a contract of employment," he said. Jack confided that he suspected I was being used. When Alan Morgan had everything they needed, there would be no further place for me.

"But Jack," I replied. "I built up the business and it's me that it revolves around. Surely, they must need me as much as I need them."

"It's not the way I see it. Hold onto the lease for security. If you do assign it to them it is against my better judgement." Those words would come back to haunt me

A few weeks went by before the lease was mentioned again. When next the Morgan manager asked I told him I would like a contract of employment first. "Oh, we don't bother with contracts. None of our men have them. We're an old-established company and treat our men fairly; it works best for everyone that way. If you do your job well for us we'll look after you." Without being totally convinced, I assured him I would see to the lease. When he left my office, I chewed it over. I felt they needed me, perhaps not for the long term but then I wouldn't need them in the future either. To show my good faith, I signed the lease transfer and posted the big brown envelope that Thursday afternoon.

About mid-morning on the following Monday I was in my office when I heard the front door open, but no one came up the stairs. After a few minutes I heard voices, then hammering. I peered over the banister to see my new boss with a man in overalls who was using a hammer and chisel on the door lock. The new boss came up the stairs and followed me into my office. "Right Ken, you are finished! Collect any personal things off this desk. The radio you put in our car will be returned to you, and we'll pay you up to the end of the month. Give me the car keys. There's no need to hand in the others as my man is changing the locks." At that he simply turned and walked out. They had obviously received the lease. Jack Mewies' words rang in my head, "Against my better judgment!"

I looked at my desk ... their desk now! Personal things? Every damned thing was personal. The desk, the chair, even the carpet I stood on. Dismissals had been made from this side of the desk. Now the tables had been turned.

I found a folder and looked around feeling a little dazed, at least the Morgan manager wasn't standing over me. I picked up a photograph of my family and a letter opener that the office girls had bought me one birthday some years before. From the wall I took a picture of me in my racing car, another of my first wagon plus one of me taking delivery of two new JCB excavators. They all went into a folder which I tucked under my arm. The girls in the main office were quiet. I couldn't even go and say goodbye as they'd changed sides to safeguard their jobs. So had my transport manager, Rod McLaughlin, who before had been so reliable and loyal.

I turned and walked slowly down the stairs remembering how excited I'd been when I agreed to take on the lease.

Morgan's joiner was putting the finishing touches to the new lock. He held the door open for me but we didn't speak. I set off on foot past what had been my reserved parking place. I had parked many special cars there over the good years: Mini Cooper, Porsche, BMW, Ferrari, how the mighty had fallen! Now I didn't even have a car. I had landed on my feet, literally rather than in a good way: it was left to my feet to carry me home.

I walked slowly up East Parade feeling that I was being watched by everyone in the garage and reception area, eyes boring into me. I didn't look back. Over to my left, steam was rising from the flue at the back of what had been Chippy Walker's fish and chip shop. I passed the old garage on the corner of Little Lane where I had worked as a bus driver for Ledgards seventeen years before. It now stood empty.

Then it was along Leeds Road, turning left towards Brook Street and taking a short cut through the Crescent pub's car park, past the rear entrance where one night after a few pints I had driven my Mini into the reception.

In Brook Street I glanced across to the opposite corner where Dutton's For Buttons now occupied the premises where Wendy's lingerie shop had stood in its heyday. I could turn right at this point and head for the Rose and Crown where I had spent such happy times over the years, sometimes with as many as fifteen of my men drinking there in the tap room after work. Often, there were so many of us that other customers complained of the smell of diesel oil.

This day I didn't want a drink or to see anyone who knew me. I felt a failure and wanted to get back to the refuge of my little rented flat and drink tea alone. I was now both car-less and job-less. If only my brother was still here. He would understand.

I made it home without seeing anyone who knew me and without having to speak to anyone. I didn't want to talk, only to think and to be alone. It was pointless going over the past analysing what went wrong. I knew what had gone wrong: the question was, what next? I'd hit the buffers but life goes on. I hadn't lost everything, I still had my health though at that moment my spirit was weak. I had to think about how to make a new living, how to earn a little money and, at the age of forty two, how to get on with the rest of my life.

In looking back, everything had been much of a struggle. Hardly ever had anything been given to me. The lesson I learned when I was a little boy was that if I wanted something I had to work for it. And work I did. Certainly, I had a touch of luck at times but nothing had been laid on a plate for me. Nothing had been easy in my past and, going forward, all I knew to expect was that nothing was going to be easy in the future!

Dramatis Personae

Employees of Ken Walker Transport and Plant Hire Ltd and Ken Walker Contracts Ltd remembered with affection:

Howard Walker	Walter Biggins	Dennis Webster
Kevin Wood	Peter Gaunt	John Goodchild
Bob Johnson	Bob Sedgwick	Bill Whittaker
Lionel Dickson	Frank Town	Walter Pye
David Scholey	Winnie Griffiths	Tony Turpin
Jim Manson	Pat Hems	Christine Spence
Horace Appleyard	Ralph Barrit	John Mierscough
Tony Rampling	Cedric Webster	Dave Harrison
Jack Rocket	Derek Symonds	John Ward
Stewart Davi	Eddie Thorne	Richard Bell
Barry Taylor	Terry Gray	David Ashbrook
Tim Roberts	Paul Dickinson	Dave Bell
Brian Glover	Chris Pinder	Peter Lister
Chris Pitt	Mrs Clapham	Rod McLaughlin
Brian Northrop	Mrs Hinchcliffe	Joe Coe
Jack Spence	John Horsman	Dave Barritt
Mick Winsor	Guy Barritt	Carl Gregg

I apologise to those missed from the list: age has had its effect.

And one I would prefer to forget: Mike Schofield

Photo taken from the railway viaduct Ilkley 1967

Brother Howard, Joan and baby Fiona

Half church felled—in error

Demolition workers in the Milligan Fields area of Cross Hills designated as a clearance area by Skipton Rural Council — have knocked down half a church by mistake.

The Cross Hills Spiritualist Church which has 28 members, stands near the fields area.

The members are incensed at what they allege is incompetence of the workers, Mrs. A. Martin, of Campbell Street, Cross Hills, who has been connected with the church for 36 years, called it "a disgrace." She said: "I think the building will have to be completely re-built."

Mr. Ken Walker, head of the demolition firm, Ken Walker Ltd., Ilkley, said "It was a pure and simple accident." He said six men were engaged on the demolition work using a bulldozer and hawsers, and knew the spiritualist church was not scheduled for demolition.

Between the church and a Scout hall were three cottages which they demolished with no trouble.

While pulling down the gable end of the Scout hall, however, a section of the gable end weighing 75 tons fell towards the church and created a strong wind which caused the thin church wall to collapse. The rest of the church was left standing, although the roof was lifted up.

Mr. Walker commented: "This is one of those freak things that could not be foreseen. Demolition work is a hazardous job and this sort of thing does happen sometimes.

"Our firm is safety conscious and we try to be as careful as we can with other people's property." He thought the wall could be repaired.

He said his firm had contacted the church trustees, and accepted responsibility to repair the damage or pay compensation.

Newspaper cutting early 70's

My Ferrari Dino early 1970

Porsche 1971-72

Demolishing railway viaduct at Mirfield 1973

Our low-loader recovers my BMW after
accident on icy road 1976

With BMW I sold to market trader 1976

Motorbike taken in part exchange 1976

East Parade after take over by Morgan